Praise for *Cracked*

'[*Cracked*] should be read by every doctor … by everyone in politics and the media, not to mention any concerned citizen.'

Peter Hitchens, *Mail on Sunday*

'Chilling reading'

Will Self, *Guardian*

'Davies's book is a potent polemic'

Bryan Appleyard, *Sunday Times*

'If, in the world of psychiatry, the DSM is Holy Scripture, *Cracked* is set to become a heretical text.'

Robert Crampton, *The Times Magazine*

'Builds a disturbing picture of a profession that is in thrall to pharmaceutical companies'

Michael Mosley, *BBC Focus*

'An eye-opening and persuasive work'

Publishers Weekly

'[A] diligent study'

Financial Times

'A well-written book … a positive contribution to the debate about whether psychiatry can become a more open practice.'

Therapy Today

'Disturbing and uncompromising'

Kirkus Reviews

'An engrossing book, full of interviews with patients and professionals'

GP Magazine

'I couldn't put the book down. It is totally engaging, as controversial as it is compelling, and as erudite as it is enjoyable … The book deserves to be a bestseller and should be read by every mental health professional.'

International Review of Logotherapy and Existential Analysis

'This is an excellent book … [it] careens, almost literally, from one psychiatric outrage to the next … I strongly recommend this book.'

Dr Phil Hickey, *Behaviourism and Mental Health*

'This thought-provoking book will make people think twice before sitting on a psychiatrist's couch or filling a prescription.'

Booklist

'This is a very well-written book – intellectually sound, but written in an accessible way … It should be read by all mental health professionals, by all politicians and policy makers charged with shaping future mental health provision.'

Dr Neil Thompson, *Social Justice Solutions*

'You will be illuminated and often shocked and certainly made to think more about how you view the children in your care. Every teacher should read it.'

International School Magazine

CRACKED

WHY PSYCHIATRY IS DOING MORE HARM THAN GOOD

JAMES DAVIES

First published in the UK in 2013 by
Icon Books Ltd, Omnibus Business Centre,
39–41 North Road, London N7 9DP
email: info@iconbooks.net
www.iconbooks.net

This edition published in the UK in 2014 by Icon Books Ltd

Sold in the UK, Europe and Asia
by Faber & Faber Ltd, Bloomsbury House,
74–77 Great Russell Street,
London WC1B 3DA or their agents

Distributed in the UK, Europe and Asia
by TBS Ltd, TBS Distribution Centre, Colchester Road,
Frating Green, Colchester CO7 7DW

Distributed in India by Penguin Books India,
11 Community Centre, Panchsheel Park,
New Delhi 110017

Distributed in South Africa by
Jonathan Ball, Office B4, The District,
41 Sir Lowry Road, Woodstock 7925

Distributed in Australia and New Zealand
by Allen & Unwin Pty Ltd,
PO Box 8500, 83 Alexander Street,
Crows Nest, NSW 2065

ISBN: 978-184831-654-6

Typeset in Minion by Marie Doherty

Printed and bound in the UK by
Clays Ltd, Elcograf S.p.A

Contents

About the author

James Davies obtained his PhD in medical and social anthropology from the University of Oxford. He is also a qualified psychotherapist (having worked in the NHS), and a senior lecturer in social anthropology and psychology at the University of Roehampton, London. He has delivered lectures at many universities, including Harvard, Brown, Columbia, Oxford and UCL, and has written articles about psychiatry for *The Times*, *The Guardian*, the *New Scientist*, *Salon* and the *Harvard Divinity Bulletin*. He is author of the recent book *The Importance of Suffering: the value and meaning of emotional discontent* (Routledge, 2011). He lives with his wife and daughter in London.

For my daughter, Rose

Author's note

I have concealed all identities and altered all real names in case-study material to protect individuals' anonymity.

Preface

The figures are startling. At least one in four of you in the UK and US will suffer from a mental disorder in a given year.* And if you are one of those lucky ones with a constant spring in your step, the odds are high that you are close to someone less fortunate. That is what the psychiatric industry tells us – we are a population on the brink. And that is why it asserts that its services are more essential than ever before. Psychiatry is a science, after all, and has the tools and knowledge at its disposal to help us when our lives break down. This is the official story we hear, the one gaining airtime in the media, the ear of National Health Service (NHS) policy-makers, and widespread dissemination through celebrity chat-shows and popular magazines. But what if the actual truth about psychiatry were not so sanguine or clear-cut as we have been led to believe? What if there is another more insidious story to be told, one that threatens all of our preconceptions? Well, an alternative story certainly does exist, a deeper and far more maddening story. And in this book I intend to tell it.

Once upon a time, psychiatry was reserved for only the most distressed members of society. This was always a small minority: people who were often removed to asylums, usually against their will, and subjected to esoteric

* This is clearly not just an American and British problem. It's estimated that approximately 450 million people worldwide have a mental health problem – people throughout the developed and developing world. (World Health Organisation, 2001)

treatments. Today, the few have become the many. Not because psychiatric wards have increased in number, but because psychiatric treatments and beliefs about mental distress have now crashed through the walls of the hospital and surged into every corner of contemporary life, affecting how we understand and manage our emotional lives. Just consider the facts. According to recent NHS figures, in 2012 alone, over 50 million prescriptions for antidepressants were dispensed to the English public. And the vast majority of these pills were not prescribed to the stereotypically 'mad' characters depicted in Hollywood movies. No, most of their recipients were just like you or me. Average people simply trying to make their way. Perhaps you are one of them. Perhaps someone you love is one of them.

Today, psychiatry's power and influence is far from abating – it's growing at a remarkable rate. And in this book I will show you why this is, paradoxically, a very bad thing for our mental health. To substantiate this claim, my method will be simple. I will investigate three medical mysteries: why has psychiatry become the fastest-growing medical specialism when it still has the poorest curative success? Why are psychiatric drugs now more widely prescribed than almost any other medical drugs in history, despite their dubious efficacy? And why does psychiatry, without solid scientific justification, keep expanding the number of mental disorders it believes to exist – from 106 in 1952 to 374 today? What is going on?

To answer these mysteries, I will leave no aspect of the industry unexamined. Each chapter will focus on a different part of the story: how the process of creating new diagnostic categories regularly strays from scientifically accepted standards; how antidepressants actually work no better than placebo (sugar) pills for most people; how negative drug trials are routinely buried and research is regularly manipulated to convey positive results; how numerous doctors have been enticed by huge rewards from pharmaceutical companies into creating more disorders and prescribing more pills; and how mass-marketing has been unscrupulously employed to conceal from doctors, patients and the wider public the ethical, scientific and treatment flaws of a profession now in serious crisis.

I have written this book to seduce a new generation away from the escalating craze for psychiatric drugs and diagnoses. I reveal through governmental, academic and interview sources that the unhappy truth about psychiatry can be explained by one startling fact: in recent decades many areas of psychiatry have become so lured by power and money that they are in danger of putting the pursuit of pharmaceutical riches and medical status above their patients' well-being. My aim is not to shock anyone gratuitously, just to report what the inconvenient facts suggest: that psychiatry, in the name of helping others, is now in serious peril of better helping itself.

During my journey researching and writing this book I have amassed a vast number of air miles criss-crossing the Atlantic, interviewing some of the leading lights of the psychiatric world. I have consulted the people who have put the profession on the map – the heads of the premier psychiatry schools, the creators of new diagnostic categories, the presidents of national psychiatric associations: the people with long and glowing entries on Wikipedia, the real movers and shakers of the profession. My aim has not been to incriminate anyone personally, merely to get at the truth. And as my eyes have gradually been opened by discoveries more worrying than I could have anticipated, I have checked and double-checked what I have heard to ensure I've got the story correct. Now that my investigations are complete, it's time to make what I have discovered more freely available. As you follow me in the coming pages, you won't always find the ride comfortable; you will encounter facts and confessions that will shock, baffle and dismay you. But there is no point sugar-coating the facts. For if things are ever to be put right, then what is required above all are people, just like you, understanding and spreading the word that a profession purporting to help us is now seriously, disconcertingly – and in both senses of the term – *cracked*.

1
Psychiatry's early breakdown and the rise of the DSM

On a chilly Wednesday morning in late January, I pass through the gates of my university after a fraught drive through London's rush hour. With two minutes left on the clock, I make my way hurriedly to the ground floor of the lecture theatre. Today I am expected to deliver my first lecture on critical psychiatry. As I enter the room it feels more close and cramped than usual, as nearly every student on the course has decided to attend (which, I must add, doesn't always happen on cold January mornings). The students are preoccupied as I approached the lectern and start quietly ordering my notes. Many of them are chatting intently, some are tapping on laptops or mobiles, while a few eager souls (in the front row, of course) quietly sit waiting for me to begin.

'Right everyone, settle down, I have a great piece of research I want you to consider. You'll like this one, trust me, so please listen closely.' I clear my throat and begin.

Some years ago during a balmy April, a group of eight academics conducted a dramatic experiment, months in preparation. As part of the experiment they individually presented themselves at different psychiatric hospitals dotted around the United States. Each academic then told the psychiatrist on duty they were hearing a voice in their head that said the word 'thud'. That was the only lie they would tell; otherwise, from that point on they would behave and respond completely normally. All of them were admitted into their respective hospitals. And all were diagnosed with serious mental disorders and given powerful antipsychotic pills. All the while they acted completely normally. The experimenters thought they would be in for a couple of days and then be discharged, but they were wrong. Most were held for weeks, and some in excess of two months. They could not convince the doctors they were sane. And telling the doctors about the experiment only compounded the problem. So it quickly became clear that the only way out was to agree that they were insane, and then pretend to be getting better.

Once the leader of the experiment, Dr David Rosenhan, got out and reported what had happened, there was uproar in the psychiatric establishment. Rosenhan and his colleagues were accused of deceit. One major hospital challenged Rosenhan to send some more fake patients to them, guaranteeing that they would spot them this time. Rosenhan agreed, and after a month the hospital proudly announced to the national media that they had discovered 41 fakes. Rosenhan then revealed that he had sent no one to the hospital at all.*

For a moment there is stunned silence in the lecture room, quickly followed by some chuckling and surprised chatter. I now have their full attention. Three or four hands shoot up.

---

* Here I paraphrase from Adam Curtis' brilliant BBC documentary, *The Trap* (2007).

'Hold your questions for now everyone. I've another series of experiments to tell you about first. These occurred around the same time as Rosenhan's experiment, and were equally devastating for psychiatry.'

These experiments explored the following question: 'Would two different psychiatrists diagnose the same patient in the same way?' To answer this, the researchers presented the same set of patients to different psychiatrists in different places, to see whether their diagnoses would match up. When the results came in, the situation did not look good. Taken en masse, they revealed that two psychiatrists would give different diagnoses to the same patient between 32 and 42 per cent of the time.[1] And this troubling result was confirmed by another series of studies showing that psychiatrists in the United States and in Russia were twice as likely to diagnose their patients as schizophrenic as their colleagues in Britain and Europe.[2] This meant that the diagnosis you could be assigned not only often depended on who your psychiatrist was, but on where your psychiatrist was located. How could you therefore trust your diagnosis, when a different psychiatrist was likely to diagnose you with something else?

I told my students about these experiments, because in the history of psychiatry they were considered game-changers. They plunged psychiatry into severe crisis in the 1970s by exposing that there was something terribly wrong with the diagnostic system. Psychiatrists were not only defining sane people as insane, but when two psychiatrists at any given time were faced with the same patient, they would assign different diagnoses nearly half the time. So why were these critical mistakes being made?

The profession was desperate for an answer. And when one finally emerged, the course of psychiatry would be altered for good. It turned out there was a serious problem with the centrepiece of the entire profession, the psychiatrist's bible – the DSM.

•

So what, you may ask, is the DSM? To answer this question, please follow me into the office of Dr Herbert Pardes, one of America's leading psychiatrists. To give you some idea of his professional standing, just consider his CV. He was former chair of Columbia University's Department of Psychiatry (the most powerful psychiatry department on the globe); former president of the American Psychiatric Association (the more glitzy US equivalent of the Royal College of Psychiatrists), and finally, former director of the largest psychiatric research organisation internationally (the National Institute of Mental Health). In short, if there were a CEO of psychiatry, then Herbert Pardes was probably it.

Pardes welcomed me into his office with an easy smile and a warm handshake, 'I'm glad we've finally managed to make this meeting happen', said Pardes kindly. 'Come on over, take a seat.'

Once Pardes and I had settled comfortably in his unexpectedly grand office, the first topic I pressed him on was the DSM. 'If you don't understand the history of the DSM', insisted Pardes, 'you cannot hope to understand modern psychiatry.' The DSM is shorthand for the *Diagnostic and Statistical Manual of Mental Disorders* and is the book listing all the psychiatric disorders that psychiatrists believe to exist. 'So the DSM contains every mental disorder with which you or I could be potentially diagnosed', said Pardes, 'and that's its significance.'

Pardes then briefly recalled the DSM's journey from its modest 130 pages in 1952 to the 886 pages it boasts today. In short, the first edition of the DSM was written in order to solve a problem that had plagued the profession for decades. Until the 1950s, psychiatrists working in different places possessed no shared dictionary in which all the disorders were clearly defined and that carefully listed each disorder's core symptoms. Without this dictionary, the behaviour that one psychiatrist called 'melancholic' or 'depressive' another psychiatrist was likely to call something else. So this made communication between psychiatrists in different places almost impossible.[3] 'If I say to another psychiatrist that I have tried the drug Thorazine on 250 people with paranoid schizophrenia', explained Pardes, 'what happens if this other psychiatrist's definition of paranoid schizophrenia is not the same as mine? Well, our discussion becomes meaningless. So the DSM was developed to try to identify and standardise the symptoms characteristic of any given mental illness – anxiety disorder, phobia, mood disorder and so on.' Every psychiatrist was then expected to learn this list so that different psychiatrists in different places would all be working from the same page.

Once the first DSM arrived in the 1950s, psychiatrists were expected to use the dictionary in the same standardised way still in operation today. For instance, if you go and visit a psychiatrist tomorrow because you're feeling down, the psychiatrist will ask you to describe your symptoms. The purpose of this is to try to work out from your symptoms what diagnosis from the dictionary you should be assigned. For example, if you report feeling tense, irritable and panicky, and that you have been feeling this way for over two weeks, then you are likely to be diagnosed with one of the anxiety disorders. Whereas if you mention that you're feeling sad, teary and lethargic and are experiencing disrupted sleep, then you are more likely to be diagnosed with one of the depressive disorders. Of course, sometimes your symptoms will not fall neatly into any single category, but rather span two or three. In this case your problem will be considered 'comorbid' – namely, that you are suffering from a disorder that is occurring simultaneously with another (perhaps you suffer from major depression as well as panic disorder). But whether your condition is comorbid or not, the diagnostic process is the same – your psychiatrist attempts to match your symptoms as closely as possible to one of the diagnostic labels listed in the book.

Now here comes the problem. And it's a problem that still afflicts psychiatry today. How does your psychiatrist know if he or she has assigned the correct diagnosis? Is there a safe and reliable way that he or she can test, objectively speaking, whether the diagnosis given is the right one? I put this question to Pardes: 'Well, one way to test whether the diagnosis is correct is to apply a scientific or biological test [such as a blood, urine or saliva test] or some other form of physical examination to assess, firstly, whether a patient has a mental disorder, and, if so, precisely what disorder they suffer from. But the crucial problem for psychiatry is that we still have no such objective biological tests.'

In other words, unlike in other areas of medicine where a doctor can conduct a blood or urine test to determine whether they have reached the correct diagnosis, in psychiatry no such methods exist. And they don't exist, as Pardes also intimated, because psychiatry has yet to identify any clear biological causes for most of the disorders in the DSM (this is a pivotal point that I'll talk about more fully in coming chapters). So the only method available to psychiatrists is what we could call the 'matching method': match the symptoms the patient reports to the relevant diagnosis in the book.

These facts, although at first glance appearing innocuous, are crucial for understanding why psychiatry, in the 1970s, fell into serious crisis. They help us explain why psychiatrists were not only guilty of branding sane people as insane (as the Rosenhan experiment revealed), but also guilty of regularly failing to agree on what diagnosis to assign a given patient (as the 'diagnostic reliability' experiments showed). Psychiatry was making these errors because it possessed no objective way of testing whether a person was mentally disordered, and if so, precisely what disorder they were suffering from. Without such objective tests, the diagnosis that a psychiatrist would assign could be influenced by their subjective preferences, and as different psychiatrists were swayed by different subjective factors, it was understandable that they regularly disagreed about what diagnosis to give. This is why these early experiments were so dramatic for the profession: they produced for the first time clear evidence that psychiatric diagnosis was at best imprecise, and at worst a kind of professional guesswork. And so without any objective way of testing the validity of a diagnosis, psychiatry was in peril of falling far behind the diagnostic achievements of other branches of medicine.

A solution was needed, and fast.

•

Under the leadership of the American Psychiatric Association (APA), the profession in the 1970s plumped for a radical solution. It decided to tear up the existing edition of the DSM (then called *DSM-II*) and start again. The bold idea was to write an entirely new manual that would solve all the problems beleaguering *DSM-II*. This new manual would be called *DSM-III*, and its central aim would be to improve the reliability of psychiatric diagnosis and thereby answer the mounting criticisms that were threatening to shatter the profession's legitimacy.*

The first step the APA took was to set about finding someone to lead the writing of *DSM-III*. The APA needed a person highly competent, energetic and daring, but also someone who had experience with psychiatric classification. After sifting through countless candidates and enduring many frustrations, the APA finally settled on a man called Dr Robert Spitzer, who was based at Columbia University's medical school. Spitzer had been a young and up-coming psychiatrist when the earlier *DSM-II* had been written, and he had also been minimally involved in that project. But most importantly, he appeared to have the drive and vigour needed to get the job done. The APA was sufficiently impressed with his qualities, so they hired him in 1974 to start work on *DSM-III*. Little did Spitzer know at

* I was often told that poor diagnostic reliability was not the only driver for the DSM's reform. There was also a need to match DSM terminology to that used in the *International Classification of Diseases* (ICD). However, Robert Spitzer, Melvin Sabshin and other leaders in the APA knew that the reliability issue was paramount and that the DSM must make that issue its priority.

the time that his appointment as Chair of *DSM-III* would ultimately make him the most influential psychiatrist of the 20th century.

The first thing Spitzer did to reform the DSM was to assemble a team of fifteen psychiatrists to help him write the new manual. This team was called the DSM Taskforce, and Spitzer was its outright leader. So in the mid-1970s the Taskforce set about writing a kind of New Testament for psychiatry: a book that aspired to improve the uniformity and reliability of psychiatric diagnosis in the wake of all its previous failings. If this sounds all very intrepid, well, that's pretty much what it was. Spitzer's Taskforce promised a new deal for psychiatry, and there was a lot of pressure on them to deliver.

So what precisely did Spitzer do to try to set things right? How was he going to make psychiatric diagnosis more reliable and scientific? His answer was simple. The DSM needed to be altered in three major ways:

- Many existing disorders would be deleted from *DSM-II*.
- The definitions of each disorder in the old DSM would be expanded and made more specific for *DSM-III*.
- A new checklist would be developed for *DSM-III* to improve the reliability of diagnosis.

Let's briefly look at each of these alterations more closely. The first involved Spitzer deleting some of the more unpopular and controversial mental disorders. These included some of the disorders introduced into psychiatry by psychoanalysis, a discipline with important differences from psychiatry (see footnote below).* In the 1970s psychoanalysis had fallen out of vogue in psychiatry, along with many disorders it had introduced to the previous DSM. One of the most controversial of these was homosexuality. Indeed, in the *DSM-II* homosexuality was listed as a mental disease. It was described as a 'sexual deviation' and was located in the same category as paedophilia.[4] While some psychiatrists felt it was wrong to brand homosexuality an illness, the main push to remove the disorder largely came from outside pressure groups including the gay rights movement. These groups asked why a normal and natural human sexual preference had been included in the DSM as a mental disease, especially when there was no scientific evidence to justify its inclusion. Surely it was prejudice rather than science that had placed homosexuality on the list?

Many psychiatrists were not so sure, but the APA, perhaps sensing the change in public mood, decided to consult the wider psychiatric community for their views. So at the APA convention in 1973 all the attending members were asked to vote on what they believed: was homosexuality a mental disorder or not? The vote was closer than expected:

---

* What is the difference between psychoanalysis and psychiatry? Or between psychiatry, psychology and psychotherapy, for that matter? It can be summarised this way: a psychologist researches different aspects of our mental lives – cognition, memory, perception, etc. They are not clinicians, unless they have undertaken a specialist postgraduate training in clinical psychology or psychotherapy (the 'talking cure'). The psychotherapist or psychoanalyst, on the other hand, has trained at the postgraduate level to treat patients with the 'talking cure' – they do not have to be medical doctors (and so do not prescribe medications). Psychiatrists are medical doctors who have later specialised in psychiatry. Some psychiatrists practise one form of psychotherapy or another but most do not, nor do they have to. Today, most psychiatrists diagnose disorders and prescribe and monitor medications.

5,854 psychiatrists voted to take homosexuality out of the DSM, while 3,810 voted to keep it in. And because the 'outers' were in the majority, homosexuality ceased to be a mental disorder in 1974 and was therefore not included in Spitzer's *DSM-III*. It was politics and not science that had removed the disorder from this list. As we continue, it's worth holding that thought in mind.

To turn now to Spitzer's second alteration, this involved making the definitions of each mental disorder more specific and detailed. The idea was that if each disorder could be defined more precisely, psychiatrists would be less likely to misunderstand the disorders and therefore misapply them to patients. The problem with the earlier *DSM-II*, Spitzer had argued, was that its definitions of disorders were too open to interpretation. So, for example, in *DSM-II* 'depressive neurosis' was defined in a single sentence: 'This disorder is manifested by an excessive reaction of depression due to an internal conflict or to an identifiable event such as the loss of a love object or cherished possession.'[5] Spitzer believed that such vague definitions explained why psychiatrists regularly gave different diagnoses to the same patient. If a word in the dictionary were poorly defined, people would not know how to use it properly. The same was the case with psychiatric diagnoses. This imprecision was why, as Spitzer said, for *DSM-II*, 'there are no diagnostic categories for which reliability [is] uniformly high … [and why] the level of reliability is no better than fair for psychosis and schizophrenia and is poor for the remaining categories.'[6] Spitzer's hope was that by sharpening the definitions there would be less scope for personal interpretation, which in turn would mean diagnostic reliability would rise.

Finally, to help improve diagnostic reliability further, Spitzer's team created criteria for each disorder that a patient had to meet in order to warrant the diagnosis. So while, for example, there are multiple symptoms associated with depression, it was somehow decided that a patient would need to have at least *five* of them for a period of at least *two* weeks to qualify for receiving the diagnosis of depression. The only problem was: on what grounds did Spitzer's team decide that if you have five symptoms for two weeks you suffered from a depressive disorder? Why didn't they choose six symptoms for three weeks or three symptoms for five weeks? What was the science that justified putting the line where Spitzer's team chose to draw it? In an interview in 2010, the psychiatrist Daniel Carlat asked Spitzer this very question:

> *Carlat*: How did you decide on five criteria as being your minimum threshold for depression?
>
> *Spitzer*: It was just consensus. We would ask clinicians and researchers, 'How many symptoms do you think patients ought to have before you would give them the diagnosis of depression?', and we came up with the arbitrary number of five.
>
> *Carlat*: But why did you choose five and not four? Or why didn't you choose six?
>
> *Spitzer*: Because four just seemed like not enough. And six seemed like too much [Spitzer smiles mischievously].
>
> *Carlat*: But weren't there any studies done to establish the threshold?

> *Spitzer*: We did reviews of the literature, and in some cases we received funding from NIMH to do field trials ... [However] when you do field trials in depression and other disorders, there is no sharp dividing line where you can confidently say, 'This is the perfect number of symptoms needed to make a diagnosis' ... It would be nice if we had a biological gold standard, but that doesn't exist, because we don't understand the neurobiology of depression.[7]

I expect that by now some of you may be scratching your heads. Wasn't the whole point of Spitzer's reform to make psychiatric diagnosis a little more scientifically rigorous? But what, you may ask, is rigorous about a committee drawing arbitrary lines between mental disorder and normality? And what is scientific about asking the psychiatric community to vote on whether existing disorders should be removed from the DSM? In other words, in the name of making psychiatric diagnosis more scientific, had Spitzer's team continued to make use of the unscientific procedures that had dogged the construction of earlier manuals?

As important as this question is, I'll refrain from answering it right now, because there is a more crucial question to be addressed first: did Spitzer's reforms actually work? Did they solve the reliability problem? I mean, if you went to see two different psychiatrists independently today, would they be likely to both assign you the same diagnosis?

In an interview for *The New Yorker* in 2005, a journalist called Alix Spiegel asked Spitzer that very question. His answer was unequivocal: 'To say that we've solved the reliability problem is just not true', said Spitzer. 'It's been improved. But if you're in a situation with a general clinician it's certainly not very good. There's still a real problem, and it's not clear how to solve the problem.'[8] Here Spitzer admits something that many within the profession agree with: diagnostic reliability, despite the reforms, is still woefully low.

According to a study published in the journal *Psychiatry* in 2007, for instance, which asked a group of psychiatrists whether they thought psychiatric diagnosis was now reliable, a full 86 per cent said that reliability was still poor.[9] It was not only their clinical experience that led them to this conclusion, but also presumably their familiarity with existing research, including work undertaken by Spitzer himself to find out whether his reforms had worked. Its conclusions were not reassuring. For example, you'll remember that I said before Spitzer's *DSM-III* two psychiatrists would give different diagnoses to the same patient 32 per cent to 42 per cent of the time. Well, Spitzer found that after his reforms psychiatrists were now disagreeing around 33 to 46 per cent of the time – results indicating the very opposite of diagnostic improvement.* And these disappointing figures are consistent with other more recent studies also implying that reliability is still poor. For example, another study published in 2006 showed that reliability actually has not improved in 30 years.[10]

•

* The psychologist Paula J. Caplan argues that one study showed that when different psychiatrists were diagnosing patients from the Axis II group of disorders (basically the personality and developmental disorders) their diagnoses were the same only about two-thirds of the time (66 per cent). Whereas for the remaining disorders they were the same only about half the time (54 per cent). See: Caplan, P.J. (1995), *They Say You're Crazy.* New York: Da Capo (pp. 197–200).

An obvious question for the British reader is whether poor diagnostic reliability is a problem in the UK? After all, in the UK we have alongside the DSM the *International Classification of Diseases* (the ICD). Perhaps the ICD leads to greater reliability than the DSM? Although this is a reasonable question to ask, when we take the research en masse, it actually shows that using the ICD leads to no greater diagnostic reliability than using the DSM.[11] This may partly explain why in countries like Britain where the ICD is used along with the DSM, many mental health researchers and professionals often prefer the DSM.[12] In fact, the National Institute for Clinical Excellence (the body that sets the clinical guidelines for the NHS) now recommends the use of the DSM over the ICD for disorders including depression.[13] Also, in my own experience of working in the NHS, the DSM is a very influential manual. But even if you wanted to dispute its precise impact, and as an article in the *British Journal of Psychiatry* put it: 'we'd still not avoid all the problems that beset the DSM [here in Britain]. Both manuals were developed and classify mental disorders in pretty much the same way. As the DSM writes: "the many consultations between the developers of the *DSM-IV* and the *ICD-10* … were enormously useful in increasing the congruence and reducing meaningless differences in working between the two systems".'[14] Herbert Pardes also confirmed this to me when recounting that 'the DSM worked very closely with the ICD to get worldwide cooperation between diagnostic categories.' In other words, diagnostic reliability is a problem for international psychiatry – whichever manual you employ, the reliability rates are broadly the same.

This leads me to one final point about the reliability problem that would be perilous to overlook: what would happen if some day reliability rates in psychiatry were to improve dramatically? This question is important because it reveals a more fundamental problem for psychiatry that it has yet to solve: even if every psychiatrist on the globe independently diagnosed the same patient with the same disorder (for example, with 'social anxiety disorder'), this would still not *prove* that social anxiety disorder actually exists in nature, that it's actually a discrete, identifiable biological disease or malfunction of the brain. You require much more than mere agreement to prove that. You need hard evidence. Unless our sciences can test whether what we agree on is objectively the case, agreement counts for nothing from a scientific standpoint. So even if psychiatrists reach high diagnostic agreement at some future point, this would not prove that the mental disorders with which they diagnose patients actually exist as valid disease entities. There need to be other procedures to establish that. So the issue is: are there other procedures? And if so, what exactly are they?

This question is so central to the entire psychiatric enterprise that I decided to ask Robert Spitzer myself.

2
The DSM – a great work of fiction?

On a sunny May morning in 2012, I catch the train from New York City. As we leave Penn Station the train slowly rattles under the Hudson River before emerging onto the wasteland of industrial New Jersey. After travelling for about 30 minutes through a bleak landscape of largely abandoned warehouses, signs of a more affluent suburbia begin to break through. With each passing mile the houses get bigger, the cars shinier and the landscape lusher, until we finally reach Princeton University.

I'm travelling to Princeton this May morning because three years earlier Dr Robert Spitzer had moved out there from nearby West Chester. His wife had taken a job at a local research laboratory, and Spitzer, now in his late 70s, had decided to embark upon one last adventure. They had chosen a large and comfortable house in the historic leafy suburbs just north-east of the university, and as my taxi pulled up outside it was clear they had chosen well.

'Come on in', said Spitzer, dressed in shorts, sandals and a loose sports top, as he led me into the living area. 'You wanna stay for lunch?'

Still reeling from my mountainous American breakfast, I struggled to say, 'Sure, that'd be nice.'

'Before we do that', said Spitzer, to my great relief, 'how

about we first sit down so I can tell you what you want to know?'

Once we had settled in our chairs, the first question I had for Spitzer concerned one of the other major changes he introduced into the DSM. What I didn't mention in the last chapter is that while he created a new checklist system and sharpened the definitions for each disorder, he also introduced over 80 new disorders, effectively expanding the DSM from 182 disorders (*DSM-II*) to 265 (*DSM-III*). 'So what', I asked Spitzer, 'was the rationale for this huge expansion?'

'The disorders we included weren't really new to the field', answered Spitzer confidently. 'They were mainly diagnoses that clinicians used in practice but which weren't recognised by the DSM or the ICD. There were many examples: borderline personality disorder was one, and so was post-traumatic stress disorder. There were no categories for these disorders prior to *DSM-III*. So by including them we gave them professional recognition.'

'So presumably', I asked, 'these disorders had been discovered in a biological sense? That's why they were included, right?'

'No – not at all', Spitzer said matter-of-factly. 'There are only a handful of mental disorders in the DSM known to have a clear biological cause. These are known as the organic disorders [things like epilepsy, Alzheimer's and Huntington's disease]. These are few and far between.'

'So, let me get this clear', I pressed, 'there are no discovered biological causes for many of the remaining mental disorders in the DSM?'

'It's not for many, it's for *any*! No biological markers have been identified.'

'Well, it's important to hear you say this, because this is something most people simply don't know. I didn't know it when I started out training as a psychotherapist. Most of my patients don't know it today. And I suspect for many people reading this interview it will come as a surprise too.* 'So if there are no known biological causes', I continued, 'on what grounds do mental disorders make it into the DSM? What other evidence supports their inclusion?'

'Well, psychiatry is unable to depend on biological markers to justify including disorders in the DSM. So we look for other things – behavioural, psychological; we have other procedures.'

Before we look at these other procedures, let me explain why you are probably surprised to hear that biological research did not guide the DSM's expansion. This may sound strange to you because we all expect psychiatry to work much like the rest of modern, mainstream medicine. In mainstream medicine a name will be given to a disease only *after* its pathological roots have been identified in the body. With few exceptions that is how general medicine operates: once you have discovered the physical origins of a problem, you then give it a name such as cystic fibrosis, cancer or Crohn's disease. But the surprising truth about psychiatry is that it largely operates in completely the opposite way. Rather, psychiatry first *names* a so-called mental disorder *before* it has identified any pathological basis in the body. So even when there's no biological evidence that a mental disorder exists, that disorder can still enter the DSM and become part of our medical culture.

---

* If you're one of the surprised or sceptical, I'll inspect this claim more thoroughly in later chapters.

Of course, the fact that psychiatry operates differently does not mean that its procedures are necessarily wrong. The only way to decide this is to assess whether psychiatry's alternative methods are scientifically valid. To find out if this is the case, I asked Spitzer to take me through the procedures his Taskforce followed when deciding whether to include a new disorder. For example, if the findings of biology didn't help the Taskforce to determine what disorders to include in *DSM-III*, then what on earth did?

'I guess our general principle', answered Spitzer candidly, 'was that if a large enough number of clinicians felt that a diagnostic concept was important in their work, then we were likely to add it as a new category. That was essentially it. It became a question of how much consensus there was to recognise and include a particular disorder.'

'So it was agreement that determined what went into the DSM'?

'That was essentially how it went – right.'

What sprung to mind at Spitzer's revelation was the point I made in the previous chapter about agreement not constituting proof. If a group of respected theologians all agree that God exists, this does not prove that God exists. All it proves is that these theologians believe he does. So in what sense is psychiatric agreement different? Why, when a committee of psychiatrists agree that a collection of behaviours and feelings point to the existence of a mental disorder, should the rest of us accept they've got it right? Perhaps, in the absence of biological evidence to convince us, they can produce other kinds of evidence to assure us that their agreements were justified? In other words, what was the evidence leading the Taskforce to agree that a new disorder should be included in the DSM?

•

Before coming back to Spitzer for an answer, let me first put this question to the psychologist Professor Paula J. Caplan, currently a Fellow at Harvard University's Kennedy School, and former consultant to two DSM committees. I interviewed Paula from my home in London in late April 2012, precisely because she has extensively assessed the evidence that guided many of the decisions the DSM Taskforce made.

One of the disorders she has focused on closely was called 'masochistic personality disorder'. Spitzer's Taskforce wanted to include this new disorder in the DSM for people who displayed 'masochistic traits' such as those thought to invite harsh treatment from others, or those leading people to seek out pain for enjoyment. Now, a crucial reason why Paula Caplan and other critics objected to these traits being called symptoms of a psychiatric disorder was because these traits were also said to be typical of women who were victims of violence. So it was thought that this diagnosis was very dangerous, not only because it could be used in courts of law to suggest that female victims of violence were in fact bringing it upon themselves (because they had a 'masochistic personality disorder'), but also because it could be used to let perpetrators of violence off the hook – they were simply doing what these women supposedly wanted.

So after much opposition from Caplan and other psychologists, the committee finally decided to rename masochistic personality disorder as 'self-defeating personality disorder' – or the neat SDPD. But the critics then argued that this change in name still implied that there was something 'self-defeating' in these victims – something compelling them in some way to invite abuse upon themselves. 'So the change in name was not really a victory at all', said Caplan to me energetically, 'since by renaming the disorder as SDPD nothing really had changed: the renamed disorder could still be used to claim that women victims of abuse, well, kind of asked for it.'

When Caplan made this point to Spitzer, he remained simply unmoved. In fact, his desire to keep SDPD was so strong, it would have been understandable had the critics retreated. But they didn't. Rather, at the last hour, Caplan devised a simple plan: 'I decided to scrutinise thoroughly the very research used to justify including SDPD in the DSM.' And here's what she found.

Firstly, she discovered only two pieces of research – a remarkably small number by anyone's standards. But as surprising as this discovery was, when Caplan actually looked at the research she became incredulous. 'It was so methodologically flawed', said Caplan animatedly, 'that it would fail an undergraduate examination. In fact, it was so full of basic errors that I actually decided to use it on an undergraduate exam in which I asked students to point out every conceivable methodological error, because his study had so many.'

For example, in Spitzer's research a group of psychiatrists at only one university, who already accepted SDPD existed, were shown some old case studies. All then unanimously agreed that the patients in them had SDPD. Caplan pointed out that just because some psychiatrists at one hospital diagnosed their patients with SDPD, that was not proof that the disorder actually exists. As Caplan said: 'all Spitzer's research proves is that a group of psychiatrists working in the same institution gave the same label – rightly or wrongly – to a given set of behaviours.'[1] It proves nothing more than that.

'But if you think that first piece of research was weak', continued Caplan, 'then consider the second piece. This involved sending out a questionnaire to a selected number of members of the American Psychiatric Association. This asked them whether the diagnosis SDPD should be included in the DSM. If they voted "yes" then they were asked to describe what they thought the characteristics of SDPD were. If they voted "no" then they were asked to return the questionnaire, blank, without any clinical data. This meant that the only data gathered about the characteristics of SDPD was data obtained from people who believed in the existence of SDPD in the first place.'

So how many psychiatrists believed SDPD to exist – how many voted 'yes'?

An official report showed that only 11 per cent of those who returned the questionnaire described what they thought the characteristics of SDPD were.[2] So essentially only 11 per cent voted 'yes', which is surely not a representative sample of the psychiatric community. But what made matters worse is that the questionnaire was also sent to many psychiatrists who already supported the diagnosis and who were deliberately screened into the study. And these psychiatrists, we can assume, made up a proportion of this 11 per cent.[3]

Caplan has therefore convincingly argued that neither piece of research justifies creating a new mental disorder. But that didn't stop Spitzer, as she said, from proudly reporting in the DSM that the nature of SDPD was defined by examining the 'data' from a single questionnaire; a questionnaire Spitzer claimed had been 'distributed to several thousand members of the APA.' 'Spitzer does not report the methodological flaws in his research,' said Caplan incredulously, 'and instead leads us to believe the creation of this disorder was based upon widespread scientific consultation and study.'

•

I have discussed at length the case of SDPD because it forces us to ask whether other disorders were included in the DSM on the basis of equally poor scientific evidence. Was this just an isolated example, or is it quite representative? To try to find out, I decided to read to Spitzer the following quotation, which claims that the research backing was not just poor for SDPD but for most of the mental disorders Spitzer's team included. This verdict comes from one of the leading lights on Spitzer's Taskforce, Dr Theodore Millon. Here's what he said about the DSM's construction:

> There was very little systematic research, and much of the research that existed was really a hodgepodge – scattered, inconsistent, and ambiguous. I think the majority of us recognized that the amount of good, solid science upon which we were making our decisions was pretty modest.[4]

Once I'd read this quote to Spitzer, I asked him whether he agreed with Millon's statement. After a short and somewhat uncomfortable silence, Spitzer responded in a way I didn't expect:

'Well, it's true that for many of the disorders that were added, there wasn't a tremendous amount of research, and certainly there wasn't research on the particular way that we defined these disorders. In the case of Millon's quote, I think he is mainly referring to the personality disorders … But again, it is certainly true that the amount of research validating data on most psychiatric disorders is very limited indeed.'

Trying not to look shocked, I continued: 'So you're saying that there was little research not only supporting your inclusion of new disorders, but also supporting how these disorders should be defined?'

'There are very few disorders whose definition was a result of specific research data', responded Spitzer. 'For borderline personality disorder there was some research that looked at different ways of defining the disorder. And we chose the definition that seemed to be the most valid. But for the other categories rarely could you say that there was research literature supporting the definition's validity.'

Spitzer's admission so surprised me that I decided to check it with other members of his Taskforce. So on a rainy English Monday I called Professor Donald Klein in his New York office to ask whether he agreed with Spitzer's account of events. Klein had been a leader on the Taskforce, and so was at the heart of everything that went on.

'Sure, we had very little in the way of data', Klein confirmed through a crackling phone line, 'so we were forced to rely on clinical consensus, which, admittedly, is a very poor way to do things. But it was better than anything else we had.'

'So without data to guide you', I nudged carefully, 'how was this consensus reached?'

'We thrashed it out, basically. We had a three-hour argument. There would be about twelve people sitting down at the table, usually there was a chairperson and there was somebody taking notes. And at the end of each meeting there would be a distribution of events. And at the next meeting some would agree with the inclusion, and the others would continue arguing. If people were still divided, the matter would be eventually decided by a vote.'

'A vote, really?' I asked, trying to conceal that I hardly felt reassured.

'Sure, that is how it went.'

Renee Garfinkel, a psychologist who participated in two DSM advisory committees, also confirmed the unscientific processes by which key decisions were made: 'You must understand', said Garfinkel to me bluntly, 'what I saw happening on these committees wasn't scientific – it more resembled a group of friends trying to decide where they want to go for dinner. One person says, "I feel like Chinese food", and another person says, "No, no, I'm really more in the mood for Indian food", and finally, after some discussion and collaborative give and take, they all decide to go have Italian.'

Garfinkel then gave me a concrete example of how far down the scale of intellectual respectability she felt those meetings could sometimes fall. 'On one occasion I was sitting in on a Taskforce meeting, and there was a discussion about whether a particular behaviour should be classed as a symptom of a particular disorder. And as the conversation went on, to my great astonishment one Taskforce member suddenly piped up, "Oh no, no, we can't include *that* behaviour as a symptom, because *I* do that!" And so it was decided that that behaviour would not be included because, presumably, if someone on the Taskforce does it, it must be perfectly normal.'

According to other members of the Taskforce, these meetings were often haphazard affairs. 'Suddenly, these things would happen and there didn't seem to be much basis for it except that someone just decided all of a sudden to run with it', said one participant. 'It seemed', another member admitted, that 'the loudest voices usually won out'.[5] With no extensive data one could turn to, the outcome of Taskforce decisions often depended on who in the room had the strongest personality. 'But the problem with relying on consensus', reiterated Garfinkel, 'is that in the discussion some voices will just get quieter, either because they don't want to fight or because they see they're the minority. And snap, that's when the decision is made.'

Admittedly, when the Taskforce lacked expertise on a particular disorder, Spitzer would consult the relevant leaders in the field. But this also led to chaotic meetings that members often found difficult to participate in. One of the few British members on the Taskforce, a psychiatrist called David Shaffer, recalled how such meetings often unfolded. '[In these] meetings of the so-called experts or advisers, people would be standing and sitting and moving around. People would talk on top of each other. But Bob [Spitzer] would be too busy typing notes to chair the meeting in an orderly way.'[6]

In an article for *The New Yorker*, Alix Spiegel recounts how two new disorders ('factitious disorder' and 'brief reactive psychosis') made it into the DSM through such disorderly consultations:

> Roger Peele and Paul Luisada, psychiatrists at St Elizabeth's Hospital, in Washington, DC, wrote a paper in which they used the term 'hysterical psychoses' to describe the behavior of two kinds of patients they had observed: those who suffered from extremely short episodes of delusion and hallucination after a major traumatic event, and those who felt compelled to show up in an emergency room even though they had no genuine physical or psychological problems. Spitzer read the paper and asked Peele and Luisada if he could come to Washington to meet them. During a forty-minute conversation, the three decided that 'hysterical psychoses' should really be divided into two disorders. Short episodes of delusion and hallucination would be labelled 'brief reactive psychosis,' and the tendency to show up in an emergency room without authentic cause would be called 'factitious disorder.' 'Then Bob asked for a typewriter,' Peele says. To Peele's surprise, Spitzer drafted the definitions on the spot. 'He banged out criteria sets for factitious disorder and for brief reactive psychosis, and it struck me that this was a productive fellow! He comes in to talk about an issue and walks away with diagnostic criteria for two different mental disorders!' Both factitious disorder and brief reactive psychosis were included in the *DSM-III* with only minor adjustments.[7]

What is striking about the construction of the DSM is that the procedures it followed often had very little to do with 'science' as most people understand the term, because, in short, the evidence was lacking. The problem here is obvious. When a group of scientists sit down to decide whether something is true, they consult the evidence. If the evidence points to a clear conclusion, then irrespective of whether an individual scientist likes it, the result has to be accepted. That is how science works. The evidence is king. But when you don't have evidence to decide the issue for you, people's opinions, beliefs, hopes and prejudices begin to intrude. In this instance, the scientist who desires a particular conclusion suddenly speaks up, argues loudly, and may, through sheer force of character, have their preferences accepted. And when there is no evidence to guide me, it can easily become largely a matter of personal or professional preference whether I vote this way or that. Voting, in other words, is not a scientific activity. It is a cultural activity. People vote for class presidents, union leaders, political parties and a host of other things. And yes, sometimes their votes are vindicated, but often they are not. Votes can disappoint. This is because a vote is not a guarantee that the thing voted for is real or true or good or certain. Votes are at best informed guesses, and at worse punts in the dark, and so when anything is voted into existence, whether it be a new leader, a political policy, or indeed a new mental disorder, the likelihood that we have got it wrong is never far away.

•

As soon as Spitzer's *DSM-III* was published in 1980, it became a sensation. The almost 500-page-long manual sold out immediately. The publisher, the American Psychiatric Association, was taken completely off guard. It took nearly six months to catch up with the orders that came flowing in. The new manual was purchased not only by psychiatrists, but by nurses, social workers, lawyers, psychologists, by anyone with any connection to psychiatry.[8] And the enthusiasm quickly spread far beyond the United States. In Britain, for example, the manual had such impact that by the end of the 1980s most British psychiatrists were being trained to use the DSM.[9] Furthermore, Spitzer's DSM categories quickly became those that guided all research into psychiatric disorders internationally. This meant that the disorders studied by researchers in Germany, Australia, Canada, Britain, India and elsewhere were those defined and listed in Spitzer's DSM. In short, the book ultimately changed the fundamental nature of research and practice within the field, not to mention the lives of tens of millions of people diagnosed with the psychiatric disorders listed therein.

And yet, as the influence of the manual spread, the truth about its construction remained obscure. Most professionals using the manual simply didn't know (and still don't know today) the extent to which biological evidence or solid research failed to guide the choices the Taskforce made. They didn't know that the definitions of the disorders contrived, the validity of the disorders included, and the symptom thresholds people must meet to receive the diagnosis were not decided by serious scientific evidence, but were the product of committee decisions that, at best, reflected the well-meaning professional opinions of a small subset of psychiatrists. In short, most people didn't know that the fundamental changes Spitzer brought to global psychiatry required only the consensus of an extremely small group of people. Indeed, as Spitzer openly confirmed to me in our interview: 'Our team was certainly not typical of the psychiatry community, and that was one of the major arguments against *DSM-III*: it allowed a small group with a particular viewpoint to take over psychiatry and change it in a fundamental way.'

'What did you make of that criticism?', I asked.

'What did I think of that charge? Well, it was absolutely true! It was a revolution, that's what it was. We took over because we had the power.'

Within a couple years, this powerful few had established for a whole new generation where the thin membrane separating psychiatric disorder from the ordinary troubles of life should be set. They had also created and defined approximately 80 new mental disorders, which very quickly became household names or, for many, established disease realities. Disorders like post-traumatic stress disorder, major depression, social phobia and borderline personality disorder gradually became as real and solid in the popular imagination as tonsillitis, shingles or the common cold. And all the while, the truth about the processes going on behind the scenes remained carefully hidden; processes that, as the next chapter will show, have dramatically increased the number of us today being branded psychiatrically unwell.

•

On the evening of my interview with Robert Spitzer, I decided to take a walk through Princeton's pristine university campus before meeting an old friend for drinks. It was a joy to be walking in the warm evening air, as only days earlier I had flown in from London and one of the wettest Aprils since records began. In contrast, Princeton was positively Mediterranean, and I couldn't believe my luck. So after walking a while I sat down on a bench, stretched out my legs still heavy with jetlag, and looked up contentedly at the dust of stars beginning to illuminate the night sky. And it was at that moment, on that bench, that a crucial realisation dawned.

It started by my recalling something Paula Caplan had mentioned to me days earlier. 'Mental disorders', she had said, 'are nothing more than constellations.' At the time I'd not given the comment much thought, but now, having spoken to Spitzer, her analogy seemed suddenly perfect. Just think about it. As far back as historical records go, we have tried to order this chaos of sparkling orbs into meaningful patterns or configurations, drawing lines between individual stars to create the constellations we know from our schoolbooks: Orion, Leo, Apus and Aquarius. Most other cultures have also engaged in this astrological map-making. Hindu, Chinese, Inca and Australian Aboriginal have all forged their unique celestial maps: this is why when someone from Bangalore or Sichuan looks up at the very same night sky as you, they identify different constellations. Their culture has taught them to read the sky differently. They see their own, not your, astral designs. And that's why Caplan's analogy now made so much sense to me: mental disorders are also man-made maps. Maps linking up our separate feelings and behaviours like astrologers do the galactic stars. One star characterises sleeplessness, another a visual hallucination, another a constant tic, a violent outburst or sexual lethargy. And when these separate items are joined with lines, a new pattern, a new disorder is forged.

Viewed from this standpoint, the DSM committee did not actually *discover* mental disorders, at least not in any traditional scientific sense. Rather, they *contrived* them, by drawing lines between painful emotional experiences. One disorder linked up fear, panic and uncontrolled bouts of anxiety (this would be called 'specific phobia'), another disorder linked up low self-esteem, lethargy, and a low capacity for pleasure (and this would be called 'dysthymia'). And so it went until 274 various patterns had all been given separate names: major depressive disorder, self-defeating personality disorder, oppositional defiant disorder, somatisation disorder, and so on. Looked at in this way, and as will become clearer in later chapters, mental disorders aren't therefore waiting to be discovered, like molecules or bacteria. They are much like the constellations, which are imposed upon the night sky. Sometimes these map-makers draw patterns that make sense, but sometimes they don't; and sometimes they make mistakes so dramatic that it's hard to put things right again.

As I stood in Princeton that balmy evening, I knew that I must now explore what happens when mistakes are made. What happens when human traits are linked up into configurations that you and I would not recognise as psychiatric disease? And if the constellations increase in number, is there a danger they will begin to colonise so much of our emotional landscape that little remains that can be called normal? This was the question I now knew I had to pursue in my next set of interviews.

3
The medicalisation of misery

In June 2011 I met Sarah Jones, a single mother of two and a care worker at a community centre in west London. Sarah had a warm smile and a welcoming manner; and as she spoke about her family and work, her love for both shone through. But when the topic turned to her seven-year-old son Dominic, she seemed suddenly overcome with anxiety. 'Dominic is a lovely boy, he really is, but last year he started getting agitated and aggressive. He was doing badly at school, being disruptive, and then he got into a fight. The school psychologist wanted Dominic to get a doctor's assessment, and I felt under real pressure to go. So after seeing Dominic for 25 minutes the doctor said he was suffering from ADHD [attention deficit hyperactivity disorder] because he had all the classic symptoms: hyperactivity, impulsivity and inattention. The doctor said medication would help. So Dominic is now on pills – and yes, he seems less distracted sometimes, but he also doesn't seem himself either. It feels like a part of his spirit has gone.' Sarah's distress was palpable. 'I just don't know what to do.'

Month on month, year on year, increasing numbers of children like Dominic are being diagnosed with mental disorders like ADHD. In fact, diagnoses of ADHD have risen so sharply in the last ten years that 5.29 per cent of the global child population is now thought to suffer from the condition (with prevalence rates in North

America and Europe pretty much equal at around 5 per cent).[1] This vaulting rise in ADHD is consistent with a growth in other childhood psychiatric disorders. If we add up the prevalence rates for all childhood disorders, for example, it's estimated that between 14 and 15 per cent of children now suffer from a diagnosable mental disorder in any given year.[2] But high as these figures may be, they pale in comparison to those relating to the adult population. For example, the National Institute of Mental Health in the US now claims that about 26.2 per cent of all American adults suffer from at least one of the DSM disorders in a given year;[3] while the Office for National Statistics on Psychiatric Morbidity in the UK reports a similar figure.[4] Effectively this means that one in four people is afflicted by a mental disorder in a given year each side of the Atlantic; a figure made more startling when you consider that in the 1950s it was more like one in a hundred, and at the beginning of the twentieth century a meagre one in a thousand. So what can account for this massive surge in mental disorders? Why in just a few decades have we apparently all become so psychiatrically unwell?

There are at least three hypotheses that mental health practitioners use to try to account for the escalating rates. As the book unfolds we will look at them in greater depth, but to give you just a quick snapshot, let me outline them briefly.

The first goes like this: as the pressures of contemporary life have increased, so too have our levels of stress and strain, leading to an upsurge in poor mental health. Now while this explanation seems reasonable enough, as we will see later, it's difficult to ascertain whether contemporary life is really so much more stressful than life many decades ago. Indeed, as many sociological studies have shown, social stress may have actually decreased rather than increased in recent years, therefore putting this hypothesis under strain.*

The second hypothesis is also problematic: it says that mental disorders have increased because today's psychiatrists are better than in the past at recognising psychiatric disease. Perhaps advances in technology now allow clinicians to more readily spot and diagnose disorders that once slipped below their radar. While this hypothesis again has some obvious appeal, its weakness is that by and large diagnostic technology has not improved: there are still no objective tests that can confirm the validity of any psychiatric diagnosis, a fact supported by the continued low diagnostic reliability rates.

To be at our most generous, then, the first two hypotheses are at best plausible explanations that can partly account for the rise in disorder rates. But what if these hypotheses do not reveal the whole picture? What if they overlook a crucial yet not-so-obvious third possibility: that psychiatry, by progressively lowering the bar for what counts as mental disorder, has recast many natural responses to the problems of living as mental disorders requiring psychiatric treatment? In other words, has psychiatry, by redrawing the line between disorder and normality, actually created the *illusion* of a pandemic?

Let's now look at this third hypothesis in greater depth.

•

---

* See Chapter 12 on recent well-being rates in Britain.

In March 2011 a group of scientists undertook a comprehensive study on nearly 1 million Canadian schoolchildren. What they did was look at the medical diagnoses that all these children had received within the period of one year. The children were between the ages of six and twelve, and the scientists were particularly interested in how many of them had been diagnosed with ADHD. Once the calculations were conducted and the results came in, the scientists were initially baffled by what they found: the precise month in which a child was born played a significant role in determining whether they would be diagnosed with ADHD.

As odd as this may sound, the figures published in the *Canadian Medical Association Journal* are plain to see. The line that charts the monthly diagnostic rates, rather than resembling a mountain range that peaks and dips from month to month, instead moves steadily and diagonally upwards from January to the end of December. To translate this into numerical terms, we find that 5.7 per cent of all boys born in January were diagnosed, compared with 5.9 per cent born in February and 6.0 per cent born in March. After that, the monthly rates rise incrementally until boys born at the end of the year are *30 per cent* more likely to be diagnosed than boys born at the start. If this figure seems startling to you, then just consider the female diagnostic rates: girls born at the year's end in December are *70 per cent* more likely to be diagnosed with ADHD than girls born in January. So what's going on here?

The clue to unravelling this puzzle has nothing to do with birth signs or weather patterns or cosmic shifts in the lunar calendar. It rather has to do with the simple fact that children in the same year at school can be almost a full year apart in actual age. This is because children with birthdays just before the cut-off date for entering school will be younger than classmates born at earlier times of the year. So in Canada, for example, children born at the beginning of the year are eleven months older than classmates born at the end of the year. This means that January children have a full eleven months developmental advantage over their December peers. And an eleven-month gap at that age represents an enormous difference in terms of mental and emotional maturity.

As I was keen to find out more about the implications of this study, I interviewed Dr Richard Morrow, one if its lead researchers.

'Well, the most important thing we noticed', Morrow said candidly, 'is that the younger kids in the classroom were far more likely to be diagnosed with ADHD because their relative immaturity was being mistaken for symptoms of ADHD.' The relative immaturity of the younger children was, in effect, being wrongly recast as psychiatric pathology. 'And this clearly explained for us', continued Morrow, 'why the younger you are in your class the more likely you are to be diagnosed with this condition. And this is happening not just in Canada, because we found that wherever similar studies have been conducted [e.g. the US and Sweden] they have reached the same results – the younger you are in your class the more likely you'll get the diagnosis – it's a pretty wide phenomenon.'

The reason why Morrow's research is so important to us is because it provides a clear example of what is known as medicalisation – namely, the process by which more and more of our human characteristics are seen as needing medical explanation and treatment. Now, while in the Canadian study it's clear that the effects of medicalisation can be deleterious, this is obviously not the case in all instances – indeed medicalisation, at best, has often been a force for good. For example, it was right to use medicine to tackle biological conditions such as Huntington's disease or epilepsy that were once unhelpfully understood as religious problems (to be healed only by prayer or church attendance). And yet there are forms of medicalisation that are clearly unhelpful, that invasively spread medical authority where it was never designed to go. For instance, 'problems' such as low achievement, certain kinds of truancy or under-performance have attracted medical diagnoses and intervention in our children, as have many normal reactions to the demands of adult life that are labelled as 'stress disorders' to be biologically explained and pharmacologically treated.

The issue of medicalisation is so crucial because it concerns where the very limits of medical intervention should be drawn. At what point does medicalisation begin to undermine the health of a population? At what point does it begin to turn what should be a matter for spiritual, philosophical or political understanding and action into an issue to be managed by medicine alone? This question has particular relevance for psychiatry. For psychiatry, as we will soon see, has been accused more often than any other medical specialism of incorrectly medicalising our normal actions and responses. The question for us right now, then, is to what extent this accusation is true …

•

In an interview for a BBC documentary in 2007, the film's maker, Adam Curtis, posed this very question to Robert Spitzer. He asked Spitzer whether the DSM had committed any errors. More precisely, he asked whether when creating *DSM-III* his Taskforce had adequately distinguished between human experiences that were disordered, and human experiences that were not. In effect, had the Taskforce, when creating their list of mental disorders, wrongly labelled many normal human feelings of sadness and anxiety as indicators of medical disorders that required treatment?

Spitzer, with noticeable regret, admitted that this had occurred. He then went on to explain why:

'What happened is that we made estimates of prevalence of mental disorders totally descriptively, without considering that many of these conditions might be normal reactions which are not really disorders. And that's the problem. Because we were not looking at the context in which those conditions developed.' (In other words, Spitzer's DSM only described the symptoms of each disorder, but never asked whether these so-called symptoms could, in some circumstances, actually be normal human reactions to difficult life situations.)

An incredulous Curtis therefore said to Spitzer: 'So you have effectively medicalised much ordinary human sadness, fear, ordinary experiences – you've medicalised them?'

'I think we have to some extent', responded Spitzer. 'How serious a problem it is, is not known. I don't know if it is 20 per cent, 30 per cent. I don't know. But that is a considerable amount if it is 20 or 30 per cent.'[5]

In this interview with Adam Curtis, Spitzer admitted that his Taskforce was interested only in the experiences that characterised the disorder. It was not interested in understanding the individual patient's life or *why* they suffered from these experiences. Because these contextual factors were overlooked, experiences of sadness, anxiety or unhappiness were often listed as symptoms of underlying disorders, rather than seen as natural and normal human reactions to certain life conditions that needed to be changed.[6]

You'll remember that I met Spitzer in his house in leafy Princeton. Well, as we sat eating lunch, I took the chance to ask him about the Curtis interview. I recounted to him his exchange with Curtis, at which he slowly put down his spoon and turned his head in my direction. It was immediately clear to me he was unwilling to elaborate on what he had previously said. It also seemed clear that he had shifted his position since that earlier interview with Curtis. While he still agreed that normal reactions were being recast as psychiatric illness, he now seemed keener to locate the cause of this problem elsewhere: not in how the DSM was constructed and written, as he had confessed to Curtis, but in how the manual is being used. As Spitzer explained:

'[In clinical practice] there is often too much emphasis placed by some on the diagnostic criteria of the DSM [in other words, if a person has 'this set of symptoms' then they have 'this disorder']. This approach ignores other things that are important when making an assessment, such as the context in which the person became ill. So there has been a move towards an over-emphasis on diagnostic criteria, and a neglect of assessing the social context in which the person is living.'

In other words, problems emerge when a psychiatrist simply tries to match the patient's experiences with one of the disorders in the book, without investigating *why* the person is suffering as they are. After all, perhaps they are suffering because they have just lost their job, or someone dear to them, or because they're struggling with their identity, with poverty, with failure in love or work – who knows, perhaps their lives just hadn't turned out as they'd hoped. There are countless understandable reasons why a person may suddenly start manifesting emotions or behaviours that can be easily misread as 'symptoms' of 'major depression' or 'anxiety disorder' – reasons that may have nothing to do with the person being psychiatrically unwell. What Spitzer told me, in other words, is that when clinicians ignore such contextual factors, they'll see mental disorders where there are none. And in these cases diagnoses are assigned unnecessarily. This of course helps us unravel what we encountered in the Canadian study – younger children in the classroom being diagnosed with ADHD. The context of their relative age had not been taken into account. When a consideration of context is omitted, in other words, damaging diagnostic oddities ensue.

•

In 1994 Spitzer's revolutionary *DSM-III* had finally reached the end of its shelf life. It was now time for it to be replaced by a new edition: *DSM-IV*. The person who replaced Spitzer as Chair of the new DSM was a psychiatrist called Dr Allen Frances. Frances was appointed Chair for many reasons – firstly, at that time he was head of psychiatry at Duke University, so he was believed to have the credentials. Also, the American Psychiatric Association made it clear they wanted someone who had dabbled in many fields.

Frances again seemed to fit the bill: not only had he trained in psychoanalysis, but he had conducted research on other therapeutic approaches, including studies of medications for depression and anxiety. Furthermore, because Frances had been minimally involved in the construction of Spitzer's *DSM-III*, he knew how diagnostic books are made and so could apply that knowledge in the construction of *DSM-IV*.

When I interviewed Frances in May 2012, his *DSM-IV* was still being used and sold around the world. This meant that apart from one minor revision in 2000, the manual he published in 1994 has for two decades shaped research and practice within the global psychiatric community.[7] What I wanted to know from Frances, therefore, was whether, with the benefit of hindsight, he felt his *DSM-IV* Taskforce had made any mistakes. In short, did his manual unleash any unintended negative consequences that he now regrets?

'Well, the first thing I have to say about that', answered Frances confidently, 'is that *DSM-IV* was a remarkably unambitious and modest effort to stabilise psychiatric diagnosis, and not to create new problems. This meant keeping the introduction of new disorders to an absolute minimum.'

What Frances meant was that his Taskforce added only eight new disorders to the main manual.* And this is indeed a modest amount considering that Spitzer had introduced around 80. Yet, from another standpoint, this claim to modesty is somewhat wobbly – it ignores that Frances included an additional 30 disorders for 'further study' in the

* Much higher standards were applied when it came to adding new diagnoses. Eight were added, out of the more than 100 proposed. Four others were reformulated. An additional 30 were included in an appendix for further study.

appendix, and that he subdivided many existing disorders. So if we include these appendix disorders and subdivisions (all of which patients can be diagnosed with), Frances actually expanded the DSM from 292 to 374 disorders.

But obviously Frances, and I believe wrongly, had chosen not to count these inclusions and subdivisions, for he continued: 'Yet despite that conservatism, we learned some pretty tough lessons – we learned overall that even if you make minimal changes to the DSM, the way the world uses the manual is not always the way you intended it to be used.'

Letting his claim of conservatism stand for a moment, I asked Frances to elaborate on what he meant by learning some pretty tough lessons.

'Well, we added a bipolar II [this is for individuals who have manic episodes who also might have a bipolar tendency]. We also added Asperger's disorder [this was to cover people who didn't have full-blown autism but who had considerable problems with autistic-like symptoms], and finally we added ADHD [for people who had attention issues coupled with hyperactivity]. And, well, these decisions helped promote three false epidemics in psychiatry.'

Trying to sound unfazed, I asked Frances to clarify what he meant by three false epidemics.

'Well, I mean we now have a rate of autism that is twenty times what it was fifteen years ago. By adding bipolar II we also doubled the ratio of bipolar versus unipolar depression, and that's resulted in lots more use of antipsychotic and mood stabiliser drugs. We also have rates of ADHD that have tripled, partly because new drug treatments were released that were aggressively marketed. So every decision you make has a trade-off, and you can't assume the way you write the DSM will be the way it'll be used. There will be so many pressures to use it in ways that will increase drug sales, increase school services, increase disability services and so forth.'

At this point in our interview I could not help but recall young Dominic and the Canadian schoolchildren, all of whom had been diagnosed with ADHD. Was the head of the team who created the modern ADHD category now admitting that potentially millions of children just like them (not to mention the adults) were being wrongly diagnosed with this and other mental health conditions?

I put the question to him directly: 'So are you saying that the way the DSM is being used has led to the medicalisation of a number of people who really don't warrant their diagnoses?'

'Exactly.'

'Can you put a figure on how many people have been wrongly medicalised?'

'There is no right answer to who should be diagnosed. There is no gold standard for psychiatric diagnosis. So it's impossible to know for sure, but when the diagnosis rates triple over the course of fifteen years, my assumption is that medicalisation is going on.'

Once in a while when conducting interviews you hear a confession that hits like a thunderclap. And this for me was one of those moments. Here was the creator of *DSM-IV* admitting that many new disorders they included actually helped trigger the unnecessary medicalisation and medication of potentially millions of people.

But is this the whole story? Could things actually be even worse than this? Frances' admission relates only to the *new* disorders he included, but what about all the *old* disorders (around 292) that he imported directly into his *DSM-IV*? After all, Frances' team significantly reformulated only four of the 292 disorders inherited from Spitzer. In other words, while Frances 'conservatism' meant many new disorders were placed in the appendix rather than in the main text, did it not also allow the continued existence of countless disorders that frankly had woeful scientific support? For example, some of the more eccentric disorders that Frances' Taskforce incorporated into *DSM-IV* (and that also, incidentally, are contained in the ICD) included: stuttering (disturbance in normal fluency and time-patterning of speech); premature ejaculation (which requires no explanation); caffeine-related disorders (caffeine withdrawal and dependency); expressive language disorder (below average language skills); social phobia (shyness and/or fear of public speaking); sexual aversion disorder (absence of desire for sexual activity); reading disorder (falling substantially below the reading standard for your age, intelligence and age-appropriate education); female orgasmic disorder (persistent or recurrent delay in, or absence of, orgasm); non-compliance with treatment (a diagnosis that can be given when the patient resists treatment); conduct disorder (repetitive or persistent violation of societal norms or others' rights); transsexualism (identifying with a gender not of your sex); and oppositional defiant disorder (for children with irritable mood swings and who overly defy authority) – to name a few.

Notwithstanding that most critics find indefensible the idea that such problems are psychiatric disorders, I asked Frances why he carried these and the other disorders from

Spitzer's DSM into *DSM-IV*. Why didn't he, as Chair of *DSM-IV*, simply remove them on the grounds that they were eccentric and enjoyed remarkably weak scientific support?

'If we were going to either add new diagnoses or eliminate existing ones, there had to be substantial scientific evidence to support that decision. And there simply wasn't. So by following our own conservative rules we couldn't reduce the system any more than we could increase it. Now, you could argue that is a questionable approach, but we felt it was important to stabilise the system and not make arbitrary decisions in either direction.'

'But one of the problems with proceeding in that way', I pressed, 'is that it assumes the DSM system you inherited from Spitzer was fit for purpose. For example, it assumes that the disorders Spitzer included, and the diagnostic thresholds Spitzer's team set [i.e. the number of symptoms you need to warrant any diagnosis] were themselves scientifically established ...'

'We did not assume that at all. We knew that everything that came before was arbitrary [Frances quickly corrects himself] – we knew that *most* decisions that came before were arbitrary. I had been involved in *DSM-III*. I understood their limitations probably more than most people did. But the most important value at that time was to stabilise the system, not change it arbitrarily.'

'So you are essentially saying that you set out to stabilise the arbitrary decisions that were made during the construction of *DSM-III*?'

'In other words', corrected Frances, 'it felt better to stabilise the existing arbitrary decisions than to create a whole assortment of new ones.'

At this point I simply didn't know what else to say. Frances, it seemed, had said it all. While his 'conservatism' had stopped his Taskforce from including excessive numbers of new disorders (if we exclude the appendix inclusions and subdivisions), it had also led him to import Spitzer's mistakes into the DSM that has now been in medical use for eighteen years and is still in use today as I write. Not only did the eccentric and non-scientifically established disorders remain, but so too did many of the low thresholds that people had to meet in order to warrant receiving a diagnosis. This meant that the dramatic medicalisation of normal human reactions to the problems of everyday life was allowed to proceed unchecked.

•

Towards the end of my interview with Allen Frances I asked him whether he felt that the problem of medicalisation would be solved some day soon. I asked this question because a new edition of the DSM (called *DSM-5*) arrived in May 2013. Will this new DSM, many years in the making, rectify the problems of the past?

'That question is crucial', replied Frances passionately, 'because the situation I think is only going to get worse: *DSM-5* is proposing changes that will dramatically expand the realm of psychiatry and narrow the realm of normality – resulting in the conversion of millions more patients, millions more people, from currently being without mental disorders to be psychiatrically sick. What concerns me about this reckless expansion of the diagnostic boundaries is that it will have many unintended consequences, which will be very harmful. The ones I am most particularly concerned about are those that will lead to the excessive use of medication, and most particularly antipsychotic medication because it leads to excessive weight gain.'

Frances was particularly disturbed by *DSM-5*'s proposal to make ordinary grief a mental disorder. While previous editions of the DSM highlighted the need to consider excluding people who are bereaved from being diagnosed with a major depressive disorder, in the draft version of *DSM-5* that exclusion for bereavement has been removed. This means that feelings of deep sadness, loss, sleeplessness, crying, inability to concentrate, tiredness and low appetite, if they continue for more than two weeks after the death of a loved one, could actually soon warrant the diagnosis of depression, even though these reactions are simply the natural outcome of sustaining a significant loss.[8]

'Reclassifying bereavement as a symptom of depression will not only increase the rates of unnecessary medication', said Frances angrily, 'but also reduces the sanctity of bereavement as a mammalian and human condition. It will substitute a medical ritual for a much more important time-honoured one. It seems to me there are cultural rituals – powerful and protective – that we shouldn't be meddling with. But by turning a normal painful human experience into a medical illness we are doing precisely that.'

'Are there any other new inclusions in *DSM-5* that worry you?'

'Yes, sure – there is the new "generalised anxiety disorder", which threatens to turn the aches and pains and disappointments of everyday life into mental illness. There is "minor neurocognitive disorder" that will likely turn the normal forgetting of ageing into a mental illness. There is "disruptive mood dysregulation disorder", which will see children's temper tantrums become symptoms of disorder. These changes will expand the definition of mental illnesses to include more people, exposing more to potentially dangerous psychiatric medications.'*

'So where do we go from here?' I asked Frances, feeling rather bleak. 'What will happen when this version goes forward?'

'I am worried that the already existing diagnostic inflation will be made much worse, and excessive medication treatment will increase. This will also lead to a misallocation of resources away from the more severely ill, who really need help, and towards people who don't need a diagnosis at all and will receive unnecessary and harmful treatment.'

'Will this do damage to the credibility of psychiatry itself?'

'Well, James, I think things have been unfortunate in that regard', said Frances pensively, 'because that's already happened.'

For one reason or another, it just felt appropriate to end our interview there …

•

The criticisms Frances expressed to me regarding *DSM-5* have now infected the wider mental health community. During 2012 a flurry of damning editorials, including two

---

* It was pointed out to me that although it was right for Frances to indicate the danger of these new inclusions, he failed however to discuss how disorders in his *DSM-IV*, like his older version of generalised anxiety disorder, similarly led to the pathologisation of many ordinary responses – in this case stress reactions.

eloquent pieces in *The Lancet* and one in the *New England Journal of Medicine*, strongly criticised the *DSM-5*'s pathologisation of grief. This chorus of dissent has been repeated in over 100 critical articles in the world press and by the appeal of over 100,000 grievers worldwide. Furthermore, in 2012 an online petition went live protesting against the changes proposed by *DSM-5*. It was endorsed by over 50 organisations related to the mental health industry, including the British Psychological Society, the Danish Psychological Society and the American Counselling Association. The arguments they advanced were similar to those made by Allen Frances: by lowering the diagnostic thresholds for warranting a diagnosis more people may be unnecessarily branded mentally unwell; by including many new disorders that appear to lack scientific justification there will be more inappropriate medical treatment of vulnerable populations (children, military veterans, the infirm and the elderly); by de-emphasising the socio-cultural causes of suffering, biological causes will continue to be wrongly privileged. The petition concludes: 'In light of the growing empirical evidence that neurobiology does not fully account for the emergence of mental distress, as well as new longitudinal studies revealing long-term hazards of psychotropic treatment, we believe that these changes pose substantial risks to patients/clients, practitioners, and the mental health professions in general.'[9]

With all this mounting pressure on the DSM to seriously mend its ways, who better to ask than the Chair of *DSM-5* whether these criticisms will have any impact. So I tried to get the interview, but unfortunately I was unsuccessful. This is because, as I would learn, all members of the *DSM-5* Taskforce have actually been forced to sign confidentiality agreements by the American Psychiatric Association, which makes their talking frankly about what they are doing legally precarious. So instead I put the question to the next best person, Dr Robert Spitzer. Did Spitzer think the *DSM-5* should stop and reconsider before going through with publication?

'Well, they have already had to postpone publication several times', said Spitzer, 'because of all the problems. So I just think the DSM committee should ask the APA for an extension until all the work has been done properly. But this is not happening, and I think it's because the APA wants it published next year [i.e. 2013] – it needs the huge amount of money sales will bring.'

Indeed, the APA has spent around $25 million developing *DSM-5* and now needs to recoup its investment, as the coffers are low. As it needs the $5 million a year the DSM makes from its global sales, the APA is now in a real dilemma, as Allen Frances pointed out: 'Will it put public trust first and delay publication of *DSM-5* until it can be done right? Or will it protect profits first and prematurely rush a second- or third-rate product into print?'

The answer came on 31 December 2012. On that fateful day, and having only minimally addressed a handful of criticisms, the American Psychiatric Association finally approved the new *DSM-5* for global publication. This means that by the time you have this book in hand, on a shelf somewhere very near you now sits the manual that will influence mental health practice for decades to come. What further damage all this will do, of course remains to be seen. But if the legions of authoritative critics are to be believed, then the future doesn't look so bright. We can expect more and more misdiagnosed schoolchildren, like those in Canada, and vastly more medicated youths, like young Dominic in London. In short, we can expect vaulting numbers of children and adults alike to become yet more statistical droplets in the ever-expanding pool of the mentally unwell.

4
The depressing truth about happy pills

When I started out working as a psychotherapist in the National Health Service, I knew nothing about the construction of mental disorders, about false psychiatric epidemics, about the out-of-control medicalisation of normality, about the disconcerting confessions of DSM chairmen, and certainly nothing about the alarming facts that I'm about to reveal to you now. Like most people inside and outside medicine, I used to think that antidepressants worked. I pretty much accepted, like everyone else, that these pills modified chemical levels in the brain in order to create improved states of mind. This was why most of the patients referred to me for long-term psychotherapy were taking antidepressant medication. The pills helped stabilise their mood to the point that they could engage more successfully in therapeutic work. That is what I was taught. That was the party line. But it wasn't long before I discovered the party line is wrong.

But how could this be? The pharmaceutical industry makes over £12.5 billion each year from antidepressant medications (this excludes the £18 billion made yearly from antipsychotic sales). Doctors are convinced of their effectiveness. The media regularly reports how these pills help millions each year. And countless patients claim that their lives would have been ruined without them. Surely it would be simply obtuse to suggest that all this money and all this enthusiasm is the product of a misleading myth? Well, that is precisely what I'm about to suggest, as solid scientific research now shows clearly that antidepressants don't actually work, or at least not in the way people think.

•

In early May 2011 I wrote to Professor Irving Kirsch, an Associate Director at Harvard Medical School and today perhaps the most talked-about figure internationally in antidepressant research.[1] When I asked whether I could see him at Harvard, he suggested that we rather meet in the UK. Kirsch, it turns out, had been a professor at the University of Hull before moving to Harvard. When working at Hull, he and his wife had become so attached to the surrounding area that they had decided to keep paying the rent on their lovely Georgian villa, which was sequestered in an urbane and picturesque hamlet just outside the city. And so one morning I set off from my home in Shepherds Bush, west London, and drove 250 miles up the M1 to rural Yorkshire.

I interviewed Kirsch in his drawing room. It was grand and congenial, like an Oxbridge senior common room, covered with authentic Georgian furnishings and illuminated by a flickering chandelier and a sweeping bay window. We settled into two plump chairs in front of the old fireplace, whose chimney breast was stuffed with newspaper to ward off the bitter Yorkshire wind.

As I surveyed the man and the scene, it was clear to me that Kirsch had travelled great distances in his life – socially, artistically, geographically and intellectually. He was a real live product of the American Dream. He was born to Polish immigrants in New York City in 1943. He'd been heavily involved in the civil rights movements of the 1960s, while also writing pamphlets against the Vietnam War (at the request of Bertrand Russell). Before becoming a psychologist in his early thirties, he'd worked as a violinist, accompanying artists like Aretha Franklin and enjoying a stint in the Toledo Symphony Orchestra. Just before gaining his PhD in psychology in 1975, he was nominated for a Grammy award for an album he'd produced that included excerpts from the Watergate Hearings.[2] His journey is, therefore, an interesting one: his life has oscillated between music, psychology, pacifism and politics – between New York, California, Krakow, Boston, and now Scorborough.

It seemed ironic to start our interview by asking Kirsch, a devoted pacifist in his youth, about a war he had recently started within the medical community, ignited by his scientific research. The war was so turbulent because so much was at stake, not only for the millions of adults and children who now take antidepressants, or for the hundreds of thousands of doctors around the globe who are now prescribing them, but also for the pharmaceutical industry that makes billions a year from antidepressant sales. What I wanted to know from Kirsch was how someone so seemingly peaceful could have created such pandaemonium.

'By complete accident', answered Kirsch with a boyish smile as he sipped tea from an antique china cup. 'I wasn't really interested in antidepressants when I started out as a psychologist. I was more taken by the power of belief – how our expectations can shape who we are, how we feel, and, more specifically, whether or not we recover from illness.

Like everyone else at the time, I just assumed antidepressants worked because of their chemical ingredients. That's why I'd occasionally referred depressed patients to psychiatrists for antidepressant medication.'

Everything would change for Kirsch after a young man called Guy Sapirstein approached him in the mid-1990s. This bright and eager graduate student had become fascinated by the placebo effects of antidepressants. What gripped Sapirstein was how depressed patients could actually feel better by taking a sugar pill if they *believed* it to be an antidepressant. This led Sapirstein to wonder about the extent to which antidepressants worked through the placebo effect, by creating in patients an expectation of healing so strong that their symptoms actually disappeared.

Once Sapirstein had outlined his interests, Kirsch knew he wanted to get on board. And so it wasn't long before both men set about investigating the question together: to what extent did antidepressants work because of their placebo effects?

'Instead of doing a brand-new study', said Kirsch, 'we decided to do what is called a meta-analysis. This worked by gathering all the studies we could find that had compared the effects of antidepressants to the effects of placebos on depressed patients. We then pooled all the results to get an overall figure.' In total, Kirsch's meta-analysis covered 38 clinical trials, the results of which, when taken en masse, led to a startling conclusion. 'What we expected to find', said Kirsch lowering his teacup, 'was that people who took the antidepressant would do far better than those taking the placebo, the sugar pill. We couldn't have been more wrong.' And if you look at the graph below you'll see exactly what Kirsch means.[3]

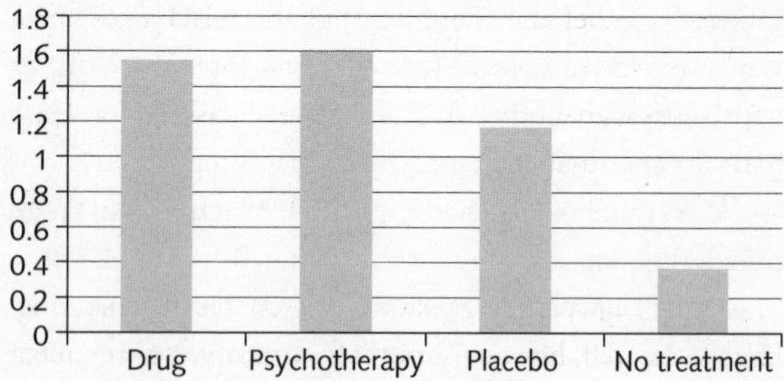

The first thing you'll notice is that *all* the groups actually get better on the scale of improvement, even those who had received no treatment at all. This is because many incidences of depression spontaneously reduce by themselves after time without being actively treated. You'll also see that both psychotherapy and drug groups get significantly better. But, oddly, so does the placebo group. More bizarre still, the difference in improvement between placebo and antidepressant groups is only about 0.4 points, which was a strikingly small amount. 'This result genuinely surprised us', said Kirsch leaning forward intently, 'because the difference between placebos and antidepressants was far smaller than anything we had read about or anticipated.' In fact, Kirsch and Sapirstein were so taken aback by these findings that they initially doubted the integrity of their research: 'We felt we must have done something wrong in either collecting or analysing the data, but what? We just couldn't figure it out.'

So in the following months Kirsch and Sapirstein analysed and re-analysed their data. They cut the figures this way and that; counted the statistics differently; checked what pills were assessed in each trial, and re-examined their findings with colleagues. But each time the same results came out. Either they couldn't spot the mistake, or there was simply no mistake to spot. Eventually there seemed to be no alternative other than to take the risk and publish their findings that antidepressants, according to their data, appeared to be only moderately more effective than sugar pills.

'Once our paper appeared', Kirsch recalled smiling, 'there was, well, how can I put it? – controversy. The most significant critique was that we had left out many important trials from our meta-analysis. Perhaps an analysis that included those studies would lead to a different conclusion?' Indeed, a professor at George Washington University called Thomas Moore pointed this out to Kirsch by revealing that his meta-analysis had assessed only the *published* trials on whether antidepressants work. Their study had therefore failed to include the drug trials left *unpublished* by the pharmaceutical companies who conducted them. Kirsch and Sapirstein had been unaware that pharmaceutical companies regularly withhold trials from publication. When Kirsch looked into how many trials this amounted to, he was aghast at what he found: nearly 40 per cent of all the trials on antidepressant drugs had not been published – a staggering amount.

I asked Kirsch what he did next. 'Well, Moore suggested we appeal to the Freedom of Information Act to get the unpublished company studies released, and once we were successful, we undertook a second meta-analysis, which now included *all* the studies – both published and unpublished.' As the results came in from this second meta-analysis, Kirsch grew even more alarmed: they showed that the results of his first study were plainly wrong.

Antidepressants didn't work moderately better than placebos – they worked almost no better at all.

•

Moving away for a moment from the cosy sitting room in which Kirsch was recounting his unsettling series of discoveries, let's backtrack a little so I can illustrate to you how the studies into antidepressants that Kirsch's meta-analysis surveyed were conducted.

To do this, imagine yourself in the following scenario. You've been depressed for at least two weeks (the minimum time needed to be classed as depressed, as you'll recall from Chapter 1). So you eventually decide to drag yourself to your doctor, who asks you if you would like to participate in a clinical trial. The aim of this trial is to test the effectiveness of a new antidepressant drug (which may cause some side-effects if you take it). Your doctor then explains how the trial will work: before you are given the antidepressant your level of depression will be measured on something called the Hamilton Scale. This is a scale that runs from 0 to 51, and the task is to work out where you sit on this scale. Your doctor explains that, to work out where you sit, the trial researcher will ask you a number of questions about yourself, such as whether you're sleeping well, whether you have an appetite, whether you're suffering from negative thoughts and so on. You'll then be given points for each of the answers you give. For example, if you answer that you're sleeping well you'll be given 1 point, whereas if you say you're hardly sleeping at all you'll be given 4 points. The more points you accumulate the higher you are rated on the scale, and the higher you are rated on the scale the more likely you are to be classed as depressed. That's how the Hamilton Scale works: if you're rated at 26 you're thought to be more depressed than if rated at 19. You've got the idea …

Now, after this initial assessment, the trial researcher will place you in one of two groups of patients and prescribe a course of pills. But there's a catch. You'll be told that only one group of patients will be prescribed the real antidepressant, while the other group will be given a placebo pill – a pill that's made of sugar and that therefore contains no active chemical properties. No one will be told which group they are in. Nor will anyone know what pill they are taking until their treatment has ended some three months later and their levels of depression have again been measured on the Hamilton Scale. Your first rating and second rating will then be compared. If your rating has gone down after treatment it means you have improved (and thus the pill has worked), and vice versa. Once the researchers gather the ratings for all patients in the trial, they can then compare the two groups to assess how superior the antidepressant is to the sugar pill in alleviating depression.

Now, imagine that the clinical trial you have just participated in contained about 500 other patients, all going through the same process as you. This of course is a significant amount, but it's still only one trial. What Kirsch did, you'll remember, is pool the results of *all* the trials he surveyed – published and unpublished. So in effect Kirsch's second meta-analysis collated the results of many thousands of patients, all of whom had been studied in trials like the one I have just described. And it was on the basis of this second analysis, as I mentioned a moment ago, that Kirsch reached the alarming conclusion that antidepressants work hardly better than placebos. Here's what his results looked like:

As in his first meta-analysis, which looked only at the published trials, Kirsch's second meta-analysis, which assessed both published and unpublished trials, revealed that *both* placebo and antidepressant groups got better. But his second meta-analysis also revealed that the difference in rates of improvement between the antidepressant group and the placebo group was insignificant. And that's the important bit. 'After surveying all the trials, we discovered that the antidepressant group only improved by 1.8 points on the Hamilton Scale over the placebo group', stated Kirsch. 'Now, this may not mean much to you. But what if I were to tell you that your score can be reduced by a full 6.0 points if you are merely sleeping better? Well, you'd rightly conclude that 1.8 is a tiny difference. And that's precisely why the NICE [National Institute for Clinical Excellence] has said there must be a difference of at least 3.0 points for the difference to be deemed clinically significant. Yet, the difference we found was only 1.8 points – totally clinically insignificant.'

Indeed, a 1.8 difference on the Hamilton Scale is barely noticeable in terms of a person's actual experience. But what was also interesting for Kirsch was that even the tiny 1.8 difference between the antidepressant and placebo groups still didn't mean antidepressants worked better than placebos. 'Just remember how the clinical trials work', Kirsch explained to me. 'You are told by your doctor you'll be given one of two pills. You are also told that the antidepressant pill will produce side-effects in most patients [like drowsiness, diarrhoea, nausea, forgetfulness, dry mouth and so on]. So what happens if after taking the pill, you start to experience some of these side-effects? Well, like most people you'll figure out that you're on the real drug. And believing you are on the real drug you'll now expect to get better. And it's this increased *expectation* of recovery that actually helps you improve.'

In other words, side-effects increase the placebo effect. And this is how Kirsch could account for the tiny 1.8 per cent improvement in the antidepressant over the placebo group.

So, in sum, Kirsch's second meta-analysis was far more dramatic than the first: it concluded that the new wave of antidepressants heralded as wonder drugs – Prozac, Seroxat (Paxil in the US), Lustral (Zoloft), Dutonin (Serzone), Cipramil (Celexa) and Effexor – worked no better than dummy pills for the vast majority of patients. There were about 10 to 15 per cent of people, the extremely depressed, for whom these pills worked in a very minor way (about 4 points better than placebos on the Hamilton Scale), but this meant, as Kirsch pointed out, that '85 to 90 per cent of people being prescribed antidepressants are not getting any clinically meaningful benefit from the drug itself'.

•

When Kirsch published his second analysis showing that antidepressants worked no better than sugar pills for the vast majority of patients, it immediately became front-page news in the most respected papers in the UK: *The Guardian*, *The Times*, *The Independent* and the *Daily Telegraph*. It made its way into newspapers and television and radio news programmes in the US, Spain, Portugal, Germany, Italy,

Britain, South Africa, Australia, Canada, China and many other countries. It was reported and debated in countless leading medical and scientific journals, including the prestigious journal *Science*. Overnight, it transformed Kirsch into a global object of media fascination.[4]

All this attention also made many in the medical community sit up and take note of his research. Just three months after his work was published, for instance, a survey was conducted on nearly 500 British doctors asking them whether Kirsch's findings would affect how they'd prescribe antidepressants in the future. Almost half of them, 44 per cent, said they would change their prescribing habits and consider alternative treatments. But this, of course, still meant that over 50 per cent intended to go on prescribing as usual. Most of these 50 per cent justified their position by arguing that in their clinical experience antidepressants do work, no matter what Kirsch's research indicates. I asked Kirsch what he made of this. 'Well, the truth is, these doctors are correct. Our research also shows that antidepressants work, but again, not for the reasons most people suppose. They work because of their placebo effects, not because of the chemical in the drug – and that's the point we were making.'

There were other criticisms of Kirsch's work: 'One we heard again and again was that the studies we surveyed must have been flawed. Some said these studies were too short to show the real effects of antidepressants. Others said that the patients studied were not depressed enough, while others said the patients were too depressed. But all these objections, taken as a whole, are very curious indeed, because the studies we surveyed were also those assessed by the regulatory agencies in the UK and US to justify approving these drugs for public use.[5] So if there were something wrong with the studies, why had the regulatory agencies in Europe and the US used them as a basis for approving these drugs?'

A further criticism, perhaps even more quixotic, was that even if the drugs don't work, it was still wrong of Kirsch and his colleagues to have published their results. Patients should be protected from findings that could undermine their faith in treatment. Kirsch disagreed adamantly: 'Without accurate knowledge, patients and physicians cannot make informed treatment decisions, researchers will be asking the wrong questions, and policy-makers will be implementing misinformed policies. If the antidepressant effect is largely a placebo effect, it is important that we know this. So that improvement can be obtained without reliance on addictive drugs which have potentially serious side-effects.'[6]

A final suite of criticisms was aimed at the methods Kirsch used. 'There were a number of papers criticising our statistical methods and redoing them', said Kirsch, 'some in appropriate ways, some in inappropriate ways, and some just making careless mistakes. But no matter how these analyses were done, nobody ever passed the 3.0 point threshold for clinical significance, which only gave additional support to our own conclusions.'

So Kirsch's research withstood the criticisms. But were there any other studies that actually replicated his findings? I put this question to Walter Brown, professor of psychiatry at Brown University, who has co-authored two studies analysing the same set of clinical trials that Kirsch surveyed.

His answer was unequivocal: 'We pretty much found the same thing as Kirsch. For a small minority of patients (the most severely depressed), our studies showed that antidepressants may have some minor benefits. But for mildly/moderately depressed patients', said Brown earnestly, 'our results confirm that antidepressants offer no advantage over placebos, alternative therapies, or even moderate exercise.' In other words, Brown's research confirmed that the vast majority of people taking antidepressants do not receive any chemical benefit.[7] 'There is no question that these drugs are over-hyped to the general public', reiterated Brown. 'The research shows they are not as good as the psychiatric establishment and the pharmaceutical industry claim they are.'

While Irving Kirsch and Walter Brown reached the same conclusions independently, so too did a major study of antidepressants that the NHS commissioned. This NHS study also declared that the difference between placebos and antidepressants is so modest that for mild to moderate depression antidepressants are not worth having at all. 'Our results were again like Irving Kirsch's', said Dr Tim Kendall, lead author of the study published in *The Lancet*. 'Our widespread comparative meta-analysis of antidepressants showed pretty clearly that the difference between the published and unpublished studies of antidepressants in children, was that for the published trials, all the drugs worked, while for the unpublished trials none of the drugs worked. And if you looked at the published and unpublished combined, you'd probably recommend the use of only one drug for childhood depression.'

At the time he was conducting that research, Kendall was also responsible for helping draw up the treatment guidelines for depression throughout the NHS. 'Once we had those figures', said Kendall, 'we asked the depression guideline group what they would conclude if they only saw the published trials, and what would they conclude if they saw the whole data set (the published and the unpublished). We found that seeing the whole data set changed their view completely. And that is the key bit: drug companies not publishing negative trials actually changes clinicians' minds.'

Given the results of studies outlined above, why do the regulatory agencies that evaluate antidepressants continue to approve these drugs for public use? Well, the key to answering this question is to realise that the regulatory agencies do not take into account the results of negative trials when deciding whether to approve an antidepressant. For example, the Food and Drugs Administration (FDA) in the United States and the Medicines and Healthcare Products Regulatory Agency (MHRA) in Britain require that a company show in just *two* clinical trials that their drug is more effective than a placebo.[8] This is the case even if there are five, ten or fifteen clinical trials showing negative results. In other words, regulatory agencies *discard the negative trials*. And they do this no matter how many there are. All they require are two positive trials to give the green light for public use.*

The FDA in the US has publicly defended what may seem to you or me a dubious approval process. In 2012, for instance, Lesley Stahl of CBS News interviewed the director

* But this is not all. For a trial to be considered 'positive', the difference between placebo and antidepressant does not have to be clinically significant, just 'statistically significant' (e.g. it can be just one or two points on the Hamilton Scale), which essentially means it can be small enough to make no real difference in people's lives.

of the unit responsible for approving antidepressants, Dr Tom Laughren. Stahl asked Laughren why the FDA requires merely two positive clinical trials to approve a drug, even though many negative trials may exist. Laughren's response was faltering and confusing:

> *Laughren*: We consider everything that we have, we look at those trials individually …
>
> *Stahl*: But how are you knowing that the two positives deserve bigger strength in the decision?
>
> *Laughren*: Getting that finding of a positive study by chance, if there isn't really an effect, is very low. That's basic statistics, and that's the way clinical trials are interpreted [by the FDA]. A separate question is whether or not the effect you are seeing is clinically relevant.
>
> *Stahl*: OK – is it clinically relevant?
>
> *Laughren*: The data we have shows that the drugs are effective.
>
> *Stahl*: But what about the *degree* of effectiveness?
>
> *Laughren*: I think we all agree that the changes that you see in the short-term trials, the difference in improvement between drug and placebo is rather small.
>
> *Stahl*: So it's a moderate difference?
>
> *Laughren*: It is a, well, it's a small – it's a modest difference.

When I spoke to Dr Tim Kendall about Laughren's admission, Kendall confessed that he'd actually seen this interview and that it had completely baffled him: 'What I do remember when listening to Laughren was that it actually sounded to me a little like mumbo jumbo', Kendall said frankly. 'I couldn't make any sense of it at all. From our point of view, whenever you're doing a trial or a meta-analysis, it is all about probabilities – about the probability that one thing works better than another, and that probability depends upon the evidence. Now, if someone conceals some of that evidence, it simply skews the result. So the idea that regulatory bodies like the FDA will continue approving drugs on the basis of only two positive trials, and are not bothered by all the other negatives, strikes me as wholly indefensible.'

Regulatory agencies in the UK, the US and beyond seem to think otherwise, and the consequence of this has been dramatic: it has allowed an inordinate yearly rise in antidepressant prescriptions. Just consider the facts: antidepressant usage has more than tripled in the US since 1986, reaching a staggering 235 million prescriptions in 2010.[9] And in Europe the situation is the same – the figures have tripled in recent years. In 2010 approximately 10 per cent of all middle-aged Europeans were taking antidepressants,[10] while in 2012 over 50 million antidepressants were dispensed in England alone.[11] In other words, despite the damning research about antidepressant efficacy, and despite the NICE recommendations that we pull back on antidepressant use, continued regulatory approval has allowed prescriptions to just keep going up and up. Of course, this raises uncomfortable questions regarding the precise relationship between the regulatory agencies and the pharmaceutical industry. Do the agencies have an incentive to set the bar so low? While I won't answer that question right now, you can be sure I'll get to it eventually …

•

I was nearing the end of my interview with Irving Kirsch when the window beside us suddenly rattled loudly from a powerful gust of Yorkshire wind. The rain had been falling for a while, forming thick sinuous rivulets down the window panes. For over an hour I'd been totally engrossed in Kirsch's story, and neither of us had cared about the deluge outside. As I turned my eyes back to Kirsch, I noticed he looked a little tired. It was time to wrap this one up, but first I had one final question to ask: 'How are things going to turn out? I mean, if serious research now shows that antidepressants work little better than sugar pills for most patients, while prescription rates still keep soaring, what's going to alter things – where do we go from here?'

'To be frank, James, I just don't know', sighed Kirsch uneasily. 'Back in the old days I used to think I was good at predicting the future, but I've lost my confidence now. I would like to think change is slow, even for the scientific community. But my hope is that change eventually occurs.' Kirsch looked pensive as he gazed out of the window. 'Perhaps in the future, twenty years from now, antidepressants will be seen as blood-letting is seen today. That would be really something. But to get to that point, well, it will take time … yes, it will take lots of time.'

I left Kirsch's house understanding why the war he had triggered within medicine was still raging so aggressively. There were forces at play that made it impossible for his findings alone to change the current state of affairs. Perhaps science wasn't in control after all. Perhaps something else, more powerful and less easy to identify, was holding up serious reform. But what could this be? On the long drive back to London, I said to myself that no matter how much more digging it would take, and how many more interviews, I wouldn't stop until I found out …

5
Dummy pills and the healing power of belief

In May 1993 a mental disorder that had been in *DSM-III* was repackaged, renamed and given new life in *DSM-IV*. It was called 'premenstrual dysphoric disorder' (PMDD) and was listed in the DSM as a mental disorder.[1] Up to 8 per cent of women were said to suffer from the condition. And the condition was apparently nasty. Its main symptoms occurred two weeks before menstruation, and included feelings of fatigue, anxiety, emotional instability, lack of interest in daily activities and difficulty in concentrating. In short, premenstrual dysphoric disorder was first presented as if it were an exaggerated form of PMT – premenstrual tension.

By the early 2000s the number of women being diagnosed with PMDD was rising exponentially. And there were some obvious reasons for this. The first was that in 1998 the Food and Drugs Administration in the US recognised the condition as an official mental disorder. This freed up doctors to start diagnosing PMDD when previously they had no disorder category to which they could match premenstrual experiences. Secondly, the pharmaceutical industry now had the green light to market the disorder and its cure. Eli Lilly was the first to step up to the plate by spending $30 million on advertising its chemical cure. The following advert by the company is illustrative of the type of commercial with which it flooded the airwaves once FDA approval was granted. It shows a woman who has lost her keys growing increasingly frustrated. The voice-over breaks through:

> Think it's PMS? It could be PMDD, premenstrual dysphoric disorder. You know, those intense moods and physical symptoms the week before your period. Sound familiar? Call to get free information about PMDD and a treatment your doctor has to relieve its symptoms. Why put up with this another month?[2]

Alongside such direct-to-consumer pharmaceutical advertising, Eli Lilly launched a marketing campaign targeting psychiatrists, gynaecologists and mental health providers, who were soon all receiving promotional materials – flyers, free samples, invitations to Lilly talks, and unsolicited visits from pharma reps. As the word spread in the medical world, diagnoses of PMDD quickly soared and so did the prescriptions.

In the mid-2000s when I met a psychotherapist called John, I was therefore unsurprised to hear that he had recently treated a patient diagnosed with the condition. Sarah, 25, began telling him her story.

'I really am not myself at the moment', she said. 'I feel so anxious and confused all the time. I just feel, well, different. It started about six months ago. I began to get these god-awful cramps before my period. It was like my guts were digesting acid. I also got these piercing headaches and I'd feel emotionally all over the place. I went to my local doctor and he sent me to a gynaecologist. The gynaecologist said he couldn't find anything physically wrong with me and so said I was probably suffering from a psychological disorder I'd never heard of before – premenstrual dysphoric disorder – and he said he could help.'

Sarah then said she had been prescribed a new drug called Sarafem. John asked her what she knew about the drug.

'Not much really', she shrugged nonchalantly. 'Apparently it helps with mood swings and other stuff. I take it every day, and I think it helps with the headaches. I don't know much more than that.'

Let me fill the gaps in Sarah's knowledge.

The pharmaceutical giant Eli Lilly makes Sarafem. Its name is a reworking of 'seraphim', a Hebrew word meaning 'angel', a word with obvious female overtones.[3] Its packaging also conjures up stereotypical female associations. The pill is encased in a pretty pink and lavender shell and is heralded by Lilly as a wonder cure for this distinctly female premenstrual disorder. So far so good. Now here comes the interesting bit. What Eli Lilly initially concealed from the thousands of women taking the pill is that the pill is actually Prozac. Chemically, Sarafem and Prozac are exactly the same. The only difference between them is that their names and packaging are different. Sarah, like thousands of other women, was taking Prozac and didn't know it.*

---

* About this case a colleague usefully pointed out: since there is no scientific evidence that there actually is a premenstrual mental illness, if taking this drug helped Sarah, then neither she nor her therapist would know why or be able to discuss why. Furthermore, by treating her based on the PMDD diagnosis, when there is no evidence that PMDD even exists, the doctor was subjecting her to experimental treatment without her knowledge or consent.

•

There are a lot of possible interpretations for why Eli Lilly engaged in what you or I might be tempted to see as corporate deception. The first is that it obviously saved the company a great deal of money. It's cheaper to repackage existing pills than it is to develop new ones. In addition, Eli Lilly's patent protections on Prozac were running out a year after Sarafem would be released, so marketing Prozac under the new trade name would effectively extend patent protections for many more years.* Money matters.

But also surface appearances matter. Women are more likely to feel comfortable consuming pink pills than they are blue pills, because of the associations attached to the different colours. As an article on drug marketing in the *Boston Globe* said at the time: 'Drug designers propose colors for a particular medicine and help make sure there are no symbolic mistakes.'[4] An example of a symbolic mistake would be making a pink Viagra, or a menstruation pill that is dark red. Symbolic mistakes occur when the colour, shape or name of a pill does not resonate with its particular consumer. There has to be a positive correspondence between consumer and product to maximise the sales effect – or so the rationale goes.

A final interpretation for Prozac's rebranding is because Prozac is associated primarily with depression. And women labelled with PMDD are not depressed. Just as the patient, Sarah, wasn't. So a new name was required to effectively strip from Prozac associations that were potentially

---

* Patent protections for most pharmaceutical products are not lifelong, but last only for around seven years.

undesirable to this new consumer group. Laura Miller, a marketing associate for Eli Lilly, put it this way:

> [Women] wanted a treatment with its own identity. Women do not look at their symptoms as a depression, and PMDD is not depression but a separate clinical entity. Prozac is one of the more famous pharmaceutical trademarks and is closely associated with depression.[5]

By rebranding Prozac as Sarafem, Eli Lilly divided the one chemical into two separate pills for two different disorders. One pill continued to be marketed as an antidepressant. The other they marketed as a so-called premenstrual corrective. A new pill was born not because a new chemical had been found, but because a popular brand had been changed.

Nathan Greenslit, a young and dynamic professor at MIT's prestigious Science, Technology and Society Program, told me: 'Eli Lilly is not alone in rebranding pills.' As we exchanged messages about Sarafem online from our respective offices in London and Boston, Nathan, who has spent years studying the pharmaceutical industry, revealed that in 1997 the FDA approved GlaxoSmithKline's antidepressant, Wellbutrin, as a smoking cessation pill. But, again, because Wellbutrin was too well known as an antidepressant to be publicly accepted as an anti-smoking pill, it was rebranded as Zyban. GlaxoSmithKline marketed them as separate drugs that targeted separate and discrete disorders: Wellbutrin targeted depression, and Zyban nicotine addiction. The website for Zyban puts it this way: 'Zyban is a nicotine-free pill. Not a patch. Not a gum.' Under the heading, 'Zyban: Helping Smokers Quit Neurochemically', the site claims that 'while it is unclear exactly how Zyban works, it is thought to act on the part of your brain that is addicted to the ingredients in cigarettes'.[6]

'As was the case with Sarafem and Prozac', Nathan wrote in an article, 'the patient-directed information does not admit that Wellbutrin and Zyban are the same drug.'[7] By giving the old drugs a makeover, they could treat complaints other than those they were designed to treat originally.

What is interesting about these interpretations as to why the rebranding of Prozac occurred is that each is so entirely plausible that it's tempting for you and me to look no further for explanations. The name was changed for reasons of marketing and money – simple as that. But what if it isn't that simple? What if something else is going on here, something far trickier to understand, but something essential to complete the picture? Hold that question in mind.

•

In the last chapter I discussed the work of Harvard professor Irving Kirsch, and how it plunged psychiatry again into crisis by revealing that antidepressants do not work for the reasons people think. He showed that they work largely because of their placebo effects, and not for the chemical reasons most people believe. But what I did not discuss in that chapter was *how* placebos work. How can it be that a sugar pill with no active chemical properties can lighten your mood or decease your anxiety? The time has come to resolve that mystery.

In the 1980s the US National Institute of Mental Health sponsored a fascinating experiment.[8] It set out to evaluate the effectiveness of antidepressants and psychotherapy in the treatment of depression. The experiment was actually very simple. Before treatment began, it asked each patient the following question: 'What is likely to happen as a result of your treatment?' When the researchers calculated the results, a startling conclusion emerged: the answer the patient gave to this question predicted their therapeutic outcome. In other words, those who expected to feel better improved the most, while those who expected little or no improvement received the least benefit from treatment. Furthermore, this result was the same regardless of whether the patient had been treated with antidepressant medication, psychotherapy or a placebo. In short, whatever the therapy patients were given, the patients with positive expectations improved most. The conclusion: expectations matter.

But if expectations matter, is there anything that can be done to increase a patient's expectation of recovery, and, in turn, their therapeutic outcome? Well, the simple answer is yes. So to understand what can be done, imagine yourself in the following scenario.

You're sitting in lecture room listening to a presentation. But you're finding it difficult to concentrate because you have a throbbing headache. Now imagine that the man sitting next to you notices that you're in pain and offers you a small white pill, quietly telling you the pill will help you feel better. After some deliberation you decide to take the pill (perhaps unwisely) and see what happens. And after a while you notice, disappointingly, that nothing happens at all. So you turn to the man at the end and ask what he gave you. He replies that he gave you a sugar pill.

So surely we now have an explanation for why the pill didn't work – it was made of sugar. That would be the obvious answer. But the trouble with obvious answers is that they tend to lead us astray. For example, we know from placebo studies that the probable reason the pill didn't work will have less to do with it being a sugar pill than with *where* it was given to you, and by *whom*. You see, the man next to you was not a medical doctor, and the lecture room is not a hospital, and these contextual factors are significant enough to affect whether the pill will work. For example, if you were to meet the same man in a hospital and believe him to be a doctor, a curious thing would happen if he gave you the same pill: its effectiveness might increase by up to 40 per cent.[9] It's the same man and the same sugar pill, but the effects are now dramatically different. And they are different because the set of contextual meanings has been changed. You are in a hospital and you believe this person to be a doctor, and so you now expect the pill to work. And because you expect the pill to work, it's more likely to do so.

The point of the above illustration is to show that cultural meanings matter. They have the power to increase or decrease, almost subliminally, our expectations for recovery and therefore the extent to which we actually improve.

But how does this insight help us deepen our understanding of why Eli Lilly repackaged Prozac? How could this research be used to explain to Sarah why the pills she was taking were simply a glammed-up version of Prozac? Well, just recall for a moment that key to the repackaging process was altering the colour of the pill. There's our clue. Prozac is green and white, while Sarafem is pink and lavender. So maybe there's something about the colour of a pill that impinges not only upon its attractiveness but also upon its effectiveness? Could the very colour of a pill help it work?

An early experiment published in *The Lancet* explored this very question.[10] What the group of researchers did was gather up 56 medical students and hand each of them a package containing red and blue pills. All the students were told was that one colour represented a tranquilliser and the other a stimulant. After taking the pills, the students were asked which set of pills were the stimulants and which the tranquillisers. The majority concluded that the blue pills were the tranquillisers and the red pills the stimulants. They reached this conclusion because when taking the blue pills they felt far less alert and much drowsier than when taking the red pills. The researchers then told the students that, chemically, the blue and red pills were exactly the same – both were made entirely of sugar.

But how could dummy pills yield such different effects? The answer is again in recognising the power of cultural meanings. For the medical students the colours red and blue held very different meanings: red means 'hot', 'up', 'danger' (meanings fitting stimulated behaviour); while blue means 'down', 'calm', 'cool', 'quiet' (meanings fitting tranquillised behaviour). The meanings attached to the different-coloured pills affected the drug's perceived action and effectiveness.

Scientists like Dr Alan Branthwaite are not surprised by the power of placebo effects. I spoke to Dr Branthwaite in early February 2012. His manner was scholarly and cautious, but as soon as I raised the topic of placebo effects he became animated: 'These effects are staggering when you first encounter them, and they still stagger me today', he said. 'The human body is so fundamentally linked to the mind, that if you can spark the right mental associations then the body responds, sometimes in dramatic and unexpected ways.'

Alan won the medical community's acclaim when he published a paper in the *British Medical Journal* on placebo effects.[11] What his study set out to discover was whether the presence or absence of a trusted brand name on a pill can affect recovery. 'So we devised a neat experiment', said Alan enthusiastically. 'We gathered up about 835 women who regularly use painkillers for headaches, and then randomly assigned them to one of four groups. And we gave each group a different pill. The first group had aspirin labelled with a popular brand name; the second group had the same aspirin but with no brand name; the third group had a sugar pill marked with the popular brand name, and the fourth group had an unmarked sugar pill. The question was, which group would improve most?'

What Alan and his team were expecting to find was a small increase in the effectiveness of the branded pills. 'But what shocked us entirely was the extent of that difference. The group given the branded placebos improved almost 20 per cent more than those with the unbranded placebos. While branded aspirins also worked significantly better than unbranded ones. So here we had striking evidence that the presence of a trusted brand name can dramatically improve a pill's efficacy, even if that pill is completely inert.'

Taking these two studies together shows how surface things that may seem inconsequential to you and me (the colour or brand name of a pill) are crucially important to the healing process. Subliminally they play with our expectations for recovery; and expectations, in fear of repeating myself, can dramatically affect outcomes.

•

To try to get to the bottom of how these meaning effects work, I spoke to Daniel Moerman, distinguished professor of anthropology at the University of Michigan. Daniel has dedicated much of his professional life to investigating how cultural meanings affect bodily functioning, and is widely known in academia as a world leader in placebo research.

I suggested to Daniel how odd it is that the meanings we ascribe to a pill can sometimes be more powerful than its active substance, especially in the realm of psychopharmacology. 'Well, James, you're an anthropologist, right? You know the power of meaning! Every culture has its symbols and objects of veneration and it's no different with us. Once for us we revered crosses and statues of the Virgin Mary, now pills and stethoscopes capture our worship. So even an inert pill can affect us because it has shape and form and a context and it has language attached. It comes in a blue box or a pink box; it's taken in a pharmacy, doctor's room or hospital with all the panoply of a thousand years of medical tradition behind it to give it overwhelming symbolic weight.'

One of Moerman's recent studies shows how the power of medical sanction should not be underestimated.[12] Medical approval is crucial to everyone, even the most critical among us. What Moerman did was gather up 117 studies of ulcer drugs published between 1975 and 1994 to discover what drugs worked best. And when the results came in he realised something astonishing. In 1975 a new ulcer drug called cimetidine was released. It enjoyed excellent clinical success, eradicating on average 80 per cent of ulcers. However, as time passed the drug's efficacy strangely became lower and lower, until today cimetidine can claim to eradicate only 50 per cent of ulcers. So what had happened? Moerman explains the deterioration by pointing out that five years after cimetidine's release, a new drug called ranitidine arrived. This competing drug was considered superior to cimetidine, and as the new drug's popularity grew, the old drug's effectiveness declined. The correlation was staggering.

Of course there are different interpretations of this (questions of changes in methods etc.), but the most compelling, and to Moerman the most plausible, is that cimetidine lost its power because as new and supposedly superior drugs arrived, cimetidine ceased to be thought of as a superior drug. Belief in cimetidine had waned, and with this so did its clinical effectiveness. 'So it's clear', said Moerman animatedly, 'meaning matters!'

•

Let's now return to our original question. We know that Sarah was unaware that the drug she was taking was Prozac. She thought that Sarafem was a specific pill developed for her specific 'problem'. Sarah was wrong. What Sarah also didn't know was that Prozac was rebranded as Sarafem more for financial than scientific reasons. But the question remains about whether Prozac was rebranded for other reasons too. Was it rebranded because the company knew that Prozac would provoke only a small placebo effect in women suffering from so-called PMDD? Did Eli Lilly turn

Prozac into a distinctly female pill to achieve a higher placebo effect in this new patient group? In order to answer this question we first have to answer a broader one: does Big Pharma more generally make use of placebo studies to manipulate higher placebo effects in patients?

I put this question to Moerman: 'In my experience people in the pharmaceutical industry are either incredibly good actors or are remarkably dense. They are good actors if they make use of these studies but pretend not to, and they are dense if they don't make use of them at all.'

So, and to use Moerman's words, is the pharmaceutical industry led by actors or dunces? I decided to cut to the chase and find out for myself. I contacted Eli Lilly's headquarters in the UK and asked whether placebo studies are consciously used to create higher placebo effects in their consumers. The head of corporate affairs replied after some prompting, stating that due to 'competing priorities' they would be unable to provide me with an answer.

Competing priorities? What did that mean? I politely wrote back asking Eli Lilly for some clarification. They responded that my questions were 'very specific' and that the person who might answer them had simply chosen to decline.

So now you understand the problem. Questions like mine are rarely answered by the industry, because there are just some things companies don't want you or me to know. Pharmaceutical companies are notoriously secretive. They have a history not only of concealing how pills are developed and marketed, but of concealing negative trials that show their drugs in a bad light (as I'll show you in later chapters). So in the absence of corporate transparency, all we can rely on is indirect evidence to answer the actor/dunce question. Let's look at some of that evidence now.

Firstly, we know that companies regularly pay academics to discuss their work with company employees and executives. We also know that these companies have conducted their own in-house studies and data-mining, and have in recent years funded the work of leading placebo scientists like Ted Kaptchuk and Fabrizio Benedetti (even Branthwaite's study of brand names mentioned earlier was pharmaceutically funded). Furthermore, the American journalist Steve Silberman recently exposed how a massive study of placebo effects (undertaken by the Foundation for the National Institutes of Health) is being funded by companies including Merck, Eli Lilly, Pfizer, AstraZeneca and GlaxoSmithKline. 'In typically secretive industry fashion', Silberman told me during our interview, 'the existence of the project itself is being kept under wraps. FNIH staffers are willing to talk about it only anonymously, concerned about offending the companies paying for it.'

During our conversation, Silberman also mentioned that a few years ago when the Public Library of Science hosted a debate about whether the pharmaceutical industry should be allowed to continue advertising antidepressants to the general public, Randall S. Stafford, a senior consultant with Merck, GlaxoSmithKline, Bayer, and Proctor and Gamble, argued that banning the ads might result in an abrupt reduction of drug effectiveness by reducing the placebo effect en masse. 'This was an astonishing and very rare admission', Silberman said to me, 'because the pharmaceutical industry won't publicly acknowledge that the placebo response is giving a boost to the drugs they make. But here we had a major consultant openly declaring that the adverts are all about generating the expectations that help increase placebo effects, and that if you cut back on the marketing the pills' effectiveness will dramatically decrease.'

Again and again we find striking correspondences between what placebo researches tells us and how actual pills are being developed. These correspondences strongly suggest that companies are taking account of placebo research when developing and marketing their pills. For instance, recall for a moment the study I quoted earlier showing that blue sugar pills create sedating effects and red sugar pills create stimulating effects, even when the pills are made of sugar. Well, a team in the Netherlands has recently researched the actual colours of the pills that you and I take.[13] And it turns out that nearly 80 per cent of all the sedative pills were green, purple, blue or white (green, purple and blue are sedating colours); while of all the anti-depressants (uppers) only 5 per cent fell into the green, purple or blue category, 40 per cent into the white category, and all the rest were coloured in 'stimulating colours'. Is it just coincidence that companies are manufacturing pills that largely match the placebo research?

Without being allowed to observe these companies at work directly (trust me, I and many colleagues have requested access countless times – but the doors remain closed), the question whether companies are manipulating placebo research must continue to hang in the air. Of course the *indirect* evidence strongly suggests that placebo research is now regularly manipulated, that pills like Prozac are not just altered for reasons of marketing and money, but because the features of Prozac, its colour, its name and its associations, would not successfully evoke the placebo response in women labelled with PMDD. Did these companies believe that women required a different pill, with different hopes and expectations attached, to get the result they wanted? I know what I think. But given the absence of direct evidence, I'll just have to leave you to reach your own conclusion.

•

'Sarah, I have a question for you', John says carefully. 'Did you know that the drug you are taking is actually Prozac?'

Sarah's head tilts sharply to one side. 'Excuse me?'

'Well, what I mean is – did you know that Sarafem and Prozac are chemically exactly the same?'

Sarah sits back for a moment, looking at John sceptically. Then a sudden wave of anxiety flashes across her face. 'You're kidding me, aren't you?'

'I'm afraid I'm not, Sarah.'

'But … but that's wrong, isn't it'? Sarah looks distressed. 'Why would they do that?'

'Well, Sarah, that requires a complicated answer.'

'But isn't Prozac for depression? I don't have depression.'

'No, you don't, or at least you didn't … The important thing is that since taking the pills you feel different. Perhaps we could spend a little time now thinking about precisely how you feel different. So before we do anything, I want to explore the role that the pills you are taking have played in how you feel now.'

'What, you mean that Sarafem may be responsible for why I feel different?'

'I don't know, it's possible. Even so, it's important for us to find out.'

'Jesus, I didn't know.'

'Well, the sad truth, Sarah, is that most people don't ...'

In the next chapter I shall reveal the strange ways in which antidepressants can profoundly change us. And I'm not talking about 'curing' us. I'm talking about how they can alter our personality, sometimes in profound and unsettling ways. So if you think the rabbit hole is already deep, it's now time to see how truly deep it goes.

6
Mental oddities and the pills that cause them

On a popular daytime TV talk show, the host, Kilroy, announces to the audience the wonders of a new antidepressant drug:[1]

> *Kilroy*: This pill could solve all your problems. It is called Prozac. And it may mean the end of depression as we know it!
>
> [*Kilroy approaches a female member of the audience and directs the microphone towards her*]
>
> *Woman*: I have been taking Prozac for two years.
>
> *Kilroy*: And what difference has that made?
>
> *Woman*: Brilliant!
>
> *Kilroy*: Oh, she is smiling. [*audience laugh*] Her eyes are lighting up!
>
> *Woman*: I feel as if I am back to normal. [*laughing*]
>
> *Kilroy*: You feel normal.
>
> *Woman*: Yeh. [*beaming smile*]
>
> *Kilroy*: You feel a better person?
>
> *Woman*: Yeh, yeh. [*smiling*]

> *Kilroy*: [*now turning to her husband*] Has it worked? You look very dubious, my friend.
>
> *Husband*: Apparently it has … I can't help being suspicious of it. [*now looking sad and uncomfortable*] I don't think she's the woman I married.
>
> *Kilroy*: Why?
>
> *Husband*: I think she has changed.
>
> *Kilroy*: In what way? [*the audience goes silent*]
>
> *Husband*: I don't know, I don't know; but there is something, there is something there that is different.
>
> *Kilroy*: OK, so she is not the woman you married. Is she a better woman?
>
> *Husband*: No … [*he looks down sadly*] … she is different.

In Chapters 4 and 5 we saw that antidepressants have effects. Mostly they have placebo and side-effects. Yet an increasing amount of evidence now confirms that for a sub-set of people they have other effects too – effects we don't yet fully understand. Like the woman on Kilroy's chat show, sometimes these pills make us different. Sometimes they sedate and numb us. And sometimes they change us in more unpredictable ways. As this chapter unfolds we will see that no matter what effects antidepressants unleash, these effects do not 'cure' us or return us to 'normality'. Instead, if we are to make any sense of their effects at all, we must regard them as we do other mind-altering substances – as propelling us into an abnormal state of mind.

By taking this view I tackle head-on one of the most powerful myths embraced by the psychiatric establishment:

that psychiatric drugs are capable of 'curing' us and are therefore distinct from recreational drugs that merely alter our state of mind. What I am going to explore now is whether this 'curing view' of antidepressants, far from capturing how these pills actually work, is rather a tale of convenience, resting upon no solid scientific basis.

•

In most British clinics and hospitals, before a patient is given psychotherapy like CBT or psychodynamic therapy, they usually undergo what is called a clinical assessment. These are interviews usually lasting about 50 minutes during which a psychologist or therapist assesses whether the patient is suitable for therapeutic work. During these interviews the practitioner notes down the patient's problem, his or her personal and clinical history, and their understanding of the patient's problem. The aim of this meeting is to gather information with which to advise the clinical team on what kind of psychological intervention is needed.

Some years back, a colleague of mine conducted one of these assessments with a 52-year-old man I shall call Toby. A few months before the assessment, Toby had lost his wife to a long-standing heart condition. Her death had left him devastated. For the first time in his life he said he could truly understand what it meant to be entirely alone. He couldn't sleep, he could barely eat, and he was regularly incapacitated by heavy bouts of grief. After being consumed by his heartache for some weeks, he decided to visit his doctor for help. He was immediately prescribed antidepressants. After taking them for four weeks, however, some odd things started to happen. In the assessment my colleague asked him precisely what these odd things were.

The first thing Toby mentioned was that he'd lost all capacity to cry. After a month on the pills, his tears had literally dried up. When my colleague asked him to elaborate, Toby responded that he no longer cried because he now experienced the memories of his wife in a different way. In short, the 'flashbacks' he used to have of his wife had now disappeared. He characterised these flashbacks as vivid bursts of recollection that would overwhelm him with the presence of his deceased wife, as if she were suddenly right there, alive and by his side. His flashbacks would typically arrive at unexpected moments: when walking home he would suddenly see an image of her smiling and opening the front door; or when lying in bed he'd hear her voice or feel her hand stretching out for his own; or when on the train he'd glimpse her in the expression of a female stranger – in a smile, a nod, a look of concern. In these fleeting moments his wife would become extraordinarily visible to him. And his body would respond with every sinew and fibre, as if she were really there. Yet she was not there. And that, he said, was what made these flashbacks so significant: their vividness meant that when they passed he'd be left with a crushing sense of loss and grief. But since taking the pills, Toby told my colleague, these flashbacks had just stopped, along with the grief they triggered. Toby wanted to know: was this new emotional drought healthy or natural?

There was also something else that the pills had changed. Before taking them, in those early weeks after his wife's death, he would regularly experience, almost daily, a dull ache growing in his chest. This would build and build, sometimes building all day, until the pressure, unable to be contained any more, would finally burst out through a deluge of tears. But, again, since taking his pills this internal pressure was somehow acting differently. Instead of finding an outlet through his tears, he said it almost now seemed to get stuck in his head, agitating his thoughts, and making him act in uncharacteristic ways. One of these uncharacteristic behaviours involved religiously counting the number of lamp-posts he passed as he walked down the street. Another involved endlessly tracing the contours of distant objects with his index finger. For Tony these acts had reached obsessive levels, but they didn't end there. He'd also become addicted to online card games, which he now played deep into the night. He'd never played these games before, let alone stayed up late on his computer. He had always preferred other activities in the late evening, like reading. But he rarely read nowadays, as serious concentration was almost impossible. As he spoke to my colleague he wondered openly whether this pent-up pressure was generating these 'obsessive activities'. Of course he couldn't be sure, but he was worried that the pills had somehow cut off his emotions and forced him into his head.

During the initial assessment my colleague dutifully noted all of Toby's insightful reflections. That was his task. That's how assessments work. What his task didn't involve was exploring if the pills were responsible for the changes in Toby's behaviour. Assessments do not afford the opportunity for that kind of enquiry. After all, if you choose to open Pandora's box, you'd better do it in therapy, where you have time to manage what may fly out, rather than in a time-restricted assessment, where you don't.

But what if my colleague had more time? What if he and Toby had met in a different environment; one that allowed for a more frank conversation about whether it was the pills Toby was taking that had affected him in the way he feared? Well, let's have a look at how such a conversation might have unfolded, in order to learn a little more about how these pills actually work and how they may have been affecting Toby's life.

One of the first questions Toby might have asked was why his emotions had become so flat. Were the pills responsible for cutting his emotions dead?

While it's difficult to be 100 per cent certain what was responsible (because these changes might have occurred even if Toby hadn't taken the pills), we do know that antidepressants have effects. Mostly they have placebo effects and side-effects. We also know that for many people they can have sedating or numbing effects – perhaps the very effects that interfered with Toby's grieving. For example, it's clear that antidepressants work differently to many drugs used in other branches of medicine. Take antibiotics and antiviral drugs, for example. When these enter the body they attack the viruses or bacteria at the root of your illness. In this sense they cure us by literally killing the problem. The same can be said for chemotherapy, which is sent into the blood to destroy the cancer cells. But antidepressants don't work in that way, because when we're talking about emotional problems there's rarely an underlying pathology, virus or disease to be cured (as I'll discuss in the next chapter). Rather, these drugs, when they do have effects, work more like substances that temporarily alter our state of mind, such as caffeine or cannabis. These pills, in other words, don't cure us – they simply change us. They can throw us temporarily into a foreign state of mind, into an altered version of who we are.

From this standpoint, antidepressant medications do not return us to health as medical pills aim to do – they rather manufacture a new state of mind, and often an unnatural state. Was it natural, in other words, for Toby to suddenly stop crying after a terrible loss? After all, the natural course of grieving is a long one, drifting away only slowly and intermittently – it's rare for it to just stop dead right in its tracks, as it did with Toby. Now, of course, it could be argued that Toby suddenly stopped grieving because his pills simply 'cured' him of an excessive emotional response. But that would be a dubious argument, not least because it assumes that grief is something we need to be 'cured' from. Rather, it makes far more sense to say that in Toby's situation the pills simply numbed his natural reaction to a deeply painful event. This interpretation is consistent with research that clearly shows that if you give Prozac to a group of healthy individuals, after a while about half of them will experience emotional blunting.[2] So the question is, what's happening to these healthy people? Well, the pills certainly aren't 'curing' them, because these people are healthy and have nothing to be cured of. Rather, these people have been thrown into a new state of mind manufactured by the drugs they've taken. This is to say, these drugs can sometimes produce effects beyond side-effects and placebo effects, but often not the effects that drug companies advertise – not healing, improving or curative effects, as they say, but mind-numbing effects.[3]

At this point Toby might raise another objection – that

if the drugs had just numbed him, what's wrong with that? Why shouldn't he take that result and run! People use substances all the time to alter their moods, the use of alcohol perhaps being the most obvious example.

The answer to this objection is, once again, that numbing things isn't curing things, or even, in the long run, helping things. It's just providing a temporary and superficial distraction, and one that may store up problems later along the line. For example, let's say you're really nervous about a party you've been invited to on Saturday night. And perhaps you're nervous because you think everyone there will be smarter than you, more attractive, or more interesting. Anyway, you get there and no one is talking to you, so you grab a drink and gulp it down. After a few minutes you relax a little and start up a conversation. And because you're feeling a little better, a little more confident, you have another drink and then another and another! Soon you're swaying all over the place, bumping into things, hiccupping and chatting to everyone. So you are now no longer nervous. But you are not your usual self either. In other words, although the alcohol has had an effect, it hasn't uprooted the reason you felt insecure in the first place. It's merely altered your state of mind so that you no longer experience your insecurity. It has replaced your feeling of inadequacy with a feeling of 'what the heck'; a feeling that's neither a natural nor a permanent product of your personality, but rather a manufactured outcome of the alcohol you've been drinking.

The alcohol has no more 'cured' you of your insecurity than caffeine 'cures' you of your tiredness. It has just changed your state of mind while you're under its influence.

And that's precisely how antidepressants work for some people – not curing us but changing us. In the case of Toby, his instinct was to cry, but the drugs seem to have cut that short. His life is the same, his loss is the same, but his reaction to life events has now been altered. Has Toby, in other words, just become like you at the party, imbibing a substance to anaesthetise his pain? If so, other serious questions have to be addressed about whether, by sedating himself, Toby is actually harming himself in the long run.

To answer this crucial question let me offer another illustration: I once worked with someone who hated his job at an accountancy firm so much that he became very depressed. He consulted his doctor and was prescribed Prozac. After a while things began to change a little for the better. At least that's how he initially felt. He started to take less offence at his boss's criticisms, he stopped stressing so much about deadlines, and he began to relax a little more socially with his colleagues. He developed that 'what the heck' attitude that some people on the drug report. So the question is: was he helped? Had the drugs made his life any better? Well, from one angle, I suppose they had: he was now slightly more tolerant of work and less conflicted about going in every day. Yet, from another angle he wasn't helped at all, because once he'd stopped taking Prozac his old dislike of work returned. Worse still, once off the drug he wondered whether he'd actually drugged himself into staying in a job he should have left years ago. Perhaps his depression was an alarm that signalled he needed to change his life. But rather than listening to the alarm, he just turned it off with Prozac, pulled up the covers and returned to sleep. This man ultimately believed that his pills had merely tranquillised him, because once he'd stopped them he faced a problem he should have confronted a long time ago.

Whether the drugs Toby was taking were also stacking up problems for him in the future is of course a possibility that any clinician should seriously explore with his or her patient. But the strange thing is, such explorations rarely happen, and there is a very simple and surprising reason why.

•

These explorations rarely happen because the vision of antidepressants I have just articulated is not the vision embraced by mainstream psychiatry. In fact, as I've learnt from experience, this version makes many conservative psychiatrists turn as red as tomatoes. But why is this so? What gets them so upset? Well, the obvious answer is that it flatly contradicts their mainstream view, which is broadly consistent with that of the pharmaceutical industry. So to understand that view, and how it differs from the one above, let's talk for a moment to Dr Joanna Moncrieff, a psychiatrist and senior researcher in the Department of Mental Health Science at University College London.

Moncrieff is today considered one of the most exciting figures in antidepressant research, earning a reputation almost as notorious as Irving Kirsch's for challenging the status quo. As I sat with Moncrieff in her university office, she was more than eager to explain to me the difference between the vision of drugs largely embraced by the psychiatric establishment (called the 'disease-centred model'), and the vision outlined above (what she calls the 'drug-centred model'). She traced their differences in the following way:

'In the disease-centred model, people are assumed to have a mental disease, a problem in their brain. And drugs are thought to be effective because they rectify or reverse that underlying brain problem in some way. This is the dominant model in psychiatry, and the one that best serves psychiatric interests. But the drug-centred model offers an entirely different way of understanding how these drugs work. It rather emphasises that drugs are drugs; they are chemical substances that are foreign to the human body but which affect the way people think and feel. They have psychoactive properties, just like recreational drugs do, which alter the way the body functions at a physiological level. So the drug-centred model does not say that psychiatric drugs heal brain problems, like the disease model claims; it rather says they alter people's states of mind in ways that may or may not be helpful.'

The interesting thing about the drug-centred model is that while there are growing numbers of psychiatric nurses, psychotherapists and clinical psychologists who accept this version of how psychiatric drugs work, at the heart of the psychiatric establishment there is still considerable resistance to this view: 'There are many psychiatrists who find the drug-centred model extremely challenging and simply don't want to hear it', said Moncrieff candidly. 'This is because it fundamentally undermines the notions upon which modern psychiatry is based: the idea that mental disorders are brain-based diseases which psychiatric drugs can remedy in the same way medical drugs remedy physical problems.'

Moncrieff's own academic research has shown that this current and widespread resistance to the drug-centred model has not always been so strong. 'Prior to the 1950s, psychiatric drugs weren't understood to act upon underlying diseases like they are today. They were seen as drugs that would pep you up. They were accepted as sticking plasters or uplifters that might at best be able to suppress symptoms for a period, but never were they seen as reversing a disease state.'

But this all changed, Moncrieff explained to me, when in the 1950s the drug-centred model began to be discredited. 'This happened because the pills being used at that time [tranquillisers like Valium and Librium] were discovered to have terrible withdrawal effects. It also became obvious that these pills had been doled out to millions of people who were unhappy with their lives, particularly women who were trapped in miserable marriages. So once people started to realise that these pills had been used to suppress appropriate emotional responses to unhappy situations, that whole drug-centred model of taking pep pills to pick you up fell into disrepute.'

Moncrieff therefore sees the rise of the disease-centred model as filling a vacuum left by the demise of the drug-centred model. 'With the growing popularity of the older antidepressants during the 1960s, 70s and 80s, the diseased-centred model began to take over', continued Moncrieff. 'This was especially the case in the 1990s when the new SSRI [selective serotonin reuptake inhibitor] antidepressants came on the scene. The drug companies were trying to capture that huge market of people who once took tranquillisers. But because the old model of how drugs work had been tarnished, they needed a new model to reassert their value and necessity. So now these drugs were cast as curing us rather than changing us. And that's where the idea of the chemical imbalance came in – it was perfect, because it implied that these drugs actually corrected a defect in the brain. If you have a brain disorder, a chemical imbalance, and this pill is going to correct that imbalance, then obviously you must take it. Few questioned whether this new way of thinking totally obscured what these drugs really do. And this unthinking acceptance of the disease-centred view has dominated mainstream psychiatry for the last 20 or 30 years.'

•

Having now heard our hypothesised discussion with Toby and my real one with Moncrieff, I imagine that some of you may be feeling a little confused. After all, only two chapters ago we saw how Irving Kirsch's research revealed that antidepressants work almost no better than placebo pills. And yet, in this current chapter, we have understood antidepressants as altering how we feel and behave. So is there a contradiction here? Can Moncrieff's view, that pills change us, be reconciled with Kirsch's view that they help us little better than sugar pills? I decided to put this question to Moncrieff.

'I actually think our work is complementary, not contradictory', Moncrieff answered decisively. 'I agree with Kirsch that the majority of benefit from these pills is due to the placebo effect. But also remember that Kirsch's research shows that active drugs can sometimes work fractionally better than placebos, especially with people who are severely depressed. And that's where the drug-centred model comes in. It can explain this small difference in terms of the psychoactive effects real drugs have. Either they produce uncomfortable side-effects that convince people they're on the real drug (which in turn makes the placebo effect greater). Or some of these drugs are so sedative that they put people into such a fog that they can no longer feel depressed or anything else.'

A recent study published in the *British Journal of Psychiatry* by a team of researchers from Oxford University strongly confirms not only the sedating nature of these psychoactive effects but also the questionable value of these effects.[4] To reach this conclusion, the researchers assessed 38 patients who had taken SSRI antidepressants for periods between three and 48 months (the average length being 23 months). The researchers then undertook in-depth interviews with all of the patients to find out how the pills affected them. The results they uncovered are so at odds with the modern myth of the 'happy pill' that it's worth giving them almost in full:

- Most participants described a general reduction in the intensity of all the emotions that they experienced, using words like 'dulled', 'numbed', 'flattened' or completely 'blocked', to capture how they felt.

- A few participants described feeling no emotions at all, while others reported their emotional experience had become more 'cognitive' or 'intellectual'.

- A few participants described how the emotions that were at times present seemed 'unreal', 'fake' or 'artificial'. And almost all participants, paradoxically, described a reduction in their positive emotions, including a reduction in emotions like happiness, enjoyment, excitement, anticipation, passion, love, affection and enthusiasm.

- Most participants also described feeling emotionally detached or disconnected from their surroundings. Most also described this detachment as extending to a detachment from other people. Specifically, they felt reduced sympathy and empathy, and felt detached during social interactions. Many participants also described an emotional detachment from their friends and family, including their partner or children.
- Almost all participants described not caring about things that used to matter to them. They cared less about themselves, about other people and about the consequences of their actions. Not caring could have both helpful and unhelpful consequences: it could reduce the sense of pressure and stress, but it could also increase the likelihood that important tasks were neglected.
- Many participants described a general feeling of indifference to things in life that used to matter to them. Some felt they just did not care as much about the consequences to themselves of their behaviour. A few participants went further, mentioning thoughts of self-harm or suicide that they related to their emotional detachment and numbness. One participant had started to self-harm in an effort to feel emotion. Many participants reported not caring as much about others, being less sensitive or courteous towards other people, having reduced concern for others' feelings, and reduced concern about other people's opinions of them. Some participants described being less concerned or even unable to care about responsibilities in their everyday lives.
- All participants experienced a reduction of intensity or frequency of negative emotions. Most considered that at some stage the reduction in negative emotions was

beneficial to them, bringing relief from distressing negative emotions like emotional distress, anger, irritability or aggression; and anxiety, worry or fear. Although this reduction was usually at some stage a relief, many participants also reported it impaired their quality of life. Participants described the need to be able to feel negative emotions when appropriate, such as grief or concern. Some were unable to respond with negative emotions, such as being unable to cry when this would have been appropriate, or respond appropriately to bad news.

- Some participants felt their personality had changed in some way. They felt they were not the person that they used to be. Participants also reported that specific aspects of their personality, and, in particular, emotional aspects, had been changed or lost. Some participants believed that at times their antidepressant had made them behave out of character. One participant believed that the medication had changed their personality permanently, having a lasting effect beyond finishing their medication.

When reading this study of how antidepressants make people feel, Toby's reaction to his pills suddenly seems less idiosyncratic. In fact, because Moncrieff is so familiar with research like that above, when I told her about Toby's experience she was completely unsurprised. 'We know these pills can have this sort of numbing effect, creating a kind of emotional disengagement', she said, 'and sometimes this disengagement can also lead to a kind of dis-inhibition. Because people aren't in touch with their normal range of emotions they can start to do odd things like the man, Toby, you're describing.'

This final point about pills making us do 'odd things' crops up again and again in the clinical research. Like Toby, or the woman on Kilroy's show, or the people surveyed in the research we've just seen, these pills can severely knock us off-centre. To illustrate this, let's have a quick look at some examples of such drug-induced behaviour, as explored by Dr Simon Sobo in his work. Sobo is a psychiatrist who has spent years documenting the strange and unwanted effects these pills can unleash.

Among the various examples Sobo provides is a female patient of his who worked as a computer consultant. She had very low self-esteem generally and at work felt she wasn't as capable with computers as her five male colleagues. She needed constant reassurance, and when things went wrong she'd punish herself with violent self-accusations. Yet on an SSRI antidepressant, things changed. She acknowledged that she wasn't as good with computers as her colleagues but that she wasn't that bad either. More importantly, she realised she was necessary to her team. She was the only one with sufficient social skills to handle their clients. She was now also able to ask questions at conferences without feeling foolish. While these changes could have been due to the placebo effect, they still seemed to her very real. She was doing things differently. However, there was a real down-side, which she experienced when coming off her pills: 'I feel like I've been drugged for two years', she said, 'and now I want to take a look at my chequebook.' She went on to report other uncharacteristic behaviour, which, from her non-drugged perspective, now seemed frankly bizarre. She had bought a puppy that she kept in an unfinished basement. While medicated she had not bothered to clean up the puppy's poo, reacting with that same 'well, whatever' attitude she'd felt at work.[5]

Sobo provides many other examples of drugs mitigating one problem but at the same time creating a plethora of others. He talks of a man who was usually very conscientious but quite anxious, quickly becoming on his pills completely indifferent to all the speeding tickets he started gathering. He also talks of a woman who began taking meds for a long-term phobia, suddenly and uncharacteristically becoming blasé about her son's diagnosis of testicular cancer. Turning to my experience, I can remember a dedicated student of mine taking meds to manage his examination terror. They lessened his fear, granted, but oddly his grades started to plummet – his fear of failure, it turns out, had been the only thing that had got him to the library. Finally, and perhaps most dramatically, a colleague of mine once told me about a seventeen-year-old girl he had worked with psychotherapeutically. She had been given pills to help with her social phobia. And yes, her confidence had minimally increased. But so too had her libido. Within two weeks she had slept with six men.

So the real question we must ask is not whether pills are leading people to change their lives, but whether they are leading people to change them in the way that is natural to them. Are these manufactured states of mind guiding people to make the right moves or decisions? Or are they stacking up more problems for them in the future, like many other mood-altering substances can do? Is it right that pills should make us feel suddenly invincible, or blasé about our son's cancer, or sexually unbridled, or indifferent to staying in a dead-end job? Is it right that they should suddenly dry up our grief for someone we love?

Joanna Moncrieff agrees that antidepressants do have effects. Mostly they have placebo effects and side-effects, yet for some patients they can have additional psychoactive effects such as numbing and sedating, which can in turn bring other unintended consequences. Moncrieff was therefore insistent that whatever effects they do have, they cannot be classed as curing effects. For her, to think of these pills as cures is a scientific and professional error. As she said: 'The idea that there is a brain disease, or a chemical imbalance or a faulty neural network that these pills correct is completely false and unsupported. You cannot therefore say that these drugs are having curative or remedial effect if the evidence doesn't support that point of view.'

As I left Moncrieff's office at University College London, I realised it was time to tackle the idea that mental disorders are rooted in brain malfunctions that can be corrected by chemical cures. Again and again, the experts were telling me that this view was incorrect – Robert Spitzer, Walter Brown, Tim Kendall, Irving Kirsch and now Joanna Moncrieff. So why was the popular and prevailing view so radically different? Why did so many people believe that the brain is at the heart of the problem? It was time for me to find out for myself precisely what the science says. What role does our biology play in our mental distress?

7
Bio-babble?

On a sunny Saturday morning in August 2003, six people entered a church in Pasadena, Los Angeles, set up a suite of computers and began sending emails around the country announcing that their hunger strike had begun. Their protest was about human rights abuses perpetrated by an institution that the hunger strikers claimed had tortured them in their youth, by incarcerating them against their will, poisoning them, firing electrical currents into their brains, branding them insane and affirming the improbability of their ever being fully sane again. To these protestors this institution is known as a system of legalised mental and emotional abuse. To most of the rest of us it is known as medical psychiatry.

In late 2011, I spoke to one of the strikers' leaders, 56-year-old David Oaks. My aim was to discover why this group had taken such drastic steps to be heard. David chose to answer my question by telling me his story.[1] As an undergraduate entering Harvard University in the mid-1970s he had great difficulty adapting to his new environment. He had been raised in a working-class family on Chicago's South Side, and so found the world of privilege at Harvard so fundamentally alien to all he had known that he struggled to find his place. He soon started experimenting with marijuana, which only deepened his feelings of estrangement and alienation. And as these difficult feelings spiralled, it wasn't long before he entered what he called an 'altered state'.

A couple of people noticed this change in him, and he was sent to the college infirmary. There they classified his experiences according to the DSM's definition of schizophrenia. He was therefore prescribed heavy doses of Thorazine, a powerful antipsychotic drug. But the drug didn't help him; in fact, it seemed only to deepen his confusion. And so by the following semester David was admitted to the famous McLean Hospital, where it was decided that what he needed was heavy sedation. But David didn't want to be heavily medicated, so the authorities did what they are entitled to do if a psychiatric patient doesn't comply with treatment. They locked him in solitary confinement and subjected him to forced drugging. The medication with which they injected him was so powerful that he could barely eat, think or move – let alone continue to uphold his spirited protest.

During one particularly agonising night locked up in solitary confinement, David became so overwhelmed with shame and disgust at the way he'd been handled that he made a lifelong pledge: 'I remember looking out through one of those impenetrable metal window screens', David recalled emotionally, 'and there and then I pounded on the screen with my fist, vowing to do something for human rights once I got out.'

Thirty-five years have now passed since that harrowing episode, but David has more than honoured that vow. After his discharge from hospital (which he secured by threatening legal action unless they released him), he graduated from Harvard University in 1977 with Honours.

Since then he has dedicated his life to protecting the rights of psychiatric patients, or as he would call them, 'psychiatric survivors'. He first worked with the Mental Patients Liberation Front, organising rallies during the early 1980s against the American Psychiatric Association's sanctioning of electroshock therapy. He also wrote for the influential *Madness Network News*, becoming one of America's foremost advocates for psychiatric patients' rights. Finally, in the 1990s, he helped found Support Coalition, now called MindFreedom, of which he is now Executive Director. Over the years this organisation has gone from strength to strength, recently being accredited by the United Nations as a non-governmental organisation with consulting status.

David's history of patient advocacy and activism is the backdrop against which we find him protesting with five other hunger strikers in that church in Pasadena. Each of the other strikers could tell their own tales of woe – some were force-fed drugs they didn't want, others were given ECT (electroconvulsive therapy) against their will, and most had suffered from the stigma and crippling side-effects of their psychiatric treatment. And so together they all sat in that church refusing solid food until their demands were met.

So what were their demands? David Oaks was forthright about this: 'We wanted something very simple – we wanted the American Psychiatric Association and two other major organisations to answer some basic questions. We wanted them to provide evidence for what we had been led to believe as patients: that the major mental illnesses are actually biologically-based brain diseases; that psychiatric diagnosis is objective; that there are chemical imbalances that can be corrected by psychiatric drugs; and that psychiatric drugs actually cure us rather than temporarily alter us like recreational drugs do.'

After sending these requests from their overheating computers, the hunger strikers sat back and waited … and … well … waited some more. Two of the organisations (National Alliance on Mental Illness (NAMI) and the Office of the Surgeon General of the United States) completely ignored the hunger strikers' requests, acting as though the whole event was just not taking place. 'Their total silence could've made the situation very sticky', recalled David, 'if the American Psychiatric Association had not finally clicked that they actually needed to respond.'

And respond they did. It came in the form of a brief 247-word PR statement declaring that the APA was committed to promoting 'the highest quality care for individuals with mental illness', and further adding that in recent years, 'there has been substantial progress in understanding the neuroscientific basis of many mental illnesses'. The APA therefore did not provide the evidence that David and his fellow protesters had specifically asked for. Instead, the APA told the strikers if they wanted to learn about the biology of mental distress, then there were three good psychiatric textbooks that they could consult for the evidence they sought.

This somewhat dismissive response would soon backfire for the APA, because what they didn't know was that the protestors had organised a scientific panel to assess the APA's response. This panel comprised fifteen senior academics and clinicians from the United States and Europe, including Professor Mary Boyle (University of East London); Professor David Cohen (University of Texas); Dr Patricia E. Deegan (Boston University); Professor Tom Greening

(UCLA) and Dr Peter Breggin (founder of the International Center for the Study of Psychiatry and Psychology). 'These guys worked incredibly hard', said David energetically, 'and yes, they went away and scoured those textbooks for any relevant studies and citations etc.'

So what did scientific panel find? Did the textbooks provide the evidence the protesters asked for? 'In short', said David, 'they did not.' Instead, the scientific panel found the books littered with confessions of failure, such as: 'The precise causes (aetiology) of mental disorders are not known'; and: 'Few lesions or physiologic abnormalities define the mental disorders, and for the most part their causes remain unknown'; and: 'Although reliable criteria have been constructed for many psychiatric disorders, validation of the diagnostic categories as specific entities has not been established'; and: 'In the areas of pathophysiology and aetiology, psychiatry has more uncharted territory than the rest of medicine …'[2]

Given that these statements hardly supported the APA's claim that modern psychiatry had made 'substantial progress in understanding the neuroscientific basis of many mental illnesses', the scientific panel sent these and other statements back to the APA, stating that they had neither found, nor once again had been given, the evidence they wanted. When the APA responded for the second time, it was clear they had become irritated: 'It is unfortunate that in the face of … [psychiatry's] remarkable scientific and clinical progress a small number of individuals and groups persist in questioning the reality and clinical legitimacy of disorders that affect the mind, brain, and behaviour.' The APA then reaffirmed that there is 'research' and 'compelling evidence' showing that *some* disorders have a strong genetic component, and that schizophrenia reveals reproducible abnormalities of brain structure. But after asking the APA, now for a third time, to provide its 'compelling evidence', not a single specific reference or piece of scientific research was provided to back up their claims. As David told me with a twinkle in his eye: 'They could not give us what we wanted because what we wanted does not exist – we knew that, they knew that, but I think they realised coming clean publicly would be a PR disaster.'

Towards the end of our interview I asked what David felt the hunger strike had achieved. 'It did not change psychiatry, that's for sure. Bio-psychiatry is now more powerful than ever in its entire history. But we did consider it a success to the extent we got our message out there. Many media outlets covered the story like the *Washington Post*, the *LA Times* and the BBC. And people saw first-hand how the APA operates – concealing information, distorting the facts, and unwilling to be held to account. We even won a real concession: the APA's final statement conceded there are no "discernible pathological lesions or genetic abnormalities" in mental disorders.[3] Now, that is something you won't hear them admit every day.'

David is not opposed to all psychiatric treatment. He recognises that in some cases drugs may help the most severely distressed in society. What he objects to is the treatment and sectioning of patients against their will, psychiatry's dubious financial dependency on the pharmaceutical industry, psychiatry's medicalisation of our most basic everyday problems, and finally, the psychiatric myth that our emotional troubles are rooted in biochemical imbalances or genetic dispositions.

As this chapter is primarily interested in the biology of mental distress, it's now time to focus more closely on that final statement about genes and biochemical imbalances. Are they indeed at the root of our mental ill-health, as much of the public have been led to suppose?

•

In the early 1960s a young medical researcher from the wrong side of Brooklyn stumbled upon an idea that would launch a paradigm shift in psychiatry. The researcher was Joseph Schildkraut, and the idea he advanced was rather simple: fluctuations in our moods may be due to chemical imbalances in our brains. To be sure, Schildkraut was not the first person to entertain this compelling idea. It had been floating around the psychiatric community in one form or another since the mid-1950s, when the first antidepressants started to be used. But for some reason when Schildkraut published his hypothesis in the *American Journal of Psychiatry* in 1965, his views took the community by storm.[4] In fact his paper, which has since become one of the most cited in psychiatric history despite its ungainly title, 'The Catecholamine Hypothesis of Affective Disorders', is now regarded as the first and clearest articulation of what is now widely called the chemical imbalance theory of mental illness.

What prompted Schildkraut to write this paper was a confluence of many things. One spur of particular note was that, while working as a researcher at the National Institute of Mental Health, Schildkraut had become fascinated with the observation that certain depressed people who did not respond well to talk therapy often seemed to improve when given certain drugs. But he, like others at that time, was uncomfortable with the 'drug-centred' view I discussed in the last chapter: the idea that psychiatric drugs were merely soothing tonics that have mood-altering effects like recreational drugs do. Schildkraut was rather convinced that they must have a more curative effect. And it was this conviction that led him to try to explain the biology of this 'curative effect' in his 1965 article. His method was to review data from many different pharmacological studies, mainly conducted on animals, which seemed to suggest that depression was due to a brain deficiency in a chemical called norepinephrine. His theory was that the two types of antidepressant most widely used at the time (the tricyclics and the monoamine oxidase inhibitors (MAOIs)), worked by increasing the amount of norepinephrine available in the central nervous system. The implication being that depression was an outcome of some kind of norepinephrine deficiency.

The first thing to say about Schildkraut's theory is that he himself called it at the time 'at best a reductionist simplification' that could neither be rejected nor confirmed 'on the basis of data currently available'. In other words, Schildkraut explicitly acknowledged that the chemical imbalance theory was just that – a theory, for which the science of the day offered no clear support. This meant that his now famous article actually *proved* nothing at all. All it did was postulate an idea; an idea that would come to captivate an entirely new generation. As the medical historian David Healy puts it:

> Despite the fact that such a hypothesis could have been proposed earlier and despite the many flaws inherent in it, this

> particular statement in 1965 came to dominate the field, set research agendas, and direct drug company efforts for the following two decades. It crystallised a split in psychiatry between biological and psychodynamic branches, each group having its own journals, its own meetings, and de facto very little to do with each other.[5]

Let's now fast-forward two years to 1967. At this time Schildkraut's theory was taken in an unexpected direction by a British psychiatrist called Alec Coppen. What Coppen argued in a paper published in the *British Journal of Psychiatry* entitled 'The Biochemistry of Affective Disorders' was that norepinephrine is not the only chemical implicated in mood irregularities. Others were crucial too, especially a neurotransmitter chemical called serotonin. But again, after reviewing all the relevant studies available at that time, Coppen, like Schildkraut before him, was still cautious with his conclusions, adding the following caveat at the end of his article:

> We must face the very real possibility that we are far from the primary disturbance in depression. The changes [in serotonin] may all be secondary to other abnormalities which have not been taken into account at all … In spite of all the numerous investigations and very exciting leads that are now opening up, we are perhaps only in a slightly better position than Sanctorius of Padua … [when he said some 300 years ago]: 'Where the bond of union is between the mind and the animal fluids God Almighty alone knows …'[6]

Coppen's theory that the 'animal fluid' of serotonin may be crucial in shaping our mental lives cleared the path for the second generation of antidepressants: the SSRIs (selective serotonin reuptake inhibitors). These newer medications included, as we have already seen, drugs like fluoxetine (Prozac), paroxetine (Paxil, Seroxat), sertraline (Zoloft), fluvoxamine (Luvox), citalopram (Celexa), etc. All of these were thought to alter mood irregularities by inhibiting the reuptake of serotonin by neurons in the brain. All of these, in other words, assumed that Coppen's theory of the chemical imbalance (this time of serotonin) was correct.

But was his theory correct? That is the crucial question. A question we cannot hope to answer without first getting a handle on some of the basics of neuroscience. I promise, I'll be very brief.

The brain is famously made up of about 1 billion nerve cells called neurons. Each of these neurons resembles a piece of string with little branches coming off it, called dendrites. The neurons don't actually touch each other, but they do communicate by discharging chemicals into the tiny gaps between them. These gaps are called synapses, and the chemicals that flood them are called neurotransmitters because they 'transmit' complex electrical messages from one neuron to another, ensuring that these neurons are in a constant and highly complex conversation. For example, and to simplify things greatly: when neuron A has received enough transmitters from surrounding neurons, it 'fires' its own transmitters to other neurons around it. When thousands of neurons are triggering each other in this way, this is called a cascade. And cascades are thought to be what facilitate our thoughts, perceptions and emotions.

Neurotransmitters are therefore widely acknowledged to be crucial to how our brains operate. This is why the chemical imbalance theory states that if there's a deficiency in these chemicals, this will impair our brain's functioning. And this is where antidepressants like SSRIs come in: they aim to increase the neurotransmitters sitting in the synapses. They do this by cutting off what we might call 'backflow'. For example, imagine waves rolling onto a beach. The waves roll in and then out. Well, that's pretty much how neurotransmitters work: they roll into the synapse, deposit their message in the neighbouring neuron, and then roll back out again. What SSRIs try to do is inhibit that rolling back action, which essentially means that more of the chemical stays in the synapse for more of the time, resulting in higher levels. Different antidepressants target different types of neurotransmitter, but broadly speaking there are thought to be three neurotransmitters that matter most: serotonin and norepinephrine, which are considered most relevant to depression; and dopamine, considered crucial for major mental illnesses like schizophrenia.

So that, in short, is the basic neuroscience behind the chemical imbalance theory. Mental illness is caused by irregularities in neurotransmitter levels that can be altered by psychiatric drugs. The theory is seductively simple, and has remained so for nearly 50 years. But what matters most to us is whether during that entire time the theory has ever been proved correct?

•

Dr Alec Coppen, architect of the serotonin theory of depression and so the intellectual grandfather of one of the most prescribed pills in history – the SSRI antidepressant – was more than happy to help me answer this question when I called him at his home in April 2012.

Being 90 years old had in no way dented his ambition – especially when it came to championing the virtues of the drug Lithium (an enthusiasm I couldn't share, given Lithium's harmful side-effects and troubled history: in the late 1800s it stopped being used to treat gout because in high doses it was fatal, while in the 1940s it was finally banned from the soft drink 7 Up because of its toxic qualities). Nonetheless, I waited while Coppen talked enthusiastically about the drug, until the moment arrived when I could jump in:

'So, Dr Coppen, do you think Lithium works because it acts upon certain chemical imbalances like serotonin?'

'Er, yes, I think there's some serotonin effect', replied Coppen, perhaps noticing I'd changed the subject.

'And since you think Lithium works on these chemicals', I continued, 'do you think this might provide evidence for the chemical imbalance theory? I mean, if drugs increase neurotransmitter levels, and drugs also treat depression, perhaps depression is therefore caused by a deficiency in these neurotransmitters. Do you believe this is so?'

'Well, yes indeed.'

'So tell me, Dr Coppen', I said, getting to the point, 'what would you therefore say to those people who argue that the chemical imbalance theory is still unsubstantiated?'

Coppen went silent for a moment, before responding in a way that surprised me: 'I think there is a lot of evidence for the theory, actually. I don't think people are working on it today because it's generally accepted.'

I was surprised to hear this, because in all my interviews with psychiatrists of different persuasions (from the most humanistic to the most biologically reductionist) this was the first time someone had said they believed there was a lot of evidence for the theory – or, in other words, that the theory was largely supported. This is not to say that there aren't people out there who actually believe this. It's just that it's rare to find anyone who will declare this position openly and without caveats. And there is a plain reason why: *the theory isn't supported*. There are three separate reasons for this that I heard again and again:

Number 1: the main evidence for the theory is arrived at deductively. Because antidepressant drugs like SSRIs act to increase our serotonin levels, and because antidepressants alleviate depression, depression is therefore probably caused by some kind of serotonin deficiency. Now, although the syllogism is deceptively neat (and therefore remarkably beguiling), critics say it's nevertheless logically flawed. In the first place, it's clear that antidepressants don't alleviate depression for the chemical reasons most people believe. As the last three chapters have shown, we can account for a positive effect of an antidepressant largely in terms of its placebo effects, not in terms of its rebalancing chemical imbalances. It's therefore wrong to say the chemical imbalance theory is supported because antidepressants work, since antidepressants probably work for non-chemical reasons.

Number 2: even if antidepressants did work for chemical reasons, critics point out that this would still not substantiate the chemical imbalance theory. If my headache feels better when I take some aspirin, I do not conclude that my headache was therefore caused by a deficiency of aspirin in my brain. Arguing deductively in this way is simply poor reasoning. After all, my headache could have been caused by one of multiple factors – noisy neighbours, a late night, too much wine and so on. All the aspirin has done is interfere with my capacity to experience my headache, rather than top up the chemicals whose deficit was its supposed cause.

Now to argument number 3 – the argument most often referred to as the strongest against the chemical imbalance theory. It goes like this: despite thousands of studies that have tried to show that a serotonin or norepinephrine deficiency is responsible for depression, not one has yet been able to provide *direct* evidence that this is so. For instance, studies of the neurotransmitter norepinephrine say very contradictory things: there are as many concluding that people with depression have *high* levels of norepinephrine as there are concluding that depressed people have *low* levels.[7] Furthermore, the largest recent meta-analysis of serotonin studies, conducted at the University of Amsterdam, has shown that low serotonin does not act as a depressant because when it was lowered in healthy individuals it produced no decrease in mood at all. As the authors summarised: 'Although previously the monoamine systems were considered to be responsible for the development of MDD [major depressive disorder], the available evidence to date does not support a direct causal relationship with MDD.'[8] These facts are consistent with earlier studies showing that special drinks that deplete serotonin and norepinephrine levels do not actually produce depressive symptoms (when depressed people take them, their mood does not worsen. When non-depressed people take them, they remain chirpy. The only slight fluctuation is found in some people who, having recovered from depression, suffered some minor 'transient depressive symptoms' but certainly not full-blown depression).[9]

Research like this not only challenges the idea that serotonin and norepinephrine are causative agents in mental illness, but is consistent with what research on the third major neurotransmitter, dopamine, also tells us. As the psychiatrist Daniel Carlat summarises:

> For years, the going explanation for schizophrenia was the 'dopamine hypothesis', because antipsychotics block the action of the neurotransmitter dopamine, it seemed reasonable to presume that psychosis must be caused by too much dopamine. You can't measure dopamine directly in the brain, but you can measure the main by-product in the spinal fluid. More than a dozen studies have compared levels of dopamine metabolites in schizophrenics. ... In most studies, there were no differences, and in a few, the levels were lower in schizophrenics, exactly the opposite of what would be predicted by the dopamine hypothesis. Other studies, looking at post-mortem brains or PET scans of living patients, have been inconclusive, partly because most of the patients have already been taking antipsychotics. This means that any alterations found in dopamine receptors are as likely to be an artefact of the medication as they are to reflect the underlying cause of schizophrenia ... it is crucial that we realise how much we know and how much we do not know. In virtually all of the psychiatric disorders – including depression, schizophrenia, bipolar disorder, and anxiety disorders – the shadow of our ignorance overwhelms the few dim lights of our knowledge.[10]

Carlat's last point is in agreement with a recent and definitive review of all basic antidepressant research published in the *New England Journal of Medicine*. This revealed that 'numerous studies of norepinephrine and serotonin metabolites in plasma, urine and cerebrospinal fluid, as well as post-mortem studies of the brains of patients with depression, have yet to identify the purported deficiency reliably'.[11] In other words, and to quote the leading journal *The Pharmacological Basis of Therapeutics*, the data for the neurotransmitter hypothesis of mood disorder 'are inconclusive and have not been consistently useful either diagnostically or therapeutically'.

In recent years such disproving research has begun to erode the profession's faith in the chemical imbalance theory. This has led increasing numbers of prominent figures in the mental health profession to declare their defection publicly. To pique your interest in this sea-change, here are a few quotations I've managed to gather:

> 'Many neuroscientists no longer consider a chemical imbalance theory of depression and anxiety to be valid.' (Dr David D. Burns, Professor of Psychiatry, Stanford University)
>
> 'Chemical imbalance is sort of last-century thinking. It's much more complicated than that.' (Dr Joseph Coyle, Professor of Neuroscience at Harvard Medical School)
>
> 'After decades of trying to prove [the chemical imbalance theory], researchers have still come up empty-handed.' (Marcia Angell, former editor of the *New England Journal of Medicine*)
>
> 'Despite pseudoscientific terms like "chemical imbalance", nobody really knows what causes mental illness. There's no blood test or brain scan for major depression.' (Dr Darshak Sanghavi, clinical fellow at Harvard Medical School)

'We do not know the aetiology of really any of the mental disorders at the present time.' Dr Carl Regier, previous Director of Research at the American Psychiatric Association)

'Research has yet to identify specific biological causes of any of these [mental] disorders.' (US Congressional Report entitled: "The biology of mental disorders, new developments in neuroscience')

'The results of decades of neurotransmitter-depletion studies point to one inescapable conclusion, low levels of serotonin, norepinephrine or dopamine do not cause depression.' (Professor Irving Kirsch, Harvard Medical School)

'We still don't know the relationship between biology and the mental disorders.' (Carol Bernstein, previous president of the American Psychiatric Association)

'Patients have been diagnosed with chemical imbalances, despite that no test exists to support such a claim, and that there is no real conception of what a correct chemical balance would look like.' (Dr David Kaiser, *Psychiatric Times*)

'As a scientific venture, the theory that low serotonin causes depression appears to be on the verge of collapse. This is as it should be; the nature of science is ultimately to be self-correcting. Ideas must yield before evidence.' (Dr Jonathan Rottenberg, *Psychology Today*)

'A simplistic biological reductionism has increasingly ruled the psychiatric roost … [we have] learned to attribute mental illness to faulty brain biochemistry, defects of dopamine, or a shortage of serotonin. It is biobabble as deeply misleading and unscientific as the psychobabble it replaced.' (Andrew Skull, Professor of History of Psychiatry, Princeton University, in *The Lancet*)

There is no point piling up more quotations. By now you get the picture: the public defections continue to mount because, after nearly 50 years of investigation into the chemical imbalance theory, there is not one piece of convincing evidence that the theory is actually correct.

So if the chemical imbalance theory is now on its knees, where can psychiatry go from here? In what biological substrate can it now locate the causes of mental disorder? Perhaps the fascinating discoveries of genetics can lead the way out of the current impasse? Let's have a look at what the evidence shows.

•

Up until about ten years ago, if you were studying any of the social sciences at university you'd have encountered a question like the following in an examination: What primarily determines whom you become – your nature or how you are nurtured? In other words, are you a product of your inherited biology or the environment in which you were raised? Ten years ago, if a student had taken a forceful side in this debate, it's possible they might still have received top marks. This is because, a decade ago, academia was still at war over the issue, making an either/or answer intellectually possible. Today, however, the situation has changed. Given the huge advances in genetics over the last ten years, the scientific community has had to fundamentally revise its position. It now broadly accepts that it's virtually impossible to understand how our biology works outside the context of our environment. This has seen the either/or debate retreat to the wings and bio/social complexity assume centre stage.

To put the new genetics in the simplest terms (which I have to say isn't easy), virtually no neurological disorders or psychological problems have been demonstrated to result from the mutation of a single gene. Rather they are now known to involve molecular disturbances that implicate multiple genes and the signals that control their expression.[12] In other words, the popular idea that so-and-so gene causes so-and-so mental trait has been surpassed by the notion that it's *interactions* between our genes and their environment that actually shape us. This is because we now know there to be thousands of molecules attached to our DNA that can literally turn our genes on and off. These molecules, or 'epigenetic markers' as they are more technically known, actually alter and develop as an individual adapts to their environment.

Dr Nessa Carey, a former Senior Lecturer in Molecular Biology at Imperial College London, summarises this new genetics to me rather well: 'We have our set of genes, but those genes can be switched on or switched off, and they can be switched on to higher or lower volume levels depending on the environmental stimuli. And epigenetics is a bit like the volume control on an MP3 player. Your MP3 player contains the tracks that you have loaded onto it; the ones you choose to play and how loudly you choose to play them, that's controlled by epigenetics.'

The equation that this new idea obliges us to embrace therefore runs something like this: because our environment affects these molecules, and because these molecules can turn our genes on or off, the environment can no longer be seen as irrelevant to how our genes determine our functioning and development.

Studies of rats have illustrated this point well. Baby rats born to mothers that displayed little affection (who licked their pups rarely) where given to foster mothers who were very affectionate (who licked them a lot). After dissection, it was clear that the affectionately-raised rats had brain characteristics different to those receiving little affection: affectionately-raised rats possessed more receptors in the neurons of their hippocampus, receptors that are considered crucial stepping-stones in slowing down the production of stress hormones. It turns out that a stretch of DNA, serving as a switch for a gene related to these neural receptors, had been suppressed in the less affectionately-raised rats. This meant that the rats receiving less affection (fewer licks) were far more stressed as adults than those who had received more. The conclusion is that adult personality differences related to stress weren't determined by genes inherited from their biological mothers, but were an outcome of how they were raised as pups.[13]

The same groups of researchers performed a related study of human beings. This involved analysing the brains of 36 people post mortem. Twelve of these people had died of natural causes, while the rest (24) had committed suicide. And of the 24 suicide victims, twelve of these had been abused as children, whereas the other twelve had not. When the brains of these three groups were compared, the group that had suffered childhood abuse again stuck out. People in this group shared the same pattern of fewer receptors linked to stress hormones as those found in the non-affectionately-raised rats. Their brains, via epigenetic changes, had reacted to the environmental abuse – leading them to grow in a direction different to brains receiving environmental care.[14]

Studies like these show that genes can be 'switched on or off' by molecules that are themselves altered by environmental factors.[15] We know, for example, that there are two genes strongly associated with hereditary breast cancer (BRCA1 and BRCA2). But we also know these genes are responsible for only about 10 per cent of all breast cancers (and that only about a further 10–20 per cent of breast cancers are related to any kind of gene or variant). This means that most women who develop breast cancer may not be hereditarily disposed to do so.[16] But even if they are hereditarily disposed, it also means they won't necessarily develop the condition. As the American Society for Clinical Oncology (ASCO) asserts, a woman with a 75 per cent chance of developing breast cancer may remain perfectly healthy, while a woman with a 25 per cent chance of developing breast cancer may eventually develop the disease.[17] Again, the presence of the relevant gene alone is not enough to account for the disease's onset. The environment influencing epigenetic factors plays a crucial role.

The complexity of the new genetics makes those who have accepted the old genetic reductionism seem flatly out of date. I remember giving a talk some years ago at a seminar at Oxford University's John Radcliffe Hospital. At one point I said that many mental health professionals regrettably used simplistic genetic reductionism to avoid the complexity of thinking through the various social, economic and environmental factors influencing who we are, what we do, and who we become.

At the end of my talk, a senior psychiatrist approached me looking none too happy. 'James, you've got it wrong', he said curtly and authoritatively. 'I have patients who are absolutely convinced their troubles are genetic, and who believe any intervention ignoring this is a complete waste of time. And most of these patients are right, especially if there is a history of depression in their family.' I remember replying that a history of family depression proves nothing definitively – perhaps the family atmosphere or culture passed on over generations was the corrosive factor. I also said that reductionist beliefs often breed a destructive attitude in many patients, leading them to think, as one of my patients put it: 'As my mother and grandmother had depression, I figure I'm biologically doomed to follow them.' This kind of fatalism, I responded, is not only scientifically unjustified but is potentially psychologically damaging – it makes people believe that no matter what they do they are genetically fated to suffer. After making my points, this particular psychiatrist merely sighed and shook his head: 'Well, James, for me most cases of depression have clear genetic markers, and even if science can't show this yet, it will do in the future.'

Statements like these are unhelpful and betray a now discredited way of thinking that dominated genetics over fifteen years ago. Back then there was great anticipation of finding singular gene mutations to account for most emotionally- or cognitively-related problems. This was inspired by a few interesting discoveries concerning what are now known as the organic brain diseases. Perhaps the best-known example is Huntington's disease. This is caused by a gene carried on chromosome 4 that destroys brain cells on the frontal lobes, leading to impairments in cognitive functioning. But these clear-cut cases in the realm of mental health are very much the exception. Most genetic influences on disease are greatly more complicated than those early pioneers of the genome project could have dreamed. For instance, in the realm of psychiatry there is no known gene or clear genetic variants for around 97 per cent of all the mental disorders contained in the current DSM and ICD. And even where genes may be implicated in disorders like bipolar disorder and schizophrenia, research now reveals such mind-boggling complexity that nothing definitive can be said. A study that scanned the genetic sequences of 20,000 normal people and then compared them with the sequence of 10,000 patients with schizophrenia, for example, revealed that over 10,000 different gene variants could have a role in the onset of schizophrenia. And this study did not take the findings of epigenetics into account (the environmentally susceptible molecules that interfere with these genetic variants).[18]

Of course, there have been periods of great excitement. In 2003, a study was published in the journal *Science* that asked why stressful experiences lead to depression in some people but not in others. After analysing 847 patients over time, it was found that those who had one or two copies of a gene variant that interfered with serotonin transport were three times as likely to develop depression if subjected to certain stressful life events, like losing a job or getting divorced. This study was thought to provide evidence of a gene-by-environment interaction, in which an individual's response to environmental stresses is moderated by his or her genetic make-up.[19] This finding generated a great deal of enthusiasm until another study, published a few years later, tried to replicate these findings by assessing over 14,000 people via a meta-analysis of fourteen studies. But the conclusion it reached dampened the previous excitement: 'This meta-analysis yielded no evidence that the serotonin transporter genotype alone or in interaction with stressful life events is associated with an elevated risk of depression in men alone, women alone, or in both sexes combined.'[20]

Nobody wants the efforts of geneticists to be frustrated. We all desire scientists to succeed and lead us out of the dark. But given the developments in fields like epigenetics (not to mention the disappointments brought about by non-replicable findings), all we can do today is embrace a position thoroughly littered with caveats. It goes something like this: where genetics plays a role in our mental lives, it does so via a given and so far undefined constellation of genes that *may* predispose a person to an *unknown degree* of vulnerability to developing a given form of mental distress *if* other social or psychological conditions trigger it, and if environmentally influenced epigenetic factors permit it. Such tentativeness is now slowly trickling through to the mental health establishment, as can be seen from the World Health Organisation's recent official statement on the causes of depression:

> Depression is a complex disorder which can manifest itself under a variety of circumstances and due to a multiplicity of factors ... biological (genetic and biochemical), sociological (stressors) and psychological (development and life experiences) factors interact to produce a picture of depression. *Research during the last fifty years indicates that there is no single factor which can explain the cause for depression.*[21] [italics added]

The WHO does not say that genes or biochemical imbalances cause depression. All it says is all anyone can say: of course our biology is implicated in mental distress, just as it is implicated in any emotional, physical or mental state that is experienced as either positive or negative. But precisely how it's implicated, and precisely to what degree, we do not as yet really know.

•

'The problem, you see', said David Oaks as he once again recalled his hunger strike, 'is that there is no proof for the things we were told: that our problems were due to brain-based diseases. And this is why the APA ducked our requests. It couldn't scientifically justify what we were led to believe as patients.'

'Do you think that patients today are receiving the same message you heard long ago?'

'I don't think, I *know*', said Oaks decisively, 'and this is misleading a lot of people into believing that only bio-psychiatry can offer a way out.'

If we therefore accept that the biological myth of mental disorders is overplayed and oversold in psychiatry, the question follows as to why this may be. I believe if we have any hope of reaching an answer it's necessary that we move away from psychiatry momentarily, in order to investigate one of the most powerful industries in contemporary society: the pharmaceutical industry. What precise role has that industry played in promoting the biological theory of mental distress, and for what end? Furthermore, who has that promotion really benefited – patients, psychiatry, the industry itself?

To those thorny questions I now turn.

8
Money and power ruling head and heart

In May 2011 the British journalist Sue Reid broke a story that would shock a nation.* It concerned a young boy from a small village nestled in the hills of Cumbria. His name was Harry Hucknall. And from initial accounts he was your average kid: he liked football, computer games and playing in the park. He had friends and was dearly loved by his family. There wasn't much to mark him out, not really. But on a Sunday night in September, that would change for good.

That evening Harry kissed his mother Jane and older brother David goodnight, carefully telling them that he loved them. He then went upstairs to his bedroom, locked his door behind him, took out a belt, tied it to his bunk bed and hanged himself. He was found after an hour, and later died in hospital. Harry was just ten years old.[1]

At the inquest into Harry's death, the coroner Ian Smith reported that Harry had at the time been taking 'two powerful, mind-altering drugs' – Ritalin and Prozac. More importantly, the coroner had found more drugs in Harry's

* What follows is a summary of that story, aspects of which I paraphrase. I have also chosen to use Sue Reid's quotations acquired through her interviews. I have done this because I was reluctant to interview Harry's family myself. Interviews ask people to revisit episodes that a family may prefer to no longer publicly discuss. And in this case, as Reid's quotations are more than adequate for my purposes, it seemed unecessary to approach them directly.

system than you would expect to find in an adult suffering from the same problem. It turns out that Harry was first given Ritalin by a child psychiatrist to help him with his poor concentration at school, and what was characterised as a 'suicide attempt' when he put a plastic bag over his head. He'd also been prescribed Prozac to help manage his feelings of depression. As the inquest continued, the image of Harry as a happy boy began to disintegrate slowly. The authorities revealed that Harry had at one point self-harmed, and was also being bullied at school (he was held down and threatened with a screwdriver on one occasion). The drugs, it seems, were prescribed to help Harry manage the powerful feelings that, presumably, his situation had stoked.

Harry's father (who had amicably separated from Harry's mother when Harry was three) was one of the last people to find out about the drugs: 'Harry was put on Prozac first, and without my knowledge', he told Sue Reid emotionally. 'I only found out about it when he came to stay for the weekend and his mother told me what dose to give him: one in the morning and one at night. "Are you crazy?" I asked her. "That's an antidepressant." I can go to work every day and pay for my child's keep, but it seems I have little say when it comes to things like the authorities deciding to give my son drugs.'

Harry's father was always unconvinced that his son's problems were psychiatric: 'He was just a kid', he said to Reid, exasperated. 'There was nothing wrong with him. He may have had some problems, but they were overstated.' For example, at school meetings about Harry, his teachers had said he was quiet. 'My son had just recently moved house and been put into a new school, where he didn't know anybody. What did they expect? Another teacher said Harry didn't laugh at his jokes. I asked Harry about that. He told me they weren't very funny.'

Reid also reports how, at the inquest, Harry's father challenged the psychiatrist who treated his son as to why he prescribed such powerful drugs. 'This doctor said that my son had a chemical imbalance in his brain. I asked him: "How do you know? Did you take chemicals from his brain?" He told me it was a theory. So based on a theory – and seeing my son five times at the most – he decided to put him on this drug, Ritalin, which is as powerful as cocaine.'

Harry's father was convinced that his son's difficulties had been wrongly medicalised and medicated. Sure, Harry had problems. But they were due to the various upheavals the boy had undergone (Harry had moved house no fewer than fourteen times), not due to deficiencies in his brain. Harry's father also believed that the drugs, rather than helping his son, had been 'a major contribution' to his suicide, stating that Harry had 'never mentioned he wanted to kill himself before the tablets'.[2]

The coroner at the inquest seemed to have sympathy for Harry's father's claims, especially since we know that Prozac can, paradoxically enough, heighten suicidal tendencies despite the fact it's marketed as an antidepressant.[3] However, the coroner could not confirm that the pills had caused Harry's death. This was largely because it's near-impossible to establish retrospectively in suicide cases whether it was the person's depression, or the drugs they were taking, or the two combined, that led them to take their life. All the coroner could say in general terms was that the combined influences of Ritalin and Prozac could not be excluded as a factor in Harry's death, and that therefore doctors should be extremely careful when prescribing these pills to ten-year-old boys.

A few months after Reid broke this story, an independent report into the events surrounding Harry's suicide was published. Its verdict was that not only had the authorities demonstrably failed to improve Harry's situation, but that there was 'evidence of poor practice throughout, which included both single agency failings and generally poor inter-agency communication and collaborative working'. It also stated that the interventions Harry had received were 'largely adult rather than child-focused' and that there was 'no evidence of Child F's [Harry's] voice being heard or his wishes and feelings taken into account by professionals working with him and his family'.[4] Furthermore, even though Harry was given exceptionally high doses of Ritalin and Prozac, he had still never been given a psychiatric assessment and had never been classed as a 'high risk' patient – this, said the report, had been a mistake. Finally, the report implicated Harry's parents, concluding that one reason why Harry was 'extremely vulnerable' and felt 'unloved and unwanted' was possibly due to his parents not putting Harry's needs before their own.

In short, and perhaps quite predictably, the report ended up levelling accusations of negligence in many directions: at Harry's parents, at Harry's psychiatrist, at the various bodies charged with Harry's care, including the local agency responsible for children's mental health (CAMHS). And this is what you'd expect in a case as complex as this: a report claiming that numerous acts of neglect, rather than a single culprit, were responsible. What you'd also expect from the report is some reference to the role psychiatric drugs played in the tragedy. But here the report is suddenly cautious: 'The issues in relation to the use of such medication and the complexities involved in treating co-morbidities remain unresolved. This is clearly a national issue and central government guidance is needed to inform and direct future medical practice.' In other words, the report assumed it was beyond its jurisdiction to comment on whether the drugs were prescribed responsibly. It also declined to comment on whether the actual chemical properties of the drugs were a causal factor in Harry's death. After all, the report's compilers were not in a position to undertake a scientific assessment of their own. But even if they were, why on earth would they? The testing of pills is a rigorous, peer-reviewed scientific process overseen by independent regulators. Surely the people who ratify drugs like Ritalin and Prozac for public use, including those undertaking the manifold clinical trials through which such drugs pass, will have therefore identified all possible dangers the drug may pose? And this information, no doubt, will be passed on to prescribing clinicians. We are talking about medical drugs, after all – and so those who supervise their development and testing cleave to the highest ethical standards, overviewing processes in which we can all confidently trust.

If this were what the report supposed, then most of us would think the supposition fairly correct. And in fact most of the time *it would be* correct – that is, *most* of the time. But there are occasions when such suppositions are fundamentally frustrated by the facts. And such occasions, as will now become clear, appear with disconcerting frequency in the realm of psychiatry.

•

In Chapter 5 we encountered research showing that antidepressants work almost no better at all than dummy pills for the majority of patients.[5] We also heard how these findings were the result of researchers like Irving Kirsch and Walter Brown performing 'meta-analyses' that assessed both published and unpublished data about the efficacy of psychiatric drugs. The fact that most of the unpublished data just happened to be negative may have led you to wonder whether companies were actively suppressing results that didn't serve their financial interests. In this chapter it's time to enter that tricky area, by acknowledging that pharmaceutical companies have histories of concealing evidence they deem inconvenient. I will show that whether this concealment is achieved by crudely suppressing negative data or by subtly manipulating research to show their drugs in the most positive light, the unpalatable truth about psychiatric drugs is that manipulation of research has been a critical reason for their popular success. In short, so many inconvenient facts have been sidelined or completely hidden that public debates that need to take place (about drugs inducing odd states, or placebo states, or long-term pathological states, or suicide states, as may have occurred in Harry's case) do not win mainstream consideration. This chapter is therefore about what the compilers of the report into Harry's death either did not know or assumed they were not in a position to address. It's about how nearly all research into psychiatric drugs is today sponsored by the pharmaceutical industry, and about how this arrangement has led to the compromise of basic scientific standards, and at worst to the outright manipulation of research with the aim of maintaining or increasing company profits. The following sad procession of industry deceptions will illustrate what I mean.[6]

The first concerns the British pharmaceutical giant GlaxoSmithKline, which conducted three studies of its antidepressant called Paxil in the US and Seroxat in the UK.* These studies investigated whether this drug could reduce major depression in adolescents. But the trials were highly inconclusive. One trial showed mixed results, another showed that Paxil/Seroxat was no more effective than a placebo, while the third suggested that the placebo may be more effective with certain children. Despite these mixed results, the company published only the most positive study, publicly declaring that the drug is effective for major depression in children. This would have gone unnoticed had an internal company document not been leaked to the Canadian Medical Association. This showed that company officials had actively suppressed negative results

* In 2013 the same company, GlaxoSmithKline, decided to support a campaign asking for all clinical trial results, both positive and negative, to be registered and made publicly available. This decision followed the US government fining the company $3 billion in 2012 for many misdemeanours including withholding negative data about its best-selling diabetes drug, Avandia. Like many pharmaceutical companies, GlaxoSmithKline has withheld disappointing clinical data regarding the efficacy and safety of certain drugs. By publishing only positive data, many pills have come to appear more efficacious and safe than they are. We can only wonder whether this dramatic turnaround was due to the fine and the ensuing humiliation. Whatever the case, the company's support of the alltrials.net campaign is indeed welcome. Whether the campaign will actually achieve the desired greater transparency, however, remains to be seen.

from one study because, as they said: 'It would be commercially unacceptable to include a statement that the efficacy had not been demonstrated, as this would undermine the profile of paroxetine [Paxil/Seroxat].' Once this information came to light, a lawsuit was filed against GlaxoSmithKline in 2004 for intentionally hiding negative findings. This was settled out of court two months later when the company paid $2.5 million for charges of consumer fraud; a meagre sum considering that GlaxoSmithKline made $4.97 billion in worldwide sales from the drug in 2003 alone.[7]

In a separate class action in 2009 the pharmaceutical company Forest Laboratories was charged by the US Justice Department for defrauding the government of millions of dollars. It appeared that top executives at the company had, for several years, hidden a clinical study showing that their antidepressants Celexa and Lexapro were not effective in children and might even pose dangerous risks to them. At worst, these risks included causing some children to become suicidal.[8] Prosecutors said that by failing to disclose the negative results, Forest had kept crucial information hidden from physicians and from the wider public, preventing them from having all the information they required to make the right treatment decisions for young children.

And again, in 2010 an article in the *British Medical Journal* showed that the drug reboxetine, marketed as Edronax by the drug giant Pfizer, is no more effective at countering major depression than a placebo sugar pill. However, Pfizer withheld negative trials from publication. In fact, data on 74 per cent of patients whom the article surveyed were actually left unpublished. The authors concluded that if the excluded data had been included, the evidence would have showed that the risks of taking the drug far exceeded the benefits. Yet reboxetine has been approved for marketing in many European countries (including the UK and Germany) since 1997, and is still being taken by thousands of people in the UK today.[9]

My final example concerns an article published by the *New England Journal of Medicine* in 2008, which confirmed in graphic terms precisely how widespread the suppression of negative data for psychiatric drugs actually is.[10] This article reviewed over 70 major studies of antidepressants' efficacy, asking which of these had been published. The answer was patently unnerving. Out of all the studies the article surveyed, 38 showed positive results for antidepressants. And nearly every one of these positive studies had been published. The remaining 36 studies showed negative results. And out of these a full 22 had been buried, eleven had been published in a form that conveyed a positive outcome, and only three had been published accurately.[11] In other words, a total of 33 negative studies had either been buried or manipulated to convey a positive outcome.

This last article is so important not only because it shows the extent to which negative data never see the light of day, but also because it reveals that psychiatric drug research is being regularly manipulated to make negative data look positive.[12] And this in turn means that companies are engaging in strategies of deception greatly more sophisticated than merely hiding negative studies.

In 2005, a report by the British government's Health Committee identified some of these strategies. The authors of the report claimed that they had heard that lax regulation and oversight had allowed pharmaceutical companies to engage in a number of practices that clearly acted against the public interest. The strategies brought to their attention included:

> … that clinical trials were not adequately designed – that they could be designed to show the new drug in the best light – and sometimes fail to indicate the true effects of a medicine on health outcomes relevant to the patient. We were informed of several high-profile cases of suppression of trial results. We also heard of selective publication strategies and ghost-writing. The suppression of negative clinical trial findings leads to a body of evidence that does not reflect the true risk:benefit profile of the medicine in question.[13]

The former chief editor of the *British Medical Journal*, Dr Richard Smith, also highlighted the proliferation of these practices in a paper entitled 'Medical Journals are an Extension of the Marketing Arm of Pharmaceutical Companies'. Here he described how pharmaceutical companies have manipulated drug-trial data in ways so initially undecipherable that, as he confessed, it took 'almost a quarter of a century editing for the BMJ to wake up to what was happening'.[14] Smith, like the 2005 government report, also outlined some of the strategies he had witnessed companies using to get the results they want:

- Conduct a trial of your drug against a treatment known to be inferior [your drug therefore looks superior].
- Trial your drugs against too low a dose of a competitor drug [your drugs look superior].

- Conduct a trial of your drug against too high a dose of a competitor drug [making your drug seem less toxic].
- Conduct trials that are too small to show differences from competitor drugs [concealing that your drug could be inferior].
- Use multiple endpoints in the trial and select for publication those that give favourable results [thus discarding results that are unfavourable].
- Do multi-centre trials and select for publication results from centres that are favourable [again discarding negative results].
- Conduct subgroup analyses and select for publication those that are favourable.
- Present results that are most likely to impress – for example, reduction in relative rather than absolute risk.[15]

It's not only the former editor of the *British Medical Journal* who has spoken out. Richard Horton, editor of *The Lancet*, wrote in 2005 that 'Journals have devolved into information laundering operations for the pharmaceutical industry'. A position also supported by the former editor of the *New England Journal of Medicine*, Marcia Angell, who lambasted the industry for becoming 'primarily a marketing machine' and co-opting 'every institution that might stand in its way'. In fact, the situation has so deteriorated that editors at *PLoS Medicine* have now openly committed to not becoming 'part of the cycle of dependency … between journals and the pharmaceutical industry'; a cycle that sees journals sometimes publishing research biased in favour of company interests.[16]

While these editor complaints are of course reassuring, the plain truth is that the problem is far from being solved. Companies are still engaging in research strategies that by most accounts involve massaging the facts, and journals still often publish this research. But to truly appreciate the extent of this problem, let me first show you in a little more detail some of the unprincipled practices that cause such consternation in senior editorial ranks.

•

In May 2000 Dr S. Charles Schulz, a psychiatrist at the very height of his powers, walks up to a podium at the annual meeting of the American Psychiatric Association and announces a breakthrough in antipsychotic research. The breakthrough amounts to the development of a new drug that has 'dramatic benefits' over its competitors. Its name is Seroquel, and because of its superiority 'patients must receive these medications first', as he later wrote in the press release.

Two months before this commanding announcement was made, the company that manufactures Seroquel, AstraZeneca, was in disarray. It had just discovered that its latest research into Seroquel had revealed that the drug was far less effective than its arch-rival, Haldol. The document containing this finding was being circulated among senior staff at the company, who were now not sure what to do. An internal email written at the time (released later by the company during litigation) captured the mood very well:

From: Tumas John TA
Sent: Thursday, March 23, 2000, 10:05AM
To: Goldstein Jeffery JM; Murry Michael MF.
Subject: FW: Meta Analyses
Importance: High

Jeff and Mike.

Here's the analyses I got from Emma. I've also attached a message I sent to her yesterday asking for clarification.

The data don't look good. In fact, I don't know how we can get a paper out of this.

My guess is that we all (included Schulz) saw the good stuff, ie the meta analyses of responder rates that showed we were superior to placebo and haloperidol, and then thought further analyses would be supportive and that a paper was in order. What seems to be the case is that we were highlighting only the good stuff, and that our own analysis [now] support[s] the 'view out there' that we are less effective than haloperidol and our competitors.

Once you have a chance to digest this, let's get together (or teleconference) and discuss where to go from here. We need to do this quickly because Schulz needs to get a draft ready for APA and he needs any additional analyses we can give him well before then.

Thanks.[17]

In this email the publications manager at AstraZeneca casts about for a solution. He knows the research into Seroquel 'doesn't look good'. Yet he also realises that Schulz has to present a paper on Seroquel at the American Psychiatric Association's meeting in two months' time. If Schulz reports the negative data, the drug is presumably doomed. A way out is needed, and fast.

What does the company do? How in just two months does it move from private despair over the failings of Seroquel to a public declaration about its exceptional advantages? Does the company rapidly undertake a new study that finally secures Seroquel's superiority? Does it reanalyse the old data only to discover that the previous negative interpretation was wrong? The company does neither. There's no time. And even if there were time, the existing data are definitive: the drug is weaker than its competitors in many areas – that, it seems, is plain for all to see.

At this point you'd probably expect the company to cut its losses and with regret publish the whole truth. But presumably there's too much money at stake, and anyway, perhaps there's another way out. Sure, it's not an ideal route to take, or even an honest one, but given the money that could be lost it has to be worth a go. The company therefore opts for a strategy known in drug research as 'cherry picking'.

Cherry picking is the name given to the process by which only some of the data from a clinical trial are 'picked' for publication and the rest ignored. The huge advantage of proceeding in this way is that you can simply pick the data that make the drug look effective while leaving aside the data that don't. This was the solution AstraZeneca chose in early 2000. Rather than admitting that after a year on Seroquel patients suffered more relapses and worse ratings on various symptom scales than patients on Haldol, not to mention that they also gained on average 5kg in weight, which put them at increased risk of diabetes,* the company rather homed in on one shred of positive data about the drug faring slightly better on some measures of cognitive functioning. And it was on the basis of these data that public claims were made that Seroquel has 'greater efficacy than Haloperidol [Haldol]'; a fact they hoped would lead physicians '[to] better understand the dramatic benefits of newer medications like Seroquel'.

The company seemed to have favoured the practice of cherry picking for some time. Indeed, in the following internal email, again released during litigation, we hear how cherry picking had been used in a previously buried trial called Trial 15:

> From: Tumas John TA
> Sent: Monday, December 06, 1999, 11:45PM
> To: Owens Judith J; Jones Martin AM – PHMS; Litherland Steve S; Gavin Jin JP
> Cc: Holdsworth Debbie D; Togend Georgia GL; Czupryna Michael MJ; Gorman Andrew AP; Wilkie Allison AM; Murry Michael MF; Rak Ihor IW; O'Brian Shawn SP; Denerely Paul PM; Goldstein Jeffery JM; Woods Paul PM; De Vriese Geert; Shadwell Pamela PG
> Subject: RE: EPS Abstracts for APA
>
> Please allow me to join the fray.
>
> There has been a precedent set regarding 'cherry picking' of data. This would be the recent Velligan presentations of cognitive function data from Trial 15 (one of the buried

* Paula Caplan argues in her article 'The Pills That Make Us Fat' (*New Scientist*, March 2008) that it's not the weight gain that necessarily causes the diabetes, although in some cases it may, but that taking the pills can directly cause diabetes even in patients who do not gain weight, which is even scarier.

> trials). Thus far, I am not aware of any repercussions regarding interest in the unreported data.
>
> That does not mean that we should continue to advocate this practice. There is growing pressure from outside the industry to provide access to all data resulting from clinical trials conducted by the industry. Thus far we have buried Trials 15, 31, 56 and are now considering COSTAR.
>
> The larger issue is how do we face the outside world when they begin to criticize us for suppressing data. One could say that our competitors indulge in this practice. However, until now, I believe we have been looked upon by the outside world favorably with regard to ethical behavior. We must decide if we wish to continue to enjoy this distinction.
>
> Best regards,[18]

Obviously, AstraZeneca decides against the ethical option. Rather it continues to risk its reputation and the health of patients by cherry picking the positive data and burying the negative data in order to sell up the advantages of Seroquel over Haldol. This finally backfired in 2010, when so many people taking Seroquel were suffering from such awful side-effects that about 17,500 of them were officially claiming that the company had lied about the risks of the drug. These claims were finally vindicated in 2010 when AstraZeneca paid out £125 million to settle a class action out of court for defrauding the public.[19]

•

Of course, cherry picking is just one practice amid a variety of goal-moving techniques employed by pharmaceutical companies. One of the most common strategies is 'salami slicing'. This is when companies not only keep negative studies hidden from professionals and the general public, but also publish positive studies many times over in different forms and locations. The problem with this practice is obvious: it creates the false impression that many studies have been conducted, and all showing positive results, when in fact all the positive studies stem from only one 'data set' or piece of research.

To illustrate the highly subtle way in which salami slicing can operate, just consider a recent study that investigated 'pooled analyses'. A pooled analysis is a study that literally 'pools' or bundles together the results of many separate and previous clinical trials – rather like a meta-analysis does. However, the crucial difference between a meta-analysis and a pooled analysis is that a meta-analysis has to include *all* the relevant studies that address a particular question, whereas a pooled analysis may 'pool' only those studies that a company chooses to include to convey a desirable outcome.

To give you an example of this strategy at work, a recent study focused on 43 'pooled analyses' conducted by Eli Lilly for its antidepressant Cymbalta (duloxetine). It revealed, firstly, that several pooled analyses were based on greatly overlapping clinical trials and presented efficacy and safety data that did not answer unique research questions, and thus appeared to qualify as salami publications. They also found that six clinical trials were used in more than twenty pooled analyses that were each published separately – meaning that data from six trials were disseminated in over twenty different places.* The authors exposing these tactics declared that 'Such redundant publications add little to scientific understanding' and rather 'better serve the curricula vitae of researchers and, potentially, goals of drug marketers' than they do 'science and patient care'.[20]

If cherry picking is choosing to publish the good data while burying the bad, and salami slicing is publishing a positive data-set many times over in different forms and locations, then another equally suspect strategy is 'washing out'. This is when a company conducts a trial comparing a placebo to an active drug but first puts all the patients on a placebo for a specified period of time *before* the trial begins. What it then does is remove from the prospective trial all those patients who got better on the placebo. In other words, if the placebo makes you feel better, you won't be included in the trial. This dubious practice is justified on the grounds that anyone who responds to a placebo is either not 'ill' enough or has already recovered. But this justification doesn't even begin to address the core problem with 'wash out': by not allowing people who are helped by the placebo to enter the trial, you artificially inflate the numbers of people responding to the active drug compared to the placebo. Again, this highly questionable practice is common in psychiatric drug research.[21]

If you still doubt whether pharmaceutical research into psychiatric drugs is not as honest as we would like to believe, consider this final study published in the *British Medical*

---

* The authors declared that as their study focused on only one drug for depression, it did not therefore support general statements that pooled analyses containing redundant data are widely spread. However, it was clear that in this instance, as the authors said, 'salami slicing appeared to have taken place with substantial frequency via pooled analyses'.

Journal. It compared the outcomes of studies funded by the pharmaceutical industry with those funded from other sources. Overall, the company-funded studies were found to be four times more likely to show results favourable to company drugs than were studies funded from other sources.[22] It appears that when companies research their own products, they get results from which the company stands to benefit. The financial rewards of moving the goal-posts, it seems, make the temptation of doing so perhaps too strong to resist.*

•

How does moving the goalposts garner huge financial rewards? The former editor of the *British Medical Journal* makes it clear that publishing a positive article in a reputable journal is the most effective form of advertising a company can get:

> A large trial published in a major journal has the journal's stamp of approval … [It] will be distributed around the world, and may well receive global media coverage, particularly if promoted simultaneously by press releases from both

* For example, as Irving Kirsch has pointed out, when drug studies are funded by the pharmaceutical industry they show positive effects for their own drugs and negative effects for their competitors. On the other hand, when these studies are independently undertaken they show results that are midway between these two extremes. For example, a team of medical researchers in New York proved that when companies study their own drugs they tend to show favourable results 75 per cent of the time, while showing favourable results to competitors only 25 per cent of the time. However, in studies that are not company-sponsored the success rate is approximately 50/50. Each company, in other words, somehow manages to 'prove' its own drugs superior even when independent research and competitors may well not. See: Kirsch, 2010: 62–3.

> the journal and the expensive public-relations firm hired by the pharmaceutical company that sponsored the trial. For a drug company, a favourable trial is worth thousands of pages of advertising, which is why a company will sometimes spend upwards of a million dollars on reprints of the trial for worldwide distribution. The doctors receiving the reprints may not read them, but they will be impressed by the name of the journal from which they come. The quality of the journal will bless the quality of the drug.

Publishing a positive article in a reputable journal is therefore paramount. But if journal editors know this, why aren't they being more vigilant? After all, the articles discussed above were all published in distinguished medical journals. Smith defends the editors by arguing that, given the growing finesse of company tactics, it's increasingly difficult for editors to spot whether they are 'peer-reviewing one piece of a gigantic and clever marketing jigsaw'. Furthermore, Smith also admits there are many financial pressures bearing down on editors to publish company trials:

> Publishers know that pharmaceutical companies will often purchase thousands of dollars' worth of reprints, and the profit margin on reprints is likely to be 70%. Editors, too, know that publishing such studies is highly profitable, and editors are increasingly responsible for the budgets of their journals and for producing a profit for the owners. Many owners – including academic societies – depend on profits from their journals. An editor may thus face a frighteningly stark conflict of interest: publish a trial that will bring US$100,000 of profit or meet the end-of-year budget by firing an editor.[23]

In other words, if drug companies were non-profit-making industries, and if journals didn't have to rely on pharmaceutical revenues for their subsistence, we might well see these dubious research practices disappearing overnight. But these, right now, are just fantastic conditionals. Even in Britain where treatment is free at the point of delivery, companies are set to make vast profits each year should the right articles appear in the right journals. And companies are, of course, very successful at making this happen, since nearly all published psychiatric drug research is in some way industry-funded. Admittedly, psychiatrists still participate in much of this research, but that's no guarantee of its quality. As the former editor of the *New England Journal of Medicine* put it, increasingly doctors are used like hired hands, just supplying the patients, collecting the data and endowing the published reports with their prestigious names and university associations. Most companies now prefer their own employees to design the studies, perform the analyses, write the papers, and decide whether and in what form to publish the results. That way the companies retain control, and therefore make use of the many subtle strategies by which their products can be cast in the best light.[24]

Money, then, is at the heart of the issue: it can galvanise companies to find ever more ingenious ways to sell up their pills, it can dull editors' critical sense by the promise of high journal sales, and it can be used to win psychiatric endorsement of a pill, should the price be right.

So let's now focus on this final point. Have psychiatrists been co-opted into supporting the pharmaceutical mega-marketing machine? And if so, in what ways have companies used their financial clout to win psychiatric support for their products?

Before I address this important question, it's only fair I first warn you: if your blood pressure is already soaring, best consult your physician before turning the page.

9
But they make us rich

Two days after interviewing Robert Spitzer in Princeton it was time to make my way to Washington DC. With each mile I travelled southward, the temperature seemed to rise a corresponding notch on the thermometer. So I spent my first morning in a local coffee shop, writing, reading, dealing with emails and periodically asking the perspiring staff to turn the air-con up.

Once eleven o'clock struck, I puffed my way along Pennsylvania Avenue, so tightly wrapped up in jacket and tie that I nearly missed the United States Capitol rising up before me like an ancient seventh wonder. That was my cue to turn right down 2nd Avenue, past the Library of Congress and the Supreme Court, towards my destination: Hart Senate Building.

The Hart Senate is where Barack Obama's office was located before he was upgraded. It now has a wall of airport-style security booths confronting you as you enter. The building had been on high alert ever since an envelope full of anthrax was posted to Senator Tom Daschle's mailbox in 2001.

Once through security, I still had twenty minutes before my interview. So I made my way to the vast central indoor courtyard whose glass-topped atrium vaults an impressive 90 feet into the air, flooding natural light into the corridors and offices below. While sitting there it became clear to me: it was hopeless to pretend I fitted in. My suit was too shabby, my hair too long, and I didn't have a Blackberry.

Senators and their aides were gliding everywhere dripping in i-technology, with suits so well-tailored and hair so neatly cropped they looked as slick and polished as the shiny marble floors. So what on earth was I doing at the US senate?

Well, I was there to find out more about a malady afflicting most of medicine today, but especially psychiatry: it relates to the fact that pharmaceutical companies are paying physicians for a variety of different reasons, and not all these payments are transparent.

This issue is vitally important because although many years ago psychiatrists did not have extensive financial links with the pharmaceutical industry, in the last twenty years the industry has become a major financial sponsor of psychiatry both in Britain and the US, with unprecedented influence over psychiatric practice and research. The facts are telling: many heads of psychiatry departments now receive departmental income from drug companies, while at the same time receiving personal income.[1] Also, nearly all research into psychiatric drugs – antidepressants, neuroleptics, tranquillisers – is now pharmaceutically financed (e.g. nearly 90 per cent of all clinical trials in the UK are conducted or commissioned by the industry).[2] Furthermore, most consultants and academic drug researchers now also receive research funding, consultancy fees and honoraria from the industry; a fact graphically illustrated by how many members of the *DSM-IV* and *DSM-5* committees have strong financial ties to the drug industry.

A recent study by the University of Massachusetts, for example, worryingly showed that of the 170 panel members of *DSM-IV*, a full 95 (56 per cent) had one or more financial associations with the pharmaceutical industry.[3]

And for the diagnostic categories for which drugs are far and away the first-line form of treatment, such as the 'mood disorders', 'eating disorders', 'psychotic disorders' and 'anxiety disorders', an average of 88 per cent of all *DSM-IV* panel members had drug company financial ties. This trend has continued with the writers of the new edition, *DSM-5* (May 2013). Of the 29 Taskforce members writing the manual, 21 have received honoraria, consultancy fees or funding from pharmaceutical companies, including the Chair of the Taskforce, Dr David Kupfer, and the Vice Chair, Dr Darrel Regier.[4] These troubling facts are consistent with those recently unearthed by Propublica, a respected watchdog charity. It revealed from the data gathered that half of the highest payments made by the pharmaceutical industry to the whole of medicine were made to doctors from a single specialism – psychiatry.[5] As Robert Spitzer said to me in our interview almost apologetically: 'Well, today it's very difficult to find somebody or a large number of people who have not had some pharmaceutical support.'

So the question that had brought me to Washington is one that should concern us all: are these financial entanglements corroding the independence of the psychiatric profession itself?

•

The person I wanted to help me answer this question was Senator Chuck Grassley, a senior member of Congress who supports intensified regulation of the mental health industry. His story is compelling. He began life as a farmer in Iowa, never intending to reach high political office. But once his local reputation spread as a spokesperson for 'the ordinary struggles of ordinary folk' he was drawn into local politics, then into State politics, before securing a place in Congress. He has now been a Senator for over 32 years, and is still a man with a mission: the moral reform of corporate America. His reputation in Washington for countering corruption is so solid that the US Justice Department now refers to him as the 'federal government's best weapon against fraud'. Little has escaped his attention: corrupt tax practices, lax regulation of government agencies, the financial irregularities of corporate elites, and more pertinently for us, the misdemeanours of psychiatry.

I was excited to meet Grassley, as his communications director Jill Kozeny welcomed me warmly and led me rather ceremoniously down a long corridor towards his office. Jill gave a tap on the door before gently pushing it open. Senator Grassley was poised ready in the middle of the room – tall, lean, senatorial, commanding. He strode towards me confidently and, with a handshake like a quarterback's, boomed with a smile: 'So you're from England, huh? Well, come on in then, take a seat, we've got a bit of time.'

It was clear that Senator Grassley and I would not be alone. The communications director and a senior assistant, busily arranging various folders and notebooks as we sat down, would be very much part of our meeting – fact-checking, jumping in with additional information, and sometimes qualifying what Grassley said. Very professional – very American.

What I wanted to know first was how Grassley became interested in the relationship between psychiatry and the pharmaceutical industry. So once a few preliminary pleasantries were past, I put the question directly to him.

'I was chairman of the Finance Committee here in Washington', answered Grassley coolly, 'and this committee pays for all of the Medicare and Medicaid medicines in the US. This gave us jurisdiction over the Food and Drugs Administration [FDA], which is the agency responsible for ensuring that prescription drugs are efficacious and safe for the public to use.'

Grassley's relationship with the FDA was initially smooth, until one rainy afternoon a whistle-blower from the agency entered his office with a barrage of disturbing revelations. 'We learned that the scientific and regulatory processes within the FDA weren't working properly', said Grassley with a growl. 'They were being compromised by a lot of people at the FDA who had too close a relationship with the pharmaceutical companies. The FDA was approving drugs for public use which some in-house scientists knew were dangerous. And when these scientists tried to speak out, the FDA put enormous pressure on them to shut up.'

Just in case you have forgotten, we encountered the FDA back in Chapter 4. Like its equivalent in Britain (the MHRA), it's the organisation that merely requires a company to show in just two clinical trials that their antidepressant is more effective than a placebo. If this can be shown, then no matter how many negative studies there have been, the drug will be approved for public use. But this issue of 'discarding the negatives' was not the problem Grassley was now referring to. He was rather alluding to a scandal concerning a drug called Vioxx, made by the pharmaceutical giant Merck. The scandal unfolded in the following way: a scientist at the FDA, David Graham, decided to go public about how the agency had ignored warnings that Vioxx was killing people by causing heart attacks and strokes (as many as 140,000 heart attacks, according to Graham). Furthermore, even before Vioxx was sent to the FDA for approval, it was clear there were questions at Merck about the drug's safety. Graham's point was that not only should the FDA never have approved the drug for public use, but the drug should never even have been submitted for approval. Once Grassley got wind of these problems, his suspicion of the dealings at the FDA was ignited, a suspicion that has in no way abated:

'Whenever I get the heads of the FDA in here', said Grassley leaning forward intently, 'I ask them all the time whether things have been put right. Every one of them sits there and promises that things are going to be changed. But we never really know until there is another scandal.' Grassley then paused as if recalling something important: 'Actually, I don't know if we've had any recent scandals or not.'

'We do!' jumped in one of his sprightly assistants. "There was another group of FDA whistle-blowers that had come to see Senator Grassley. The FDA got wind of it, so they hacked into these scientists' personal email accounts to monitor the discussions they were having with Senator Grassley.'

'And that reminds me', boomed Grassley, banging the chair with his fist, 'we are going to get the FDA director in here to pursue that, right? Because they aren't even answering our mail yet. So what have they got to cover up?'

It was these struggles with the FDA that led Grassley to turn his attention more specifically to the doctors themselves, especially those who work as academic researchers within universities. This group is crucially important to the pharmaceutical industry, because they have the power and influence to alter the opinions and prescribing habits of the wider community of practitioners. When a university professor or leader in the field speaks up on behalf of a drug, other doctors listen. And this is why companies actively and aggressively recruit their services: doctors simply trust them more than they do company reps. The companies themselves even have a term for these influential doctors: 'KOLs' (Key Opinion Leaders). But given the potential conflicts of interest involved in being both a psychiatrist and a KOL, psychiatrists who work in universities are expected to report any income they receive from pharmaceutical companies for research, speakers' fees or work on advisory panels. Grassley was interested in whether this reporting system was working within the universities. Were doctors accurately reporting their industry income? He undertook an investigation to find out.

What Grassley first discovered was that when financial disclosures were being made, they were usually kept secret. As he put it in a speech delivered to the Senate floor in 2007: 'If there is a doctor getting thousands of dollars from a drug company, payments that might be affecting his or her objectivity, the only people outside the pharmaceutical industry who will probably ever know about this are the people at that very university.' A further and more serious problem he encountered was that the universities were terrible at keeping track of who was being paid what. 'The reason why the universities weren't checking things', said Grassley to me heatedly, 'was because the National Institute of Health wasn't paying much attention to how the universities were conducting their affairs. This meant that the only people who knew whether the reported income was accurate or not were the actual doctors receiving the money.'

This problem first became apparent after Grassley sent a letter to the University of Cincinnati asking how much money the drug companies had been paying to one of their psychiatrists, Dr Melissa DelBello. Grassley had become interested in DelBello ever since her work on bipolar disorder in adolescents had been discussed in the *New York Times*. Her study, which was funded by pharmaceutical company AstraZeneca, showed that Seroquel (yes, Seroquel again) was particularly effective for treating bipolar disorder in children. This study, which helped put Seroquel on the map, led to DelBello being hired by the company to deliver promotional talks to other psychiatrists about the virtues of the drug. When DelBello was asked by a reporter at the *New York Times* how much she'd received for this promotional work, she replied curtly: 'Trust me, I don't make much.'

But Grassley wanted to know how much. So he contacted her university to find out. The university disclosed that a year after DelBello's influential study was published, AstraZeneca paid her over $100,000 for lectures, consultancy fees, travel expenses and service on advisory boards. In the year after that she received a further $80,000 for the same services. In subsequent years (between 2005 and 2007) DelBello was also paid a further $238,000 by AstraZeneca. The problem was that for that same period she had reported earnings of only $100,000 to her university. As DelBello had not been reporting her industry income accurately, were other doctors doing the same? Grassley cast his net further to find out.

The next person Grassley caught was totally unexpected. His name was Professor Charles Nemeroff, and he was Chair of Psychiatry at Emory University – one of the most prestigious psychiatry departments in the US. Now, the thing about Nemeroff was that for many years he had been widely accorded almost rock-star status in American psychiatry, being referred to as the 'Boss of Bosses' by a leading psychiatric journal due to his voluminous drug research and many charismatic public appearances. Behind the glamour, however, another story was waiting to be told – one that again would be written by Grassley.

In short, officials at Emory University had been aware for some time that Nemeroff was slippery when it came to declaring company income. In 2004 a fourteen-page university report had asserted that Nemeroff had committed 'serious' and 'significant' violations of university policy when it came to stating his conflicts of interest (this seemed to have been linked to his receiving money from sitting on no fewer than 26 different pharmaceutical advisory boards). Rather than severely sanctioning Nemeroff, the university seemed only to give him a gentle tap on the knuckles and let the matter slide.[6] This would prove to be a mistake, as Nemeroff's misdemeanours would simply continue. For example, Nemeroff later published an article in the very journal of which he was editor-in-chief. In this article he gave a glowing endorsement to a treatment device made by a company from whom he was also receiving consultancy fees – fees that he did not declare (something he put down to a 'clerical error'). Then another scandal broke regarding a book he had co-written that taught family doctors how to treat psychiatric disorders (largely with psychiatric drugs).

While the preface disclosed that the authors had received an 'unrestricted educational grant' from a major pharmaceutical company, it did not acknowledge the true extent of company involvement, which included the company paying a writing firm to develop the outline and text of the book, drafts of which were sent to the pharmaceutical company for 'sign-off' and 'final approval'. It was argued by many critics that obviously Nemeroff had been paid by the company to put his name to a book that largely promoted company products.

As these and a series of other alleged infringements continued, the university seemed none the wiser. That is, until Grassley's investigation began to shed light on Nemeroff's accounts. As the figures came in, Grassley discovered that between 2000 and 2007 Nemeroff had earned a staggering $2.8 million in personal income from drug companies, while declaring income of only $1.2 million to university officials. This included receiving from GlaxoSmithKline a full $960,000 of personal income between 2000 and 2006, while he'd declared only $35,000 to Emory. But what disturbed Grassley more was that at the same time as receiving money from GlaxoSmithKline, Nemeroff had also been given a grant worth $3.9 million (paid for by the taxpayer) to study psychiatric drugs made by GlaxoSmithKline – the very same company from which he had received nearly $1 million in personal income.

'So I got the president of Emory in here', said Grassley pointing his finger angrily, 'and I asked him what are you going to do about this! He sits where you are and tells me that he'll stop Nemeroff from getting any more federal grants for research while at Emory. But Nemeroff is senior professor who is used to getting grants, so that's no good for him. So what does Nemeroff do? He moves to another university [Miami], where he is made the new Chair of psychiatry.' Grassley then turned to one of his assistants: 'Now that reminds me, we've gotta find out whether he's still getting federal grants down at Miami!'

'Sure', said one of the assistants eagerly, 'we'll look into it!' (After the meeting I decided to look into it. Nemeroff had just been given another grant from the National Institute of Mental Health for a huge sum of $2 million. His move to Miami had obviously paid off.)

'There were other outstanding examples too', said Grassley crossly. The most prominent of these concerned another grand patriarch of the industry – the Chair of Psychiatry at Stanford University, Dr Alan Schatzberg, who also at the time of Grassley's investigation had just been made President of the American Psychiatric Association. What Grassley discovered was that Schatzberg controlled more than $4.8 million worth of stock in Corcept Therapeutics, a company he co-founded and that was testing a drug called mifepristone for psychotic depression. At the same time Schatzberg was the principal investigator on a National Institute of Mental Health grant that included research on mifepristone. He was also found to be co-author of three papers about the drug. When Stanford was challenged about Schatzberg's position, the university released an ill-advised statement declaring that it saw nothing amiss with his arrangements. This seemed an unreasonable claim to make, since Schatzberg was the principal researcher for a drug from which his company stood to make millions if it were proved effective. Once the team at Stanford realised that Schatzberg's position was indefensible, it released another statement a month later saying it was temporarily replacing Schatzberg as principal investigator to eliminate any 'misunderstanding'.

As Grassley's investigation unfolded, he exposed more and more psychiatrists for similar infringements. Some of the more prominent culprits included Joseph Biederman of Massachusetts General Hospital (colloquially known as the 'King of Ritalin'), who was reported to have earned $1.6 million in consulting fees from drug companies between 2000 and 2007, most of which was not disclosed to Harvard University officials. There was also Dr Frederick Goodwin, former director of the National Institute of Mental Health, no less. He was reported to have earned at least $1.3 million between 2000 and 2007 for marketing lectures to physicians on behalf of drug companies. He did not disclose this to relevant parties such as national media outlets, where he'd been invited to speak publicly about drugs. There was also Dr Karen Wagner, Professor at the University of Texas, who was reported to have failed to disclose more than $160,000 in payments from GlaxoSmithKline, disclosing only $18,000. Then there was Dr Thomas Spencer, Associate Professor of Psychiatry at Harvard Medical School. He was reported as failing to disclose fully his at least $1 million in earnings from drug companies between 2000 and 2007. Another culprit at Harvard Medical School was Dr Timothy Wilens, who reported to Harvard that he had earned several hundred thousand dollars in consulting fees when in fact he had earned at least $1.6 million.[7]

Grassley's investigation slowly revealed that there was hardly a bank left in the country into which some senior psychiatrist hadn't deposited unreported pharmaceutical cash. And as disturbing as this may be, what troubled Grassley more was that not one of the psychiatrists listed above had actually broken the law. This is because there is no current law (either in the US or the UK) prohibiting psychiatrists or doctors from inaccurately reporting what money they receive. Of course, false reporting may be frowned upon within the professional community, and may even be sanctioned by a particular university, just as Emory sanctioned Nemeroff at the prompting of Grassley. Even so, while no actual law was broken, the fact that the University of Miami still employed Nemeroff as Chair of Psychiatry while knowing his financial entanglements raises serious questions about the double-edged relationship some universities have with industry money. For not only do individual psychiatrists benefit from company income – so do many university research centres that rely on the industry funds their researchers bring in. Nemeroff is a huge industry player, winning pharmaceutical grants with consummate ease, which makes him supremely attractive to psychiatry departments, especially since (as in the US and the UK) there is almost no departmental funding available to underwrite research, and also very limited government or federal funds.

Pharma fills an important funding gap – but again, does it do so at a price? Pharmaceutical companies, after all, are businesses, not charities. Their bestowals can't be classed as disinterested handouts; rather they are investments from which companies expect a definite return. The question, of course, is if universities begin to feel obliged to deliver on that investment, is there a danger they'll lose some of their independence and start doing and saying things advantageous from the company's standpoint?

•

To address this concern, let's now consider the case of a professor of psychiatry called David Healy, who teaches at the University of Wales. For many years Healy had been investigating whether antidepressants can cause suicidal tendencies and violent behaviour in patients. Such was the significance of his research as well as his growing international reputation that in 2000 he was formally offered the prestigious position of Clinical Director of the Mood and Anxiety Programme at the University of Toronto. Before he started his post, he was invited to the university to deliver a lecture on mental illness and addiction. During his lecture Healy argued that much research 'demonstrating' the value of antidepressants was unconvincing, and that in rare cases these drugs can lead to suicide. The lecture seemed to go well, and he returned to Britain feeling satisfied with his performance. But two months later an email from Toronto dropped into his inbox, retracting the university's previous offer. The reason the university gave to Healy was that his work, as his lecture indicated, 'was not compatible with the development goals and clinical resources of the department'. Healy was at first bemused by this change of mind, then wondered whether it had anything to do with his openly criticising the pharmaceutical industry.

Healy did some digging, and his suspicions were compounded after discovering that Eli Lilly, the company whose antidepressant he'd critiqued in his lecture, was a significant contributor to the University of Toronto. It turns out that it supported 52 per cent of the budget for the Mood and Anxiety Disorder Clinic that Healy would have run, as well as having given $1.5 million to the clinic's fundraising campaign. Healy also discovered a precedent that the company would remove its financial support if anti-Prozac comments or publications were made by the clinic. Putting two and two together, Healy began to suspect that the university had pulled its offer because it feared that he, by critiquing Eli Lilly, would threaten an important funding source.

And so with the full backing of the Canadian Association of University Teachers, he sued the university. He argued that by retracting his job offer, perhaps because his views were potentially economically inconvenient, the university had essentially sent the message that certain viewpoints are undesirable – in short, Healy argued, they had violated the principle of academic freedom.[8] Perhaps sensing the negative media attention this case would whip up, the case was finally settled out of court for a substantial but undisclosed fee (which, incidentally, Healy donated to charity).

This particular story illustrates how company ties may compromise not only the integrity of institutions but also that of individuals working within those institutions. After all, the decision to retract Healy's post was made not by an anonymous centralised computer system but by individuals who presumably had personal and institutional interests to protect. When push came to shove, it appeared that Healy rather than Eli Lilly was sacrificed, which raises questions about whether accepting pharmaceutical money comes at the cost of retaining one's full institutional, research and clinical independence.

Whenever I put this question to a psychiatrist, the response I receive invariably depends on whether he or she is a recipient of industry money. Those who are recipients, perhaps unsurprisingly, regularly sidestep the idea that taking industry money is potentially corrupting, and rather point out that the pharmaceutical industry is now virtually the only source of funding for research into new psychiatric drugs. How can a researcher therefore hope to study new drugs without having financial industry ties? Many also stress that engaging in promotional activities, such as speaking on behalf of company drugs, is a professional obligation: if a drug works, then psychiatrists have a responsibility to disseminate this knowledge to the wider medical community and beyond; and as such dissemination takes time, it's only right that psychiatrists should be remunerated. A similar argument is also used to justify accepting fees for company consultancy work: as psychiatrists are mental health experts, why should they deny companies their expertise? To deny their expertise surely means to debar the industry from a vital source of guidance and knowledge, they argue.

Psychiatrists who have rejected company money often scoff at these arguments, regarding them as rationalisations that physicians use for having put themselves in a compromised position. They argue that if all research into psychiatric drugs is pharmaceutically sponsored (and therefore often interfered with by company employees), then the funding system simply has to change. Furthermore, if psychiatrists feel the need to promote drugs or consult for companies, then let them do so – as long as they either do the work for free or donate their payments to charity.

Taking money, the critics argue, too easily leads to the subtle corrosion of professional independence, which in turn can lead to putting company interests above the interests of patients. For instance, some psychiatrists now use pharmaceutical money to supplement their salaries – often by very generous amounts. These supplements can ease many financial burdens. But the danger here, of course, is that once you have become dependent on such annual payments, you have to keep doing whatever you're doing to ensure these payments don't dry up. Usually this means doing and saying things that are cost-effective from a company's point of view, because companies will rarely continue to invest in doctors from whom they don't expect to profit. Critics therefore insist that to take from the pharmaceutical purse is to enter a Mephistophelian pact; one that gradually and often unconsciously erodes the recipient's capacity to think and act objectively.

Dr Carol Bernstein, ex-president of the American Psychiatric Association, referred to this matter when I interviewed her at New York University's medical school in 2011. When I raised with her Grassley's investigations, her response was unequivocal: 'If you're getting money and benefits from doing something, there's going to be tremendous psychological incentive to keep doing that thing, whatever it is, even if it's not science. … Brilliant scientists were in bed with the pharmaceutical industry and I think that they just got corrupted because you get all this money and you get all these perks and you stop thinking objectively. The purpose of pharma, yes, it's to do with research, but it's an industry whose purpose is to make money. So they're going to do whatever they can to make money.'

When I quote this statement to industry-paid psychiatrists, the responses I get are interesting. Many of them acknowledge the dangers, then reassure me that, unlike others, they're on top of it. Others simply shrug as if to say, 'What else can we do? The industry is our primary sponsor.' This position seemed to be close to that offered by Dr Ian Anderson, the Chair for the current NICE guidelines into how depression should be treated throughout the NHS. I interviewed Anderson because he had recently altered a clause in the NICE guidelines that I believe can allow pharmaceutical companies to claim that antidepressants have 'statistically significant' benefits over placebos, even though the 'significant' difference could be as low as a single point on the Hamilton Scale. I was concerned that this alteration gave the green light for companies to continue to make inflated public claims about the benefits of antidepressants when in reality the benefits could be completely clinically insignificant. Towards the end of the interview, I said: 'I must ask you, Dr Anderson, have you ever received money from the pharmaceutical industry for consultancy research grants, conferences, honoraria, etc.?'

'Yes, yes I have', Anderson replied.

'But you can see how it may appear to people', I continued. 'On the one hand you are creating guidelines for how depression should be treated in the NHS, while at the same time you've received pharmaceutical money. Furthermore, you have now controversially removed a threshold that may allow companies to make inflated claims about the power of their drugs. You can see how easy it is to make an argument that there's a bit of a cosy relationship going on here ...'

'There is no perfect solution to individual corruption', answered Anderson, 'if I can put it as strongly as that. We are all influenced by different things to different degrees. I think one of the problems is that because some of the cutting-edge developments in psychopharmacology are tied in with industry, there is a danger [by severing these ties] of throwing out the baby with the bathwater.'

Anderson sits on the fence. But this position would be more acceptable if we knew for certain that industry money did not bias the judgement of its recipients. The problem is that we can't be so certain. For example, there were two recent separate investigations of what happened when many hospital doctors were given corporate all-expenses-paid trips to seminars at popular vacation sites. Although these doctors said the gifts would never influence them, the investigations revealed that from the period after they had received their invitations they significantly increased prescribing the promoted drugs.[9] A further study by the *New York Times* analysed the prescribing habits of psychiatrists in Minnesota. This found that on average, psychiatrists who received at least £3,000 from makers of newer-generation antipsychotic drugs appeared to write three times as many prescriptions to children for the drugs as psychiatrists who received less money or none.[10]

Research like this is still scant on the ground, and it only charts the effects on prescribing habits, not on doctors' clinical values, beliefs and research practices. Nonetheless, it does flag up what many people intuitively sense to be the case: that it's harder to retain your independence when you receive money from a company with a vested interest in your taking a position profitable to them.

•

Given the Grassley investigations discussed above, UK readers could be forgiven for thinking that dubious pharmaceutical entanglements are mainly an American problem and that in Britain we have escaped the worst excesses of industry involvement. This was certainly what I believed until I started digging more deeply back in the UK.

First off, it wasn't long before I realised that regarding transparency laws, Britain is still far behind the US. Recent legislation initiated by the Obama administration (called the Physician Payment Sunshine Act) will, as of August 2013, oblige all drug and medical device suppliers and manufacturers to track and report all payments made to physicians and teaching hospitals. This move towards greater transparency has been accorded a significant boost since full oversight for the Act's implementation has been given to Senator Grassley. Also, the American Medical Student Association has now set up a system requesting all medical schools to report how many faculty members receive pharmaceutical money.[11] Today you can find online which US universities are tightening their policies on drug ties, and find out how many faculty employees have acknowledged having these ties. These measures are attempts to balance the need for drug companies to recruit the expertise of doctors, with the public need to know whether a psychiatrist is saying something because it's the best medical advice or because he or she has a financial interest in saying it.

So in the US there may be a glimmer of light on the horizon. But what about in the UK? In 2011 the Association of the British Pharmaceutical Industry's code of practice was updated to include new requirements for companies to declare, as of 2013, payments to doctors for attending medical congresses. These changes are of course welcome. But you also have to read the small print. This code does not include the obligation of companies to disclose payments to doctors for research and development work, including the conduct of clinical trials. Nor does it include a requirement for companies to disclose funding given to doctors for research. Furthermore, the code only asks companies to disclose the total yearly amount paid to all of the doctor-consultants who have provided services.[12] Most significantly, it does not request companies to disclose the individual names of these consultants. Nor do companies have to disclose the names of doctors who have received speakers' fees or hospitality and sponsorship for attending meetings and conferences.[13]

In short, if you want to know how much pharmaceutical money your psychiatrist has received this year, short of asking for their personal accounts (and good luck with that), you have little hope of ever finding out.

What about British universities? Under the Freedom of Information Act (2000) I made requests to eight universities, chosen at random, to disclose whether their psychiatry department or psychiatric faculty had received payments from the pharmaceutical industry. These universities were: Oxford, Cambridge, Manchester, Liverpool, The Institute of Psychiatry (King's London), University College London, Newcastle and Edinburgh. So what emerged? Well, two universities declared they hadn't gathered the figures; a third declared (it turns out wrongly) that their psychiatrists had received no money; I'm still awaiting the figure from another university; and the remaining four declared that members of their psychiatry faculty had received pharmaceutical payments. Here is a breakdown.

- The psychiatry department at the University of Newcastle took over £5.5 million from the industry in the years 2009 to 2012 (this figure was only for research funding and does not include payments received by individual psychiatrists for consultancy work and speakers' fees – so the final figure will presumably be far more.)
- The psychiatric department at the University of Oxford had received £687,000 from the pharmaceutical industry from 2009 to 2012 (again, this figure does not include payments received for consultancy work and speakers' fees).
- The division of psychiatry at the University of Edinburgh received £1.59 million in research funding over the last three years (again, this figure does not include payments for consultancy work and speakers' fees).
- The Institute of Psychiatry reported receiving £1.87 million between 2009 and 2012 (once again, this does not include payments for consultancy work and speakers' fees).

None of the above universities would disclose their psychiatrists' private industry income for consultancy work, speakers' fees etc. And in many cases this was simply because the university did not request this information. As

Liverpool University put it, psychiatrists 'are not required to report individual payments to the University so we don't hold any information which could be provided in response to this part of the request'.[14] But even if universities make a commitment to gathering this information, that is no guarantee that all employees will play ball. For example, one senior British psychiatry department declared to me that their faculty had reported no payments at all, even though there was a responsibility for the faculty to do so. Yet after a mere five minutes searching online, I discovered that at least three of its senior psychiatrists had declared receiving pharmaceutical money in their published research. After I wrote back to the university to point out this discrepancy, a week later they sent another email reaffirming curtly: 'As we have stated, we are not aware of any academic staff receiving payments from pharmaceutical companies and this would include all academic staff both currently and previously employed by the university.' The phrase 'we are not aware' makes it hard not to conclude that these psychiatrists, based at one of the most prestigious departments in the UK, had simply not reported their income to university officials.

The troubling truth is that neither universities nor pharmaceutical companies in the UK are obliged to declare under any kind of legislation the following critical information: the names of individual psychiatrists and what pharmaceutical money they receive for research funding, consultancy work, speakers' fees, hospitality, educational activities, sponsorship, honoraria and so on …

Without this vital information we cannot check whether the eye-watering payments Grassley discovered in the US are also being issued in the UK. And this is particularly worrying since we know that payments are being made. What we don't know is how much and to whom. So if you therefore think we are far ahead of the US in our transparency laws (or that, even if we are behind, we are still 'probably more trustworthy than the Americans', as one interviewee put it), I urge you to consult the facts and seriously think again.

•

I left Senator Grassley's office and headed down the National Mall, that long covering of greenery stretching out from the US Capitol towards the Lincoln Memorial. As I walked close to the shade of the trees, I couldn't shake one of Grassley's final comments from my mind: 'Good luck with how your work is received', he had said, with a hint of warning in his voice. It was almost as if he were saying, don't expect an easy ride. So I started recalling some of the responses I'd already received whenever people asked about this book. Did they signal trouble ahead? Well, mostly the responses were genuinely encouraging. At other times, sure, they were non-committal. But then again, occasionally I did indeed receive reactions that verged on hostile: 'Why are you taking on the community?' an older associate asked suspiciously. 'Hasn't psychiatry got its house in order since the problems of the 1970s?' Another man at an academic conference seemed incredulous, telling me that critiquing psychiatry was 'a risky business' and asking: 'Have you read Freud's *Totem and Taboo*?' (This question, if you don't know the book, implied that my true motive for challenging psychiatry could be an unconscious desire to take a pop at 'authorities'.) Then there was a gala dinner at my old university where a young cardiologist asked me about my research. After giving him a few ins and outs, he said half-jokingly, but also tellingly: 'Why, are you a scientologist?'

I of course understand these reactions. Medicine is a profession to which we all feel we owe enormous debt, and in which we ought to be able to trust fully. When one of its specialisms is challenged, it would be naive to expect everyone to take it well. So mostly I just let the more provocative comments slip, treating them as data to be stored rather than as invitations for dispute. After all, I have never felt troubled by authority per se, but only with its abuse. Power itself is neither good nor bad. It's how it is used that matters. What disturbs me, and I suppose what disturbs us all, is when the powerful, in the name of serving others, begin to use their power to serve themselves. This is what enrages us about political expense scandals, or free press abuses of privacy rights, or old-boy networks protecting their own. Call us idealistic, but we are right to feel consternation when people start wielding the privilege of power self-interestedly.

As I continued on my way towards the Lincoln Memorial, there was one final comment still on my mind, one that had stood out from all the rest. A psychiatrist I had interviewed early on in this project put it to me frankly: 'Don't you practise psychotherapy, so don't you have competing interests? Any critique of psychiatry is surely a goal scored for psychotherapy?' This got me thinking. Psychotherapy and psychiatry, after all, do compete for limited resources, both in the private and public sector. So a book like this, which exposes the weakness of psychiatry, could potentially be seen as inadvertently serving the psychotherapeutic profession (leading to increased employment for people like me). And yet, to be clear, I am also a social anthropologist (a profession from which I earn my living), and as an anthropologist I have never taken an either/or position with respect to psychiatry and psychotherapy. I have been critical too of psychotherapy's limitations and excesses – something my previous academic work makes clear.[15] After all, my professional aim has never been to put the interests of a single professional group within the mental health industry first, but only ever the interests of patients. Furthermore, although I have worked as a psychotherapist in organisations like the NHS, I have never received any money for the clinical work I have undertaken. So far I have worked only voluntarily.[16]

At the Lincoln Memorial, I stood for a moment pilgrim-like at the foot of an icon. Lincoln had fascinated me ever since reading his letters as a teenager. He had always been conflicted by power – reluctant to assume it, watchful of those wielding it, and consummately observant of its potentially corroding effects. As I sat in the shade on the Memorial steps, looking back soberly towards the Capitol, one of Lincoln's sayings came to mind: 'Nearly all men can stand adversity', he had written, 'but if you want to test a man's character, give him power!' This quotation now seemed thoroughly apposite to what Grassley had revealed only moments ago: a psychiatrist warrants criticism to the extent that his or her character has failed the test of power. But I also knew that this general notion applies to institutions as well as to individuals; institutions that, for one reason or another, have similarly failed the test of power.

How this notion applies specifically to psychiatry is a matter I shall explore next.

10
When science fails, marketing works

In the years following the release of Prozac in 1988, the pharmaceutical industry fractured into ever-greater warring fragments. The ensuing battle concerned which company would gain the greatest share of a rapidly emerging market opportunity: the demand for a brand-new wave of antidepressants believed far superior to earlier psychiatric drugs. This market would be worth billions of pounds annually to any company able to convince doctors and the wider public that it manufactured the most efficacious pill. As company after company charged in to win its market share, different versions of these new antidepressants arrived year on year – Prozac, Effexor, Seroxat, Lustral, Cipramil – each claiming to be better than the last.

Given the vast amounts of money at stake, it's little surprise that companies developed increasingly sophisticated marketing techniques to persuade people that their drugs worked best. In places like Britain where the pharmaceutical industry was prohibited from directly advertising its pills to the public, it instead had to rely solely on what is generally called physician-directed marketing. This meant that general practitioners (GPs), psychiatrists, academic researchers and psychiatric nurses all became targets of elaborate promotional exercises by which the profile of a particular drug could be raised and the number of prescriptions increased. The seriousness with which companies took these marketing offensives is illustrated by the huge sums they spent. At the height of the marketing war, the industry invested twice as much money in promoting its pills as it did in researching and developing them. For instance, in the mid-2000s companies were spending £1.65 billion on drug promotion in Britain each year. This investment is evidenced by how quickly marketing departments in the pharmaceutical companies expanded. The ex-editor of the *British Medical Journal* stated, for example, that between 1995 and 2004 there may have been a 59 per cent increase in the number of employees working in pill promotion, while jobs were actually cut in drug research.[1] Because a large proportion of these vast resources were used in promoting antidepressants, it's safe to say that during the 1990s and 2000s the British public's escalating familiarity with these drugs was largely a product of the pharmaceutical marketing machine.

What kinds of strategies did companies use to promote their pills so successfully? In what kinds of tactics did they so heavily invest to achieve their financial goals? How did the pharmaceutical industry, in other words, manage to transform an obscure set of SSRI antidepressants in the early 1990s, which really didn't work too well and were dangerous in many ways, into one of the most widely prescribed species of drug in medicine today?

•

In early 2001 a young psychiatrist called Daniel Carlat, like thousands of other psychiatrists at the time, became embroiled in this drug marketing war.[2] The particular battle in which he got tied up concerned a new antidepressant called Effexor, developed by the pharmaceutical company Wyeth. During the early 2000s the company was on a promotional offensive to convince practitioners across Europe and the US that Effexor was superior to its competitors. Unlike the existing SSRI antidepressants, which just targeted serotonin levels, Effexor was rather a 'dual reuptake inhibitor', which meant it targeted two neurotransmitters (serotonin and norepinephrine). Wyeth claimed that Effexor's dual action rendered it superior to its SSRI competitors. And so the Wyeth sales reps worked to the same simple objective wherever they went: convince the doctors you visit that Effexor is best.

On a nondescript afternoon in 2001, one of these sales reps would confidently stride into Dr Daniel Carlat's office with an enticing offer in hand. Would Carlat be willing to give some talks about Effexor to other doctors? Sure, he'd be paid for the talks (between £300 and £500 per hour), and sure, he'd receive some training. But the training really wouldn't take long – and he'd be paid for that too. All he needed to do was turn up at a hotel in New York in a few weeks' time and attend a two-day crash-course on Effexor. Then he'd be ready. His stay would also be very comfortable: all expenses paid of course. What's more, he needn't leave his wife at home – her ticket was paid for too.

'I was extremely flattered by this offer', Carlat confessed to me as he recounted the drug rep's visit, 'especially since I'd been out of the academic setting for so long working in a small community.' Indeed, since finishing his psychiatry residency a few years earlier, Carlat's career had remained decently modest. 'I'd been working half-time in an in-patient unit and half-time in my own private practice', said Carlat. 'I was just spending my time enjoying meeting patients and learning my craft.' Carlat enjoyed no glitzy pharmaceutical links or perks, even though he knew lots of other psychiatrists had been enticed by them, something he first noticed when still training as a psychiatrist at medical school: 'I realised back then there were a lot of doctors and academics who were doing work with pharmaceutical companies, either doing research or just jetting around the country, or even the world, giving different kinds of presentations. Their lifestyle appeared very glamorous. And there was an unspoken sense among the psychiatry trainees that this was the lifestyle to one day chase after too.'

Perhaps a seed had been sown back then, because a few weeks after the Wyeth rep stepped into Carlat's office, Carlat and his wife would step off the plane in New York. They would make their way to a luxurious hotel in the heart of Manhattan, where a Wyeth attendant with a dazzling smile would greet them. She would hand Carlat a conference pack, containing a schedule of talks as well as invitations to various dinners and receptions, and, surprisingly, two tickets for a Broadway musical. Despite the pang of conscience Carlat felt at having so much money lavished on him, he couldn't help but feel, well, kind of special. How very distant his small-town practice now suddenly seemed from the glamorous world into which he had been invited.

In between the dinners and entertainment events, Carlat eagerly attended the talks, which were delivered by some leading lights in antidepressant research. Firstly, there was Dr Michael Thase from the University of Pittsburgh. He was the global authority on Effexor, and one of the most respected psychiatrists in the United States. Thase's task was to report the findings of his huge meta-analysis, which included studies covering more than 2,000 patients. Thase's results were so impressive that Carlat soon understood why they were taking the world of psychiatry by storm. Effexor achieved a remarkable 45 per cent remission rate, which in ordinary terms meant that 45 per cent of patients experienced a complete disappearance of symptoms. With results like these Effexor far excelled the existing SSRIs (whose remission rate was only 35 per cent) and placebos (remission rate 25 per cent). If these figures held true, then for the first time in modern psychiatry, one antidepressant stood out from all the rest. Not only would this revolutionise what doctors would prescribe, it would also increase Wyeth's profits by billions of dollars a year. Could Thase's results be trusted?

Thase was determined they could. And to prove this he would spell out carefully to the crowded room of psychiatrists the main objections to his research, so he could impressively rebut each in turn. The first objection he addressed was that Wyeth had funded his meta-analysis. Did this not create a conflict of interest that may have biased his study? Thase was adamant. He and his team had consulted all the data and not cherry picked the results most favourable. They had abided by the strictest scientific standards, ensuring that their objectivity could not be purchased – it was as simple as that.

Another objection was that Effexor had only been compared to one SSRI – Prozac. So presumably other SSRIs may perform better. Thase was ready for that one too. Since the original study, he had analysed data about Paxil and other

SSRIs. And as luck would have it, these also showed similar advantages for Effexor – case closed. The final objection concerned why Thase had chosen to measure 'remission' rates over the more usual 'response rate'. The difference was subtle but important. For instance, 'a response' is achieved when a patient experiences a 50 per cent improvement on the Hamilton Scale (e.g. moving from 30 points before treatment to 15 points after treatment), while 'remission' is defined as complete recovery (in Thase's study this meant achieving a score of 7 or below on the Hamilton Scale). Had Thase chosen to measure remission over response because it would make Effexor look superior? Carlat couldn't work it out, until Thase addressed the issue head-on: no matter where you put the cut-off rate for remission (7 points, 6 points, 9 points, etc.) Effexor always came out on top. With each rebuttal the audience grew more convinced.

Thase received eager applause for this impressive display, and the next speaker made his way to the podium: a psychiatrist called Norman Sussman, a professor at New York University. Sussman was a typical front-man – more charismatic and personable than the academic Thase. He was also an expert populariser, demonstrating fluently to the psychiatrists the most effective manner in which they could communicate the great news about Effexor to doctors up and down the country.

And so the talks continued until, by the end of the weekend, the attendees had been thoroughly dosed with a mixture of genuine education and effective sales techniques. If any lingering doubts remained, well, there was no need to dwell on them now: the last night of the conference had arrived, and what's more, there was a surprise waiting: for

Carlat it came in the form of a small envelope containing $750 – 'it was now time to enjoy the city', as Carlat put it.[3]

When Carlat returned to his small practice in Newburyport, there were already two messages from Wyeth reps waiting on his answer machine. Obviously the company wanted to begin its promotions in earnest. Carlat would deliver his talks once or twice a week during his lunch breaks. This time suited everyone, including the reps, who could use the occasion to entice bigger audiences with offers of free lunch. Sometimes there'd be just a small gathering of doctors and nurses, sometimes a crowded conference room, and at other times just Carlat and a single physician. While each setting was different, one thing never changed: there was always a drug rep present, scrutinising Carlat's performance and occasionally giving him notes after a talk: emphasise this, don't worry about that, enjoy yourself more, you're doing well. Before his talk the reps would also advise Carlat on the prescription habits of the various doctors he'd be addressing that day. They obtained this crucial information from data-mining companies that accessed prescribing data recorded at pharmacies. These data were repackaged and sold on to companies like Wyeth so they could tailor their sales strategies accordingly. The whole operation was very slick, and Carlat was beginning to feel uneasy.

First off, he soon realised that his £300–£500 an hour came at a price. 'When I was sitting in New York I could never have imagined the huge pressure I'd be under to perform in those talks in a certain way', Carlat said to me. 'When you are being paid a significant amount of money to promote a pill, and when you know that the reps are going to decide whether to invite you back depending on whether the doctors will prescribe Effexor after your talk, the question is how that pressure affects you. Does it cause you to highlight the advantages inappropriately and to downplay the side-effects? Did the promise of more money actually affect the content of what I was telling those doctors? I struggled with those questions.'

These struggles deepened as Carlat began to encounter more criticisms of Effexor. New data seemed to show that the remission rates for the drug were far less impressive than Thase had reported in New York – more like 5 per cent better than SSRIs instead of the reported 10 per cent. Also, Carlat realised that Thase's meta-analysis may have been a victim of some of the methodological games I discussed in Chapter 8. For example, some patients enrolled in the original Effexor studies had taken SSRIs in the past and had presumably not responded well. This meant that the study population might have included patients who were already treatment-resistant to SSRIs, therefore giving Effexor an inherent advantage. Finally, the majority of studies Thase assessed in his meta-analysis were fairly short-term – only six or eight weeks long – so there was a possibility that if the clinical trials had been longer (e.g. six months or a year), the response and remission rates of the SSRIs compared with Effexor's would have turned out to be the same.

Although Carlat knew that this crucial information invited 'the kinds of methodological discussion that may really be important for doctors to hear', he kept this highly relevant information out of his talks. He feared that if he mentioned it, the reps wouldn't invite him back. But at the same time he also realised 'by not mentioning them I was committing sins of omission'. Carlat began to struggle seriously with the ethics of his position – a struggle very soon deepened by two events.

The first occurred at a lunchtime meeting when Carlat was talking about Effexor to a group of psychiatrists. One psychiatrist took issue with Carlat's view that high blood pressure was relatively uncommon with low doses of Effexor, stressing that in his clinical experience Effexor's record on hypertension was pretty poor. Carlat was caught off-guard and struggled to respond. Sure, back in New York Thase had actually briefly addressed the blood pressure problem. But Carlat was also aware that 'while there are data to support the position that the drug is safe, when you really dig more deeply into the data, the full story isn't quite as cut and dried'. In other words, Carlat had been trained to talk about Effexor's weakness in a way that would reflect best for the drug, and in a way that would be most likely to encourage doctors to try it out. 'This did not mean the company ever told us to deny these side-effects exist', said Carlat, 'only that you just had to talk about the side-effects to physicians in a way that wouldn't alarm them. And you'd also have to couch them in a way that would convince doctors that Effexor was worth trying even before, in some cases, safer medications had already been tried.'

The disagreement forced Carlat to acknowledge that he was spinning the study's results in the most positive way possible, while playing down the limitations of the data. 'I thought to myself', said Carlat frankly, 'that I'm ultimately doing more of a disservice by discussing the data in simplistic terms than I am serving these doctors in educating them about the drug.' His style had to change. He would have to be more upfront. Then came the second event.

'I decided in one talk to say that the studies of Effexor were very short, and that if they'd been longer it's feasible that the competitors of Effexor may have caught up. But when I made that point in front of the doctors, the drug reps did not look very happy. The next day I had an unexpected visit from the district manager of Wyeth, who said the reps had told him that in my last talk I didn't seem so enthusiastic about his "product". He then looked at me closely and asked – "Have you been sick?" I was shocked. It was as if the only possible way I could not be enthusiastic about his product was if I were somehow ill – not on my game.' That encounter was decisive for Carlat: 'It laid bare for me my role from the standpoint of the company, which was to be a marketer for their drug. And to the extent that I said anything that was in any way negative or not glowingly positive about their product I was less and less useful to them, even if what I were saying was accurate. That was the tipping point when I decided to stop giving promotional talks.'

When I asked Carlat whether he believed his talks influenced the prescribing habits of the doctors he addressed, he was unequivocal: 'I would be astonished if my talks did not significantly affect their prescribing behaviours. And the reason I say that is I was talking to primary care doctors and family practitioners who are not specialised in psychiatry. To them I was an expert simply educating them about the benefits of Effexor. So they just assumed, well, as he's saying it, it must be true, and I should try prescribing it.'*

* Carlat continued: 'This is why companies hire physicians. Over the years, companies have found by trial that a physician pitching a drug is much more effective to the bottom line than the drug being pitched by a rep. The reasons

This indeed, was the intended effect. And if 'Key Opinion Leaders' like Carlat didn't achieve this effect, there would be tangible consequences. As Kimberly Elliott, who handled Key Opinion Leaders for a number of pharmaceutical companies, put it: 'Key opinion leaders were salespeople for us, and we would routinely measure the return on our investment, by rating prescriptions before and after their presentations.' She continued: 'If that speaker didn't make the impact the company was looking for, then you wouldn't invite them back.'[4]

•

There are many startling things about the case of Dr Carlat, but it raises the question about one particular strategy that I think is essential to how the pharmaceutical industry markets its pills. This involves exploiting the highly hierarchical nature of the medical profession, in which an almost caste-like system of professional rank arranges the relations between its various 'levels'. Junior doctors defer to registrars, who defer to consultants, who in turn bow to their more senior consultants. This pyramid of ascending seniority sees each rank sitting atop and enjoying authority over the ranks below. Companies therefore know that if they are to convert the pyramid's base, they must first convert those at the top. They must recruit senior psychiatrists like

for that are obvious. When you listen to a drug rep you know you are listening to a salesperson, whose incentive is to make a bonus based on your prescribing. But when you listen to a colleague physician, even though you know that he or she is being paid by the company, there is a tendency to trust that person, to believe that it would be somehow uncouth for a fellow physician colleague to have the same kind of financial motivation the drug reps have.' (interview, August 2012)

Dr Michael Thase and Dr Norman Sussman to convince less senior doctors like Daniel Carlat to spread the message to the wider ranks of medical students, junior doctors, primary care physicians and GPs. This latter group is especially important because the vast majority of antidepressants are not actually prescribed by senior psychiatrists, or even by psychiatrists at all, but by family doctors and GPs who listen carefully to the advice psychiatrists provide.[5] After all, your kindly and overworked local GP has little time to scrutinise all the research relevant to every drug that he or she daily prescribes, and so is reliant on what more senior people like Thase impart through medical journals, and on what less senior doctors like Carlat impart during their visits.

This strategy of paying Key Opinion Leaders like Thase and Sussman to ensure that community preferences align as closely as possible with company interests sheds a bit of light on why Senator Grassley found so many senior psychiatrists receiving eye-popping amounts of industry money. An endorsement from a top researcher at a senior university will benefit your brand far more than a thousand company reps could ever do. This is especially the case if their endorsement is itself published in a journal of high repute, which has often led drug companies to brazen excesses to recruit journal support. And I'm not just talking about providing financial incentives for editors to publish company-sponsored research (as in Chapter 8) or designing, conducting and writing research to which academics then merely put their names (a practice known as ghost-writing) but about strategies that go even further. One recent case saw the drug giant Merck, for example, pay an undisclosed sum to the international academic publishing house Elsevier to produce several volumes of a publication that had the look of a peer-reviewed medical journal, but actually contained only reprinted or summarised articles – most of which, unsurprisingly, presented data favourable to Merck products.[6]

While feeding the top of the food chain is a crucial company marketing strategy, this doesn't mean that the junior ranks are left alone. They are not only visited by pharma reps and by speakers like Carlat (albeit perhaps in fewer numbers than in Carlat's day), but they too can be invited to all-expenses-paid conferences or 'continuing medical education' events where experts discuss new treatments. They are also regularly sent free drug samples in the hope that their prescribing habits will alter, and are sometimes asked to find patients for drug trials while being offered strong financial inducements. At the same time they are subjected to a barrage of adverts for psychiatric drugs placed in medical journals.[7] Company marketing directives should therefore be a matter of serious concern for the general public, not least because it would be naive to suppose that marketing campaigns have played no role in inflating prescriptions (the over 50 million antidepressant prescriptions in England in 2012 cost the taxpayer well over a quarter of a billion pounds).[8] After all, if these marketing strategies didn't work, you'd hardly expect pharmaceutical companies to keep investing in them.

•

While the prescribing figures in the UK are high, in the US they are higher by around 13.5 per cent. To put this figure into perspective, this means that in 2011 there were around

746 prescriptions of antidepressants per 1,000 people in the UK, while in the US there were around 843 prescriptions per 1,000 people.[9] Naturally, there will be many socio-cultural factors contributing to why the US prescribes more antidepressants, but once again we cannot dismiss the role of marketing. After all, the US is one of only two countries (the other being New Zealand) where direct-to-consumer advertising of psychiatric drugs is permitted. This means that in the US adverts for antidepressants can be placed freely on trains and buses, on billboards, in magazines, on television and on the internet. The pharmaceutical industry takes this form of advertising very seriously, spending billions of dollars on it every year.[10] And it justifies this huge expenditure both as a wise investment and in terms of its providing an important public service; one that increases public awareness of undiagnosed disorders such as depression and that therefore alerts people to problems that may otherwise go untreated. Countries that reject direct-to-consumer advertising often offer the counter-argument that the education of patients and physicians is surely too important to be left to the pharmaceutical corporations, whose ability to produce unbiased information can't be guaranteed. Consider, for example, the following series of US adverts, all of which make scientific-sounding claims that don't stand up to serious scientific scrutiny.

In a recent advertising campaign for a drug called Abilify, which is prescribed to people diagnosed with bipolar disorder and depression, a commercial claimed that it works in the brain 'like a thermostat to restore balance'.[11] The print advertisements also claimed that: 'When activity of key brain chemicals is too high, Abilify lowers it …

When activity of key brain chemicals is too low, Abilify raises it.' Another example was the widely televised Zoloft commercial, which again plays on the chemical imbalance idea. It states that 'Prescription Zoloft works to correct this imbalance', even though not a single piece of research has ever confirmed what a so-called 'correct' chemical balance looks like. Then there's the advert for Paxil that says: 'Just as a cake recipe requires you to use flour, sugar and baking powder in the right amounts, your brain needs a fine chemical balance in order to perform at its best.' Advertisements for other big-selling antidepressants such as Prozac and Lexapro have made similar claims, again in the absence of scientific support.[12] One of the first direct-to-consumer pamphlets produced by Eli Lilly for Prozac, for example, stated that: 'Prozac doesn't artificially alter your mood and it is not addictive. It can only make you feel more like yourself by treating the imbalance that causes depression.' The fact that the chemical imbalance theory has never been proved doesn't seem to matter to these corporations, who have made their public assertions as though they were based on scientifically established certainties.*

In these cases it's clear that pseudo-scientific claims are being misused to sell the idea that our problems are largely biological in origin and so best remedied with costly biochemical solutions. In 2011 I encountered a particularly brazen example of how far such misinformation will go. In a video promoting antidepressants on the American

---

* Irving Kirsch speaks of a brochure issued by the US National Institute of Mental Health, which states that 'depressive illnesses are disorders of the brain' caused when 'important neurotransmitters – chemicals that brain cells use to communicate – appear to be out of balance' (Kirsch, p. 81).

Psychiatric Association's website, we overhear a father reflecting upon his son's depression and how it led to a catastrophic end. The father says:

> 'I did not understand that depression was a disease. If he'd been a diabetic I'd have gotten him insulin. I told him "get over it, you'll feel better later". I used to think medication was mind control. When he stopped his therapy he got worse. When maybe he could have been helped.'

The most chilling part comes at the end of the video when the father turns to his other son and says forlornly, 'I have got some bad news about your brother ...' – implying that his untreated depressive brother had finally taken his own life.[13]

This promotional video drives home a number of misleading messages that play on public fear and confusion around mental health issues, while exploiting viewers' trust of medical experts. These messages imply that depression is a disease like any other physical disease (a view that research doesn't support); that medication is really the only solution (another unsupported view); and finally, that not giving your child medication may lead to their death (a gross overstatement by all measures). This video therefore taps into our anxiety that if we don't defer to drug treatments then we have only ourselves to blame if tragedy ensues. This kind of pseudo-scientific scaremongering should have no place in respectable medicine or even in medical marketing, but research now indicates that such tactics are used in adverts for psychiatric drugs more than in adverts for any other type of medication.[14]

It's not just scientific authority that has been misappropriated to sell pills. Any authority will do – including the authority of celebrity. In a popular commercial for the antidepressant Paxil, the British company GlaxoSmithKline paid the American football player Ricky Williams a huge figure to discuss his 'social anxiety disorder'. Elsewhere, GlaxoSmithKline has Williams saying: 'It's amazing how much I've grown and how much I've changed and how much I went through. And of course I owe a lot of that to Janey, my therapist, and Paxil.'[15] So it seems that Paxil not only corrects your chemical imbalance but also helps you to grow into a better person. The irony is that while this advert was being disseminated, GlaxoSmithKline was busily burying data about Paxil's ineffectiveness for certain groups.

What should concern Americans more is that all the adverts above were approved by the Food and Drugs Administration (FDA). But even when the FDA has to step in to ban a particular drug advertisement (as it eventually did with the even more misleading commercials for Sarafem), those adverts will still have been aired. This is because, contrary to what many people believe, the FDA does not assess pharmaceutical advertisements before they are released. Instead, it only monitors advertisements once they are disseminated, which means that fraudulent messages can still do the rounds (and so do their work) before they are axed.[16]

While many doctors are savvy about the cozening claims of 'pharma fraudulence', the evidence is that these ads still have a significant impact on doctors' prescribing habits as well as expanding the antidepressant market.[17] This is because consumers are influenced by the adverts and then go to their doctors to demand the promoted pill, which doctors in turn prescribe. An innovative study published in *The Journal of the American Medical Association* demonstrated this by gathering together a group of pseudo-patients who were trained to behave as patients. They were sent to different primary care physicians to see what would happen if they asked for a particular drug. The results were revealing. Out of the 100 pseudo-patients who asked their doctors for Paxil, a full 32 received Paxil, while out of the 99 pseudo-patients who just made a general request for any antidepressant, only six received Paxil – indicating that what doctors prescribe is significantly affected by what patients demand.[18]

While direct-to-consumer-advertising is prohibited in Canada, the UK and the rest of the European Union,[19] pharmaceutical companies still manage to get their message across to the public in these countries, often via the more circuitous routes of media and internet resources. For example, in the UK today there is an ever-growing number of mental health professionals who receive money from drug companies while at the same time contributing to public debates in prominent newspapers and online magazines, often presenting in these contexts positive messages about antidepressants.

The problem here is that audiences rarely know about these industry ties, because media outlets are not obliged by law to report them. To give you just one example: In 2011 I read an article published on BBC NewsOnline extolling the virtues of antidepressants.[20] What concerned me was not its recommendation for wider antidepressant use, but that the citation at the foot of the article stated that the author had 'given lectures on behalf of a number of pharmaceutical companies'. When I further researched these company ties I found that the citation omitted to mention that the author had actually received consultancy fees and honoraria from many pharmaceutical companies including Janssen-Cilag, Eli Lilly, AstraZeneca, Bristol-Myers Squibb, Otsuka and Wyeth. The thousands of people who read this article were not informed that this author was a paid pharmaceutical consultant.

After I pressed the BBC, the Health Editor finally conceded to change the citation to reflect this potential conflict of interest (it can now be seen at the foot of the article at the time of writing). Changing the author's citation was a welcome implied admission that full disclosure is the proper course of action. But would this single admission stop similar mistakes being made in the future? I wrote to the BBC Trust requesting that BBC NewsOnline enshrines in its editorial policy the obligation to disclose whenever authors on mental health issues have financial industry links. I also included an online petition that I had started, which in the first few days of going live was signed by over 1,000 mental health professionals (psychologists, counsellors, psychiatrists and psychotherapists). I explained to the BBC Trust why this issue was so important to us, citing further evidence where BBC NewsOnline had failed to declare its antidepressant commentators' financial ties on many occasions. For example, in 2009 alone, I found the following cases:

In the article 'Antidepressants "Work Instantly"' (October 2009), the same Dr Michael Thase who trained Daniel Carlat in New York was quoted supporting antidepressants. We weren't told that he has acted as a consultant to AstraZeneca, Bristol-Myers Squibb, Cephalon, Cyberonics, Eli Lilly, GlaxoSmithKline, Janssen, MedAvante, Neuronetics, Novartis, Organon, Sepracor, Shire US, Supernus and Wyeth; that he is on the speakers' bureaus of AstraZeneca, Bristol-Myers Squibb, Cyberonics, Eli Lilly, GlaxoSmithKline, Organon, Sanofi-Aventis and Wyeth; and has equity in MedAvante. In the article 'Antidepressants Not Overused' (September 2009), Dr Ian C. Reid was extensively quoted, again supporting the prescribing of antidepressants. We weren't told that he has received consultancy and speaker fees from Sanofi-Aventis, Wyeth UK, Eli Lilly and AstraZeneca. In the article 'Drugs Can Help Mild Depression' (May 2009), Tony Kendrick was also extensively quoted supporting antidepressant use. Again, we weren't told he receives fees and funding from Eli Lilly, Lundbeck, Servier and Wyeth pharmaceuticals.

Upon discovering these and other undeclared interests, I argued that the BBC (albeit unknowingly) was in effect permitting the pharmaceutical industry to promote and/or advertise antidepressants via its paid consultants on its website, by not informing readers as to their paid status. I requested that the BBC Trust take action to ensure that the public will be better protected from such editorial mistakes in the future.

It took ten months for the Trust to respond. I finally received a reply on 19 November 2012 from Francesca O'Brien, Head of Editorial Standards at the BBC Trust. In short, it stated that the committee found the issue I raised very 'thought provoking', but nevertheless believed my concerns to be covered by the current guidelines. Even so, it agreed that if the guidelines needed to be more explicit they would 'consider' their amendment at the time of the next revision. In the meantime they would ensure that the BBC's Director of Editorial Policy and Standards, David Jordan, would remind BBC News of its obligations to make careful editorial judgements about signposting any potential conflicts of interest among its contributors.

The result could have been better (there's no admission that the current editorial guidelines fail to oblige editors to cite financial conflicts of interest). But on the other hand it could also have been worse (they will consider revising the guidelines at the next revision, while right now reminding editors of their obligations). So all that remains is to continue to monitor BBC News articles closely to ensure that these obligations are kept, as well as to continue lobbying for a change of guidelines at the next review. As for the countless other news outlets regularly reporting on antidepressants – well, things look far less sanguine. Short of a national media commitment to making these ties entirely transparent, we must continue to be wary of what we read in the news.

•

When we pull together the facts of all the preceding chapters, an underside of psychiatry begins to emerge with which most people are unfamiliar. The underside is that whenever someone ostensibly benefits from a psychiatric prescription, the pharmaceutical industry and many within psychiatry benefit too. The question must be, therefore, who benefits more? Once again, where you sit will determine your answer. After all, those who enjoy industry ties usually defend their importance robustly, stating that they inform research and facilitate the creation of better drugs, which in turn can only better serve struggling patients. But that is not the story here – ours reports a different version of events; one that gets far less publicity and one to which you must decide for yourself how far you are willing to subscribe. That alternative version in its most unvarnished form is:

The categories of mental disorder (rather than painful experiences themselves) are psychiatric constructions and not scientifically discovered biological entities. As these categories have greatly proliferated in number in the DSM and ICD, psychiatry has reclassified more and more of our natural human behaviours and feelings as psychiatric disorders requiring treatment. By doing so, psychiatry has not only expanded its jurisdiction over more of us (one in four of us apparently now suffers from a mental disorder), but has also, by inflating the number of mental disorders, created a huge market for psychiatric treatments. The preferred treatments are pharmaceutical treatments such as antidepressants and antipsychotics. But the emerging reality is that these treatments don't actually work in the way most people believe. In the case of antidepressants, mostly they have placebo effects, powerful side-effects, and sometimes mind-numbing effects. But never do they have curing effects, largely because for the vast majority of disorders listed in the DSM there is no discernible 'disease' that these pills target and treat. These inconvenient facts are not generally known, partly because pharmaceutical corporations have promoted misinformation through concealing negative data, through powerful marketing campaigns costing billions of pounds a year, and through conducting research that regularly chops the figures in ways advantageous to company interests. One reason why psychiatry has tolerated this more than it should is because too many doctors, research centres and researchers, and too many DSM committee members – that is, too many leaders within the psychiatric profession – have had their objectivity compromised by the pharmaceutical funds upon which they have come to depend.

I offer the above as a hypothesis that the facts of the preceding chapters oblige us to take very seriously. But however far you subscribe to this hypothesis, there is one proposition that I think most of us, wherever we stand, would find very hard to discount: that 'biological' or 'pharmaceutically sponsored' psychiatry has slowly, imperceptibly but most assuredly begun to alter the way many of us now manage, respond to and experience our emotional discontent. Precisely what form this alteration has taken, and what its implications may be, is a matter that I will pursue in the next chapter.

11
The psychiatric myth

In the late 1890s it was time for a brilliant young medical student called Carl Gustav Jung to decide his professional future.[1] What branch of medicine would Jung specialise in? The decision was difficult, as every door was open to him. If he chose one of the more established branches of medicine, his future would enjoy all the trappings of financial security and professional prestige. But then Jung was never a conventional man; and what's more, through marrying into a wealthy family he could afford to make unconventional professional decisions. So Jung followed his inclination, and decided to do something that his peers, his seniors and his family believed to be very foolish. He chose to specialise in psychiatry.

Why on earth, they asked, would he do that? After all, psychiatry at that time had still not been established as a legitimate medical specialism. It suffered from very low status among the medical professions for a variety of reasons. In the first place, psychiatric treatment just wasn't very successful. While researchers and doctors practising general medicine were gaining headway in understanding and treating the disorders of the body, psychiatry continued to slumber far behind in its clinical success rate.[2] Furthermore, the subject matter of psychiatry (our internal mental lives) was far less accessible to medical study and treatment than were the disorders of the physical body. The mind was decidedly more complicated, not least because its problems could be caused by multiple factors – spiritual, moral, environmental, social – not easily explained by biological malfunctions. Psychiatrists were dealing with something different, and were struggling to know what to do. This was the state of affairs in the late 1800s when Jung shocked those close to him by choosing psychiatry. Little did he know that the fortunes of psychiatry would soon change dramatically.

A key player in this change was a doctor called Emil Kraepelin. In the early 1900s, Kraepelin gained international repute by arguing that our emotional problems were not really problems of the soul or the mind or anything else that was difficult to pin down scientifically. Rather, underlying every mental disorder, he claimed, there was surely a specific brain or biological pathology. If psychiatrists were to treat mental problems successfully, therefore, they should direct their efforts at finding these underlying biological malfunctions. With the help of this new biological vision Kraepelin believed that psychiatrists would not only be finally free to explore new procedures that treated mental distress via the body, but would also be better able to align themselves with the general medical preference for biological explanations and treatments. Psychiatry, went the argument, was like the rest of medicine – it had just been looking in the wrong place. Jung might not have made a poor decision after all.

Kraepelin's biological convictions gave momentum to the development of a barrage of new psychiatric treatments during the first half of the 20th century. In the 1920s these included interventions not for the squeamish:

surgically removing parts of the patient's body, their teeth, tonsils, colons, spleens and uteri. The rationale for these highly painful and sometimes fatal treatments was that bacteria living in one of these bodily areas caused mental illnesses. So, it was thought, if you remove the body part, you cure the problem. As Joanna Moncrieff's work makes clear, this was the thinking behind other similar treatments being reported at this time in reputable psychiatric journals as reasonable cures for mental illness.[3] These included injecting patients with horse serum; using carbon dioxide to induce convulsions and comas; injecting patients with cyanide; and giving them hypothermia. Again, psychiatrists used these procedures to target the underlying virus or disease that they were convinced must be at the root of the trouble. Another treatment was malaria therapy. This involved injecting the patient with the malaria parasite in the hope that the high temperatures malaria produced would kill the virus then thought to be responsible for mental diseases. You won't be surprised to hear that the effects of this therapy were often devastating, as many patients failed to recover from the malaria.[4]

Because success rates of these early treatments were so poor, a suite of new procedures was developed during the 1930s. These included treatments like insulin coma therapy: putting patients into a coma for two hours with high doses of insulin, and then suddenly waking them with glucose. The aim here was to generate in patients powerful seizures, which were thought to be somehow therapeutic. After this procedure, granted, patients might seem to be or in fact feel calmer, but they would often show memory loss and other neurological abnormalities such as loss of speech. Five per cent of all patients actually died from this treatment, so once again psychiatrists found themselves grappling for alternative treatments.[5]

Hope was kindled in the 1940s with the development of what was called at the time a ground-breaking new psycho-technology – known as the lobotomy. This involved surgically removing parts of the brain that were thought responsible for acute mental distress. This new treatment was so widely celebrated in psychiatry at the time that its inventor, António Egas Moniz, was actually awarded the Nobel Prize in 1949.[6] Thirty to forty thousand people in the US had been lobotomised by the 1970s before the treatment was finally abandoned because of its appalling effects, which are still being experienced by thousands of people alive today.

Fortunately, however, as lobotomies decreased, other treatments were ushered in. One that grew in popularity during the 1940s (and still in use) is electroconvulsive therapy (ECT), which was brought to popular attention by the cult classic book and film, *One Flew Over the Cuckoo's Nest*. This procedure involves inducing severe seizures in depressed patients by administering intense electric shocks to the brain. Although many psychiatrists still swear by the healing effects of this controversial intervention, their claims about success are more than offset by the reams of research illustrating ECT's pernicious effects, poor remission rates and responsibility for widespread neurological damage.[7] Furthermore, recent reviews of ECT research have not shown significant differences between real and 'fake' ECT after the treatment period (fake ECT administers no electricity at all, without the patient's knowledge). On the contrary, research assessing the improvement rates of fake versus real ECT after six months has actually revealed a 2-point difference on the Hamilton Scale *in favour* of the fake treatment – suggesting that if ECT has any positive effects at all these are largely placebo effects.[8]

The point of listing some of psychiatry's more outlandish treatments is that they all won impetus and legitimacy from psychiatry's enduring conviction that there must be a physical basis for mental disorder. As you will recall, this originated with Kraepelin's assumption: if our emotional maladies are biologically caused, then that is where our treatments must be directed. Of course, for psychiatrists such as Carl Jung, who felt that these practices verged on barbarianism, there were alternatives. Jung was a part of a growing tribe of psychiatrists in Europe, the UK and the US who rejected Kraepelin's biological vision and embraced the more interpersonal and less invasive talking cures. During the 1940s, 50s and 60s this group became very powerful indeed, especially in American psychiatry. In fact, the Taskforces of the first and second editions of the DSM (in the 1950s and 60s) largely comprised these psychoanalytically-oriented psychiatrists. But the talking cure and biological psychiatry were always strange bedfellows, and always antagonistic. After all, psychotherapists did not share the same biological convictions that Kraepelin used to save psychiatry from complete obscurity in the early 1900s – convictions that helped align psychiatry, intellectually at least, with neighbouring biological streams of medicine.

Therefore, when criticisms of psychotherapy gained momentum in the 1970s the ground was set to reject the talking cure and once again embrace Kraepelin's early vision. This was reflected by the fact that Spitzer's *DSM-III*

Taskforce included only one psychoanalyst, as Spitzer put it to me, as 'a token gesture'. This neo-Kraepelinian revolution, as it was called, was given a significant boost by allegedly exciting new developments in drug treatments. As I discussed in Chapter 5, in the 1950s drugs were seen at best as soothing tonics, but as drug company involvement in psychiatry gained pace in the 1970s, 80s and 90s they were soon marketed as medical cures that targeted and cured discrete diseases. Many senior psychiatrists legitimated this view in medical journals and the popular media – at the same time as receiving handsome rewards from the drug companies.

The drug revolution solved many problems for psychiatrists. The profession could now put a legacy of embarrassing clinical failures and devastating treatments to rest, and embrace drugs as the first line of treatment. Psychiatry now possessed the psycho-technologies that not only brought it in line with the rest of medicine, thus increasing psychiatry's status in the eyes of other medical doctors, but that also rendered psychiatrists distinct from the barrage of psychologists, counsellors, pastoral counsellors, marriage and family therapists and other psychotherapists who were beginning to flood the treatment market in the 1980s and 90s. Psychiatrists were largely the only professionals, after all, who had legal authority to assign psychiatric diagnoses and prescribe psychiatric drugs. And so long as these activities remained predominantly in their hands, their distinctiveness and authority was assured. Furthermore, psychiatrists now had a new and immensely powerful ally – the pharmaceutical industry – whose financial sponsorship would see the profession move from a medical backwater during the middle of the 20th century to one of the most powerful medical specialisms by its close. In short, the drug revolution benefited psychiatry in many ways: ideologically, professionally and financially. It's no wonder that many psychiatrists now regard the pharmacological revolution as a high point in psychiatric history.

Yet there were serious problems with this revolution. And I'm not referring to those I have already covered (drugs not working as well as claimed; reductive biological theories remaining unsubstantiated; normality being medicalised through successive DSM and ICD manuals; and pharmaceutical industry sponsorship corrupting medical objectivity). No, I'm talking about something far less easy to identify, and for that reason far more difficult to challenge. I'm talking about how once this new biological vision began to seep into popular consciousness it started to alter our understanding of the very nature of emotional suffering itself. In order to explain precisely what I mean by this, I'll have to be a little philosophical for a while. I assure you this momentary change in tone has nothing to do with authorial indulgence, but is a necessary preface to all that follows in the remainder of this book.

•

So let me start. As the idea began to take root that different forms of emotional suffering are essentially *biological* problems best treated with pills, psychiatry committed itself to stripping much emotional suffering of its spiritual, psychological and moral meaning. After all, if mental suffering is a result of biological misfortune then it must be a purposeless experience best swiftly removed. As this new 'negative vision' of mental suffering began to gain currency, many previous and more positive cultural associations attached to suffering (for example, that it can be purposeful and necessary if handled productively) began to lose their hold. As I have written about and defined the differences between negative and positive visions of suffering elsewhere, let me quote those statements here:

> The positive vision holds that suffering has a redemptive role to play in human life; as if from affliction there can be derived some unexpected gain, new perspective or beneficial alteration. If this vision could have a motto then Thomas Hardy captured it well: 'If a way to the better there be, it first exacts a full look at the worst.' The positive vision of suffering, thus considered, sees pain as a kind of liminal region through which we can pass from a worse to a better place. A region from which can thus be derived something of lasting value for individual life. But the negative vision of suffering, on the other hand, asserts quite the opposite view – namely, that little of value can come of suffering at all. It says there is no new vista or perspective to be gleaned at its end, nor any immured insights to be unlocked from its depths. It is thus something to be either swiftly anaesthetised or wholly eliminated, for what good is an experience whose most obvious features are pain and inconvenience.[9]

While this negative view of mental suffering is still controversial today, it has nevertheless served psychiatrists well because it fits so neatly with their biological myth of mental distress: since mental suffering is largely caused by biological problems, it is by implication largely purposeless. It's therefore right and proper to mitigate it in any way possible.

And insofar as pills can achieve this, to deny their usage would be a basic dereliction of duty. This simple equation gave many psychiatrists a growing sense of confidence in their own moral and clinical authority, as well as a rationale for claiming to be better equipped than other professionals to help improve our mental health. But this equation also has its faults. As we have seen, the view that mental suffering is caused by our biology still does not enjoy scientific backing. And this has led many critics to argue that the biological view is less a realistic scientific picture of events than a convenient professional myth.

To explore this criticism further, we must first unpack what is actually meant by the term 'myth'. To do this, let me share with you an event that a friend once told me concerning his five-year-old daughter.

He was driving her home along a country road late one clear summer's night. She had been looking out of the car window quietly the whole time, and after about twenty minutes she finally spoke up. 'Daddy', she asked with great seriousness, 'why is the moon following us home?' The poetry of the question took him so off-guard that he mumbled something about near objects seeming to pass by quicker than distant objects, because of relative distances and so forth. His daughter wasn't impressed: 'Daddy, I think the moon is following us home because it's lonely.' With this conclusion she appeared satisfied – she picked up her book and started humming contentedly to herself. She now had her myth.

We are not so different from that little girl. We seek myths to settle crucial questions for which we have no clear answers, but about which we feel we need answers so that we may turn our attention to other things. This is why every society throughout time has had its multifarious myths about all aspects of life: about where we are from, about where we are going, about why we are here, and so on. Myths help soothe our anxiety about some of our most fundamental human uncertainties. Take one of the greatest uncertainties of all – what happens to us after death. This issue provokes such universal anxiety that anthropologists haven't found a single community upon this vast globe that doesn't have a myth about the afterlife. One community speaks of ethereal angels awaiting us at pearly gates, another of a cosmic mother we'll all return to after death, another of gambolling ancestors welcoming us with barrels of manioc wine. The myths are everywhere, all telling fantastically different stories, but all in effect serving the similar purpose of providing explanations for questions that if left unanswered could drive many of us to mad distraction. Myths speak to the realms of life that matter most, including 'whence comes and how goes our suffering' – a matter for which, in contemporary Western societies, we turn to psychiatrists for help.

But surely the help that bio-psychiatry offers is located in something more substantial than myth? After all, apologists argue that psychiatric notions are scientific, not mythic; that they are a product of scientific investigation, not human imagination. Critics are keen to retort that this is clearly not the whole story. Many psychiatrists' claims are no more substantiated than are the claims of religion. This is because, in so many areas that they survey, psychiatrists do not prove things but *decide* things: they *decide* what is disordered and what is not; they *decide* where to draw the threshold between normality and abnormality; they *decide* that biological causes and treatments are most critical in understanding and managing emotional distress. Granted, many of these decisions are informed by research, yet none of these decisions or the research on which they are often based is free from the subjective persuasions of the players involved, while much of the research is methodologically poor – DSM definitions are not fashioned in scientific laboratories but in contentious committee rooms; drug research cannot be fully impartial when it's wedded to drug company interests; and the profession's commitment to the biological vision of our mental lives can't be shorn from psychiatry's historical struggle for biomedical status.

That many of psychiatry's claims cannot be scientifically substantiated has led critics to state that it's therefore no more objective than many traditional systems of belief. Take systems like Shintoism, Confucianism, Shamanism or Christianity, for example. Each of these systems offers explanations about the causes and meaning of suffering, about what is normal or abnormal, sick or healthy, mad or bad. And all these systems say different things about the experiences they try to explain and manage. What is seen as wrong, pathological or odd in one society simply isn't regarded that way in another. In what sense, then, can we say that our own psychiatric system has somehow transcended culture to reach a more universal and truthful vision than all the rest?

Abstract questions like these are always best answered by looking at concrete examples on the ground. So let's now look at one such example – the experience of hearing voices. As I have written elsewhere, in a society where this experience is chiefly associated with mental illness, any individual harassed by these visitations must also contend with the difficult idea that he or she is psychologically unwell; an idea that, if believed by the hearer, is likely to generate additional anxiety as well as compound with each new episode the hearer's sense of abnormality. This means that in societies where these experiences are perceived negatively, individual sufferers will not only struggle with the experience itself but with the consequences of how these experiences are socially perceived, defined and managed. But in a community where 'hearing voices' does not invite the same cultural suspicion, or where these voices are seen, as in the *poleis* of ancient Greece, as possible signs of divine inspiration, the hearer is believed to be less mentally afflicted than potentially blessed. The individual subject to this more favourable cultural diagnosis will invariably possess a far less tortured relationship with their internal voices, and will therefore be freer from the burdens of shame and angst attending our first individual. This is to say, an experience that can mark you as unhinged in one society can mark you as inspired in another. And because how we are marked can shape how we feel, when trying to make sense of any human experience we must always relate it to the dominant myth that defines and pronounces upon this experience.[10]

This comparison reveals a major danger with psychiatric diagnosis. As soon as you're assigned a diagnosis of 'depression' or 'anxiety disorder' or 'attention deficit disorder' you become a protagonist in a larger myth – you now have a mental disorder that marks you as a patient. You have entered into a social contract in which you are now socially positioned as dependent on psychiatric authority.

From then on it's harder to think of yourself as a healthy participant in normal life, or as a person in control of your own fate. You have a psychiatric condition that has seized control, set you apart, and made you dependent.

Admittedly, for many people being diagnosed will bring initial relief (at least someone has named your suffering, and so presumably can treat it. When you're in that kind of pain, the promise of any kind of help brings relief). However, many other ways of responding to suffering can also bring initial relief (psychotherapeutic, spiritual, religious, etc.) and these may not always entail the unfortunate side-effects of being labelled psychiatrically unwell. For instance, patients' complaints about the burden of their diagnosis are widely documented in the mental health literature. This is because we know that being diagnosed can bring additional stresses that accompany self-identifying as different, disordered and in need of medical help. In other words, receiving a diagnosis can have negative secondary effects that are not always anticipated at the start.

In the work of the psychiatrist Marius Romme, there is a particularly striking example of precisely what these effects can be. Romme was working with a 38-year-old woman who had been diagnosed with schizophrenia. This woman had been hearing voices for a long time, but her antipsychotic medication was just not helping her. After enduring many years of failed drug treatment and the awful negative effects her medication caused, she was finally on the brink of suicide. But then one day she unexpectedly took a turn for the better, appearing much happier and more optimistic than before. This sudden change followed her reading a book by the psychologist Julian Jaynes, which argued that the ancient Greeks were different from modern Western individuals in that they regularly understood their inner thoughts as coming from the gods. Whether Jaynes' theory stood up to academic scrutiny didn't matter to this patient. All that mattered was that the book provided her with an alternative myth of her internal world. So she decided that she was probably an ancient Greek rather than a schizophrenic. And it was this simple change to the myth she embraced that altered her whole relationship to her voices – making her feel less frightened of them, less odd, and consequently less alone.[11]

So the myth we embrace affects how we read and experience our psychological states. This means that changing the 'myth' through which we understand such states can be just as therapeutic as taking a pill or undergoing therapy. Consider, for example, another significant change many patients report once they reject the psychiatric view: they often no longer experience the stigma that accompanies being identified as psychiatrically unwell. This is an important point, because a popular justification for the biological vision of our emotional troubles is that it reduces the stigma of mental disorder. After all, if a patient has a biological disorder they cannot be blamed for the way they are. Groups like the National Alliance on Mental Illness in the US and SANE in Britain take this position: the biological myth helps sufferers because it indicates to others that they are not responsible for their predicament. They are like anyone else with a medical condition, and so should not be seen or treated otherwise.[12]

While in theory this position is sensible enough, in practice things seem to unfold very differently. Many people experience negative secondary effects from their diagnosis, either concealing the diagnosis from others out of shame (which can compound their isolation) or becoming so identified with their label that they regularly declare it to others, which can in turn invite real rejection. For example, research now shows that today's most popular public perception of mental disorder is that it's biological in origin.[13] This is particularly problematic in the light of recent research revealing that patients whose emotional problems are believed to be caused by brain disorders are treated far more harshly by the average person than patients believed to have problems caused by social or psychological factors. A research team at Auburn University revealed this troubling fact by asking volunteers to administer mild or strong electric shocks to two groups of patients if they failed at a given test. The results were alarming: the patients believed to have a brain disorder were shocked at a harder and faster rate than the patients believed to have a disorder that was social or psychological in origin, suggesting that we may attract harsher treatment when our problems are considered in brain-based terms.[14]

Results like these are obviously alarming but not entirely unexpected. After all, we know from other research that people who are believed to suffer from biological abnormalities are seen by the average person as more unpredictable and dangerous than 'normal' people. Such perceptions have also been shown to lead 'normal' people to avoid interacting too closely with the 'mentally distressed' – an avoidance that can, once again, compound the sufferer's isolation.[15]

Studies like those above show that being diagnosed with a psychiatric condition – with depression, anxiety, or one of the more severe disorders – often comes with powerful cultural baggage, especially when our suffering is perceived as being rooted in our biology. Paradoxically, then, the worldwide psychiatric campaigns whose goals are to reduce stigma associated with mental illness by asserting that it's just like any other biological disease may well have helped bring about the very opposite of what they intended.[16]

There is another crucial question. You may be wondering if I have exaggerated the extent to which the dominant myth in psychiatry is biological. Surely psychiatry takes into account the relevance of factors that are non-biological in nature?

The first thing to say is that many psychiatrists do in fact recognise, at least in principle, that the causes of mental distress can be various mixtures of social, biological and psychological factors.[17] This view has been captured in what is dubbed the 'bio-psycho-social' model of suffering, which states that these diverse factors interact to precipitate and perpetuate emotional distress. The problem with this view, however, is that psychiatric treatment has, in spite of it, increasingly preferred biological treatments since the 1980s. As the British psychiatrist Professor Christopher Dowrick put it:

> … the biopsychosocial model has little substance beyond the descriptive, and in everyday general practice is viewed mainly as necessary rhetoric. In reality, general practitioners work to what I have characterised as a 'bio(psycho)' model of health care. We tend to see acute physical problems as most appropriate for us to deal with, followed by chronic physical and psychological problems. But we generally

> consider social problems to be inappropriate for medical attention, and can become irritated if we are presented with too many of them.[18]

While Dowrick suggests that the 'bio-psycho' model now dominates, others argue, and with justification, that even the 'psycho' arm of psychiatry is on the decline. As a recent president of the American Psychiatric Association admitted, psychiatry has allowed the 'bio-psycho-social model to become the bio-bio-bio model' – meaning that prescribing pills is all that most psychiatrists now want to do.[19] The British psychiatrist Duncan Double also confirmed this to me when he bemoaned that even those who most ardently avow a bio-psycho-social view often tend at bottom to put the biological first in their treatment practices. So while the bio-psycho-social model exists theoretically, in practice it's far from being realised. This is borne out by the fact that pill treatments are up, long-term psychotherapy is on the decline, and psychiatrists rarely make social interventions. In short, bio-psychiatry advocates do not necessarily advance their negative model of suffering by way of their theoretical pronouncements, but by way of their clinical practices. This is demonstrated by the fact that biological treatments are generally preferred.[20]

•

The growing dominance of the bio-psychiatric myth of suffering poses many serious questions. Is this domination leading increasing numbers of us to view our suffering in entirely negative terms, as something to be erased or anaesthetised at all costs? After all, as diagnostic thresholds lower, and as the number of disorders increases, more and more realms of emotional distress are being daily recast as medical malfunctions to be psychiatrically eradicated. Are we therefore replacing traditional philosophical and religious ways of managing and understanding distress, which once saw meaning and opportunity in many forms of suffering,[21] with a starker technological view that sidesteps the bigger humanistic questions: cannot much suffering that is now medically managed often be a necessary call to change (and therefore a message to be heeded rather than anaesthetised), or the organism's protest against harmful social conditions (therefore requiring a social or psychological rather than a chemical response), or a natural accompaniment of our psychological development (therefore having vital lessons to teach if managed responsibly and productively)?[22] Is psychiatry's essentially negative view of suffering, in other words, yet another manifestation of a wider cultural obsession with using emotional anaesthetics – pills, alcohol, retail therapy, escapist activities – as the principal consumables for managing emotional distress? And if so, in what way is the idea that we can consume our way out of psychological difficulty a myth that is economically convenient not only for psychiatry and the drug industry, but for the wider capitalist system in which we all live?

However you choose to answer these questions, they have to be relevant to any radical rethinking of psychiatric practice today. This is because psychiatry as a system does not float above culture. Its ideas and preferences shape, reflect and respond to the dominant cultural shifts of our time. But psychiatry's cultural embeddedness is not just pertinent for the regions in which it was developed. This is because, in recent years, Western psychiatry has aggressively expanded into new lucrative markets – China, India, Indonesia, South America, Eastern Europe – rapidly converting whole new parts of the globe to our culturally specific modes of misery management. What happens, then, when a system made in the US or the UK is exported to communities that have never before embraced our medicalised view of emotional suffering? By exporting our remedies can we be confident that we are really helping to heal the world?

Before you begin to formulate an answer, I ask you to first consider the bizarre series of facts that I'm about to reveal to you; facts that require us to take a journey to destinations somewhat farther afield.

12
Psychiatric imperialism

On a sunny afternoon in 1994, a fourteen-year-old schoolgirl called Charlene Hsu Chi-Ying collapsed and died on a busy Hong Kong street. Nothing untoward appeared to have precipitated her death. She had just been walking home from school as usual. A coroner was called in to investigate Charlene's body. He was immediately disturbed by what he found. She weighed only 75 pounds. But worse than that, her heart was tiny – weighing just 3 ounces, half the usual size for a girl her age. In fact, her body looked so emaciated that nurses at the local hospital actually mistook her corpse for that of a woman in her nineties. A public inquest was immediately undertaken to work out what had happened. What it revealed seemed shocking: Charlene had done something then practically unheard-of in Hong Kong – she had starved herself to death.

After Charlene's death a chilling series of events started to unfold in the city. Young women suddenly seemed to begin copying Charlene's self-starving. First it was one or two, but very quickly the numbers began to rise dramatically. What was initially considered an isolated event now appeared to be turning into a city-wide minor epidemic, and nobody could understand why. What was going on in Hong Kong?

That question led one of America's foremost investigative writers, Ethan Watters, to fly to the city in hope of unravelling the mystery.[1] As he had undertaken his preliminary research, he knew exactly where to start his investigation: with one of Hong's Kong's leading eating disorder specialists, a physician called Dr Sing Lee. Lee had made a career working with patients suffering from eating disorders, and was knowledgeable about the events preceding and following Charlene's death. As Watters' conversations with Lee took place, the key facts surrounding Charlene's death began to become clear. And here is what Watters found.

After Charlene's death, there was uproar in the Hong Kong media. A young schoolgirl dying in such a public way, under such odd circumstances, was bound to make irresistible news. 'Girl Who Died in the Street was a Walking Skeleton', one headline rang out; and another: 'Schoolgirl Falls Dead on Street: Thinner Than a Yellow Flower'. As article after article reported the facts, most also asked the same burning question: what was the meaning of this strange disease that led a bright young local girl to stave herself to death?

As the question was turned over again and again in Hong Kong's media, the phrase 'anorexia nervosa' began to be heard. Until this time anorexia was a little-known condition in the city, readily recognised only by a few Western-trained psychiatrists. But as the public wanted to know more, the expertise of psychiatrists was recruited in discussions that started appearing in women's magazines and daily papers. Educational programmes were also soon set up in schools to increase awareness of the disorder. A youth-support programme was initiated, called Kids Everywhere Like You, which included a 24-hour helpline for children struggling with eating irregularities. As these forces gained momentum in Hong Kong, the disorder was slowly put on the map. The word was getting out that anorexia nervosa was not just a Western disease – the youth of Hong Kong were susceptible as well.

As public awareness of anorexia grew in Hong Kong, so too did the number of anorexia cases being reported. For instance, psychiatrists like Lee, who before Charlene's death had seen only about one case of self-starving a year, were now seeing many cases each week. As one typical article noted, eating disorders were now 'twice as common as shown in earlier studies and the incidence is increasing rapidly'. And as a headline in the *Standard* echoed when reporting on a study documenting this rise, 'A university yesterday produced figures showing a twenty-five-fold increase in cases of such disorders'.[2]

Watters was desperate to know why a disorder like anorexia, once practically unknown in Hong Kong, could suddenly become a local epidemic. The first answer he considered was that the growing media attention had brought to public attention a widespread problem that had always been there but carefully hidden, making it easier for doctors to recognise and diagnose the disorder. Perhaps until that time people didn't feel they had permission to report their anorexic experience; perhaps the new discourse had given a voice to a disorder long kept underground. But as compelling as this explanation initially seemed, for Watters it didn't appear to fit the facts. In the first place, if there had always been many cases of anorexia in the non-clinical population, then schools, parents, psychiatrists and paediatricians would surely have spotted it. After all, anorexia is not something that sufferers can easily hide, given its very obvious symptomatic signs. So Watters considered another explanation: perhaps as Western notions of female beauty became dominant in the media, the accepted physical ideal had begun to transmute. As women encountered more images of slim so-called paragons of perfection, they simply felt pressurised to make their bodies conform. But again, the evidence didn't support this. After all, Western depictions of featherweight beauty didn't rise hand-in-hand with anorexia cases. These depictions were widespread long before the anorexia epidemic broke out, and so could not account for the sudden explosion of cases. Watters was therefore convinced that something else was going on, something less obvious, something perhaps even more disturbing. The question that continued to plague him was what could this 'something' be?

•

Before we pursue that question further, let us first journey a few thousand miles from Hong Kong, and a little way back in time, to investigate another odd series of events that I had been independently studying in Britain. The time I was focusing on was the late-1980s, when another strange psychiatric contagion seemed to be spreading. During this time increasing numbers of young women started arriving in clinics displaying severe and disturbing wounds. Some had gashes on their arms and legs; others had marks from scalding, burning, hitting and scratching, or were missing clumps of hair. What linked all these cases was that other people weren't inflicting these wounds. No, the young women were inflicting them upon themselves.

As the 1990s and 2000s unfolded, cases of such 'self-harming' behaviour continued to increase dramatically. A study on the mental health of college students found empirical evidence that at one university the rate of self-injury doubled from 1997 to 2007.[3] And when the BBC reported on self-harm in 2004, it bemoaned the escalating rates in Britain: 'One in 10 teenagers deliberately hurts themselves and 24,000 are admitted to hospital each year.'[4] A later BBC investigation also found that the number of young people being admitted to hospital for self-harm was up 50 per cent in five years (2005–2010).[5] What began as a tiny number of cases in the late 1980s had suddenly exploded beyond most people's comprehension. The urgent question was, once again, how could this be?

By the mid-2000s many conventional explanations had been advanced. Dr Andrew McCulloch, chief executive of the Mental Health Foundation, put one as follows: 'The increase in self-harm … may be visible evidence of growing problems facing our young people, or of a growing inability to respond to those problems.' Susan Elizabeth, director of the Camelot Foundation, similarly pointed out: 'It seems the more stresses that young people have in their lives the more they are turning to self-harm as a way of dealing with those stresses.' Professor Keith Hawton, a psychiatrist at Oxford University, also joined the fray: self-harm is rising because 'pressures have increased and there's much more expected of young people'.[6]

Statements like these by the mental health establishment boiled down to the simple idea that self-harming was on the up because teenage life-satisfaction was down. But today, with the benefit of hindsight, this explanation appears unsatisfactory. Firstly, it's not so clear whether teenage life in the late 1980s was so much easier than it was in the late 1990s, the period during which self-harming really began to rise. On the contrary, there's strong evidence that social conditions for teenagers during the 1990s, if not significantly improving, at least did not decline. For instance, sociologists at Dartmouth and Warwick Universities showed that, overall, general well-being in Britain actually flat-lined during the 1970s, 80s and 90s, rather than plummeted.[7] And an independent study conducted at the University of York (commissioned by Save the Children) concluded that: 'While overall the UK can claim that life is getting better for children, child well-being continues to be mixed: the list of improving indicators is more or less equal in length to the list of deteriorating/no change indicators.'[8] So the situation was not ideal. But nor did it seem to be declining in the 1990s and 2000s, a fact undermining establishment claims about why self-harm was on the rise. Perhaps there was something else at play – something that has escaped mainstream attention.

To explore some possible alternatives, I called Professor Janis Whitlock, a specialist in self-harm behaviour at Cornell University. Whitlock has dedicated much research to trying to work out what makes this particular behaviour attractive to young people at a particular time: 'In some of our early work we found evidence of self-harming back in the early 20th century', said Whitlock, 'but all among severely traumatised people like war veterans. How it shows up among otherwise normally functioning kids in the 1990s I think says a lot about our culture, what is going on in that time and place.'

The aspect of culture that Whitlock focused on was how popular depictions of self-harm grew exponentially during the 1990s and 2000s. In a recent study, her team focused on representations of self-harm in the media, in popular songs and in movies from the 1970s until 2005.[9] What they found was that between 1976 and 1980 there was only one movie depicting self-harm behaviour, while there were no references to it in popular songs. But between 2001 and 2005 depictions and references rose sharply, appearing in 23 movies and 38 songs. Furthermore, when charting the rise of news articles on the issue, between 1976 and 1980 they found only eleven articles featuring self-harming, while between 2001 and 2005 this figure had soared to a whopping 1,750 articles. Was the growth of popular references to self-harm simply reflecting a growing epidemic? Or were these references actually helping spread self-harming behaviour?

I put this question to Whitlock: 'My educated guess was that it was the latter. In the late eighties I don't think self-harm was out there as an idea, so mostly the average kid's response was "Eww, why would you do that?" But when you hear people like Christina Ricci and Johnny Depp and Angelina Jolie talking about their experiences of it, the idea can become normalised ... And once an idea becomes part of the repertoire of possibilities, it can easily gain traction.'

This is especially true when behaviours like self-harm gain authoritative recognition from institutions like psychiatry, something that was also occurring during the 1990s. For instance, in 1994 self-harm was for the first time given prominence in the DSM as a symptom of borderline personality disorder. This meant that a behaviour once peripheral to psychiatric discourse was now part of the psychiatric canon, potentially making media conversations about the behaviour easier to facilitate, because there was now a legion of qualified experts who could explain it to a concerned public. For example, was it merely coincidence that after self-harm entered the DSM in 1994 the number of popular articles on self-harm trebled, increasing from 485 articles in the four-year period before its inclusion to 1,441 in the four-year period after?[10] 'In many of the media articles we assessed', said Whitlock, 'sure, there was just plain sensationalism, you know: "Look at what is going on!" But in others there was now a serious attempt to understand what was happening, and of course people turned first to the clinical world to do that.' Whitlock gave me an example of how popular US news channels like NPR recruited psychiatrists to discuss self-harming. 'These would have been classic venues for exporting a psychiatric framework and language of self-harm, and may have helped it enter public consciousness too.'

Since the rise of media reporting and psychiatric recognition of self-harm appeared to coincide with its escalating rates, one question seemed to me inevitable: was psychiatry, by giving prominence to self-harm in the DSM, helping endorse the idea that self-harm was a legitimate way through which young people could express distress? And was this endorsement, coupled with the increasing media reports on self-harm, somehow contributing to its higher prevalence?

This was the very same question plaguing Ethan Watters as he attempted to understand why anorexia soared in Hong Kong after Charlene's death. Was there something about psychiatric recognition of the behaviour, coupled with growing media attention, that was partly responsible for self-harm's escalation? Watters soon realised that in order to answer this question, another matter needed settling first: if psychiatric and media publicity of a disorder could actually increase its occurrence, how did this process actually work? What were the mechanisms by which growing cultural awareness of a condition could lead to its proliferation?

To unravel this mystery let's return to Watters in Hong Kong, who was now on the brink of finding an answer.

•

As Watters continued his conversations with the eating disorders expert Dr Sing Lee, a key piece in the jigsaw at last slotted into place. One day in Lee's office in downtown Hong Kong, Lee told Watters that he had become gripped by the work of the eminent medical historian, Edward Shorter, who had written many articles on the history of anorexia. What Edward Shorter was at pains to point out in his writing was that rates of anorexia, and the form anorexia took, had never been stable in the general population. Its form and prevalence had fluctuated from period to period. For example, in the mid-1800s anorexia didn't actually exist as a distinct medical category. It was rather regarded as one of the symptoms of a broader condition then called hysteria. This catch-all term characterised a suite of symptoms, usually afflicting middle- and upper-middle-class women, which included things like uncontrollable tics, muscular paralysis, fainting fits, bouts of vomiting, and in many cases a complete refusal to eat food. But in 1873 an expert in hysteria, the French physician Ernest-Charles Lasègue, came to the conclusion that self-starving warranted its own official designation, as it was often a stand-alone condition. Lasègue coined the term 'anorexia' and also drew up a thorough description of its core symptoms and a template guiding physicians in their diagnosis and treatment of the condition. It was clear that Lasègue's work at last provided a model, as Shorter put it, 'of how patients should behave and doctors should respond'.[11] The question now was whether Lasègue's work was related to a rise in the disease?

Even though there were no epidemiological studies of anorexia rates in Lasègue's day, what Shorter noticed was that anecdotal reports suggested that once anorexia became part of the medical canon, its prevalence increased too. While in the 1850s the disorder was still confined to just a few isolated cases, after Lasègue's work it wasn't long before the term 'anorexia' became standard in the medical literature, and with this cases climbed. As one London doctor reported in 1888, anorexia behaviour was now 'a very common occurrence', giving him 'abundant opportunities of seeing and treating many cases'; while a medical student confidently wrote in his doctoral dissertation 'among hysterics, nothing is more common than anorexia'.[12]

This rise in anorexia was fascinating to Shorter because it closely followed the trajectory of many other psychosomatic disorders he had studied during his historical investigations; disorders that were also not constant in form and frequency but came and went at different points in history. This led Shorter to theorise that many disorders without known physical causes did not behave like diseases such as cancer, heart disease or Parkinson's, which seemed to express themselves in the same way across time and space. Rather, disorders like anorexia seemed to be heavily influenced by historical and cultural factors. For example, if a disorder gained cultural recognition, then rates of that disorder would increase. This challenged the conventional view that a disorder could proliferate after being recognised by medicine because doctors could now identify something previously off their radar. While it was no doubt true that once doctors knew what to look for, diagnostic rates would inevitably increase, for Shorter it was also essential to consider the powerful role that culture could play in the escalation of some disorders. Shorter was convinced that medicine didn't just 'reveal' disorders that had previously escaped medical attention, but could actually increase their prevalence by simply putting the disorder on the cultural map.

To explain how this could happen, Shorter made use of a very interesting metaphor – that of the 'symptom pool'. Each culture, he argued, possessed a metaphorical pool of culturally legitimate symptoms through which members of a given society would choose, mostly unconsciously, to express their distress. It was almost as if a particular symptom would not be expressed by a given cultural group until the symptom had been culturally recognised as a legitimate alternative – that is, until it had entered that culture's 'symptom pool'. This idea helped explain, among other things, why symptoms that were very common in one culture would not be in another. Why, for example, could men in south-east Asia experience what's called *koro* (the terrifying certainty that their genitals are retracting into their body), but not men in Wales or Alaska? Or why could menopausal women in Korea experience *hwabyeong* (intense fits of sighing, a heavy feeling in the chest, blurred vision and sleeplessness), but not women in New Zealand or Scandinavia? For Shorter the answer was simple: symptom pools were fluid, changeable and culturally specific, therefore differing from place to place.

This idea implied that certain disorders we take for granted are actually caused less by biological than cultural factors – like crazes or fads they can grip or release a population as they enter or fade from popular awareness. This is not because people consciously choose to display symptoms that are fashionable members of the symptom pool, just that people seem to gravitate unconsciously to expressing those symptoms high on the cultural scale of symptom possibilities. And this of course makes sense, as it's crucial that we express our discontent in ways that make sense to the people around us (otherwise we will end up not just ill but ostracised). As Anne Harrington, Professor of History of Science at Harvard, puts it: 'Our bodies are physiologically primed to be able to do this, and for good reason, if we couldn't we would risk not being taken seriously or not being cared for – human beings seem to be invested with a developed capacity to mold their bodily experiences to the norms of their cultures, they learn the scripts about what kinds of things should be happening to them as they fall ill and about the things they should do to feel better, and then they literally embody them.'[13] Psychiatric contagions do not spread through conscious emulation, then, but because we are unconsciously configured to embody species of distress deemed legitimate by the communities in which we live.

One of the reasons people find this notion of unintentional embodiment difficult to accept is that such processes occur above our heads – imperceptibly, unconsciously – and so being unconscious we fail to spot them. But if you still doubt the power of unconscious embodiment then just try the following experiment. Next time you're sitting in a public space where there are others sitting opposite you, start to yawn conspicuously every one or two minutes, and do this for about six minutes. And all the while keep observing the people in your vicinity. What you'll almost certainly notice is that others will soon start yawning too. Now, there are many theories why this may happen (it's due to our 'capacity to empathise', or to an offshoot of the 'imitative impulse'). But the actual truth is that no one really knows why for sure. All we do know is that those who have caught a yawning bug usually don't know they have been infected. They usually believe they are yawning because they are tired or bored, not because someone across the way has just performed an annoying yawning experiment.

Such unconscious forms of infection have been captured in many different theories developed by social psychologists. One theory of particular note is what has been termed the 'bandwagon effect'. This term describes the well-documented phenomenon that conduct and beliefs spread among people just like fashions, or opinions or infectious diseases do. The more people who begin to subscribe to an idea or behaviour, the greater its gravitational pull, sucking yet more people in until a tipping point is reached and an outbreak occurs. When an idea takes hold of enough people, in other words, it spreads at an ever-increasing rate, even in cases when the idea or behaviour is neither good, nor true, nor useful.

Take the following experiment as an example. Imagine that a psychologist gathers eight people around a table, but only one of the eight people is not in on the experiment. That person is you. Everyone else knows precisely what is expected of them. What they have to do is give a prepared answer to a particular question. The question is: which of the three lines in the box on the right most closely resembles the line on the left?

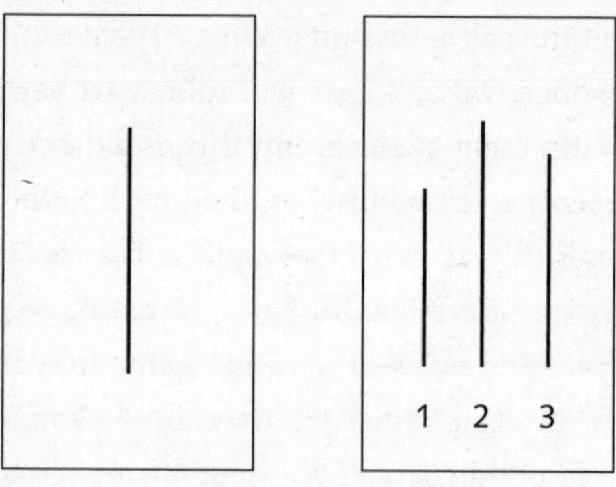

Easy, right? And of course, if you're sitting in a group where everyone is told to answer correctly, it's almost 100 per cent certain that you will answer correctly too. But what would happen if you were put in a group where a sufficient number of members have been told to give an incorrect answer with sufficient forcefulness to many such images? Well, the odd thing is, as unbelievable as it sounds, at least one third of you will begin to give incorrect answers too. You will conclude, for instance, that the line in the box on the left resembles the lines numbered 1 or 3 on the right.

The psychologist Solomon Asch demonstrated this bemusing occurrence by conducting this very experiment. His aim was to show that our tendency to conform to the group is so powerful that we often conform even when the group is wrong. When Asch interviewed the third of people who followed the incorrect majority view, many said they knew their answer was wrong but didn't want to contradict the group for fear of being ridiculed. A few said that they really did believe the group's answers were correct. This meant that the group's opinion had somehow unconsciously distorted their perceptions. What Asch's experiment revealed was that even when an answer is plainly obvious, we still have a tendency to be swayed in the wrong direction by the group. This is either because we don't want to stand alone or because the bandwagon effect can so powerfully influence our unconscious minds that we will actually bend reality to fit in.

Because Asch showed that it didn't take much to get us to conform to a highly implausible majority conclusion, the question is: what happens when we are asked to conform to something discussed as real and true by powerful institutions like the media and psychiatry? The likelihood is that our rates of conformity will dramatically increase. And this is why the historian Edward Shorter believed that when it came to the spread of symptoms, the same 'bandwagon effect' could be observed. If enough people begin to talk about a symptom as though it exists, and if this symptom is given legitimacy by an accepted authority, then, sure enough, more and more people will begin to manifest that symptom. This idea explained for Shorter why symptoms can dramatically come and go within a population – why anorexia can reach epidemic proportions and then suddenly die away, or why self-harm can suddenly proliferate. As our symptom pool alters, we are given new ways to embody our distress, and as these catch on, they proliferate.

After reading Shorter's work, Dr Lee began to understand what had happened in Hong Kong. Anorexia had escalated after Charlene's death because the ensuing publicity and medical recognition introduced into Hong Kong's symptom pool a hitherto foreign and unknown condition, allowing more and more women to unconsciously select the disorder as a way of expressing their distress. This theory was also consistent with another strange change Dr Lee had noticed. After Charlene's death it wasn't just the rates of anorexia that increased, but the actual form anorexia took. The few cases of self-starving that Lee treated before Charlene's death weren't characterised by the classic symptoms of anorexia customarily found in the West, where sufferers believe they are grossly overweight and experience intense hunger when they don't eat. No, this particular set of Western symptoms didn't match the experiences of the anorexics Lee encountered before the mid-1990s: then, they had no fear of being overweight, did not experience hunger, but simply had a strong repulsion for food. This all changed as Western conceptions of anorexia flooded Hong Kong's symptom pool in the mid-1990s. Young women now began to conform to the list of anorexic symptoms drawn up in the West. Like Western anorexics, those in Hong Kong now felt grossly overweight and desperately hungry. As part of the Western symptom drained eastwards, the very characteristics of anorexia in Hong Kong altered too.

Ethan Watters now understood that Lee's discoveries in Hong Kong could be used to help partly explain a whole array of psychiatry contagions that could suddenly explode in a population. The only problem was that Western researchers were loath to recognise how the alteration of symptom pools could account for these contagions. As Watters writes:

> A recent study by several British researchers showed a remarkable parallel between the incidence of bulimia in Britain and Princess Diana's struggle with the condition. The incidence rate rose dramatically in 1992, when the rumours were first published, and then again in 1994, when the speculation became rampant. It rose to its peak in 1995, when she publicly admitted the behavior. Reports of bulimia started to decline only after the princess's death in 1997. The authors consider several possible reasons for these changes. It is possible, they speculate, that Princess Diana's public struggle with an eating disorder made doctors and mental-health providers more aware of the condition and therefore more likely to ask about it or recognise it in their patients. They also suggest that public awareness might have made it more likely for a young woman to admit her eating behavior. Further, the apparent decline in 1997 might not indicate a true drop in the numbers but only that fewer people were admitting their condition. These are reasonable hypotheses and a likely explanation for part of the rise and fall in the numbers of bulimics. What is remarkable is that the authors of the study don't even mention, much less consider, the obvious fourth possibility: that the revelation that Princess Diana used bulimia as a 'call for help' *encouraged* other young women to unconsciously mimic the behavior of this beloved celebrity to call attention to their own private distress. The fact that these researchers didn't address this possibility is emblematic of a pervasive and mistaken assumption in the mental-health profession: that mental illnesses exist apart from and unaffected by professional and public beliefs and the cultural currents of the time.[14]

As I was nearing the end of writing this chapter I called Ethan Watters at his home in San Francisco to ask if we should be concerned about this professional 'cultural blindness', especially at a time when Western psychiatry is being exported to more and more societies globally as a solution for their problems. 'When you look around the world to see which cultures appear to have more mental illnesses and are more reliant on psychiatric drugs', answered Watters, 'you do get the impression that we in the West are at one end of the scale in terms of being more prone to mental illness symptoms. But if that is due partly to our cultural agreement about what mental illness is, what in the world are we doing giving them all our techniques and models? Especially when other countries clearly have better recovery rates from these illnesses than we do?'

This question for Watters was rhetorical – he had his answer. But before we unpick what Watters knows, we first must consider one final collection of methods by which Western ideas of distress, contained in manuals like the DSM and ICD, are now infecting global populations. These methods have nothing to do with the subtle alteration of local symptom pools, but rather with the intentional exportation of Western models and treatments by the pharmaceutical industry.

•

In early 1999 the Argentinian economy went into a tailspin. Poor economic management throughout the 1990s meant that many years of mounting debt, unemployment, increasing inflation and tax evasion culminated in a catastrophic three-year recession. By December 2001, things had become so bad in Argentina that violent riots had reached the capital, Buenos Aires. But as people were approaching breaking point, they were not only taking to the streets to express their despair, they were also turning up en masse at local hospitals, complaining of debilitating stress.

As the social suffering continued to mount in Argentina, two major pharmaceutical companies were at the same time grappling for the market share: the multinational Eli Lilly and the local company Gador. What both companies knew was that mounting stress presented a great sales opportunity. As the situation deteriorated on the ground, both companies actively engaged in powerful marketing campaigns. These involved many of the marketing techniques I talked about in Chapter 9, where companies learn from prescription records about which doctors their sales campaigns should target. As both companies aggressively competed for the market share, slowly but surely a clear winner started to emerge – the local pharmaceutical company, Gador. Its unlicensed copy of Prozac soon became the most widely used antidepressant in Argentina, while Eli Lilly's Prozac, which was the same price as Gador's version, strangely languished in sixth place. Was there something about Gador's marketing campaign that gave it the edge?

Professor Andrew Lakoff, an anthropologist studying antidepressant usage in Buenos Aires during the 1990s, had become particularly interested in how both companies were marketing their chemical solutions. When I interviewed Lakoff in late 2012, it became quite clear that the companies did things differently: 'There was a legendary drug rep at Gador', said Lakoff, 'who told me that he was somewhat dismissive of the marketing strategies that purely focused on crunching numbers and data mining of prescriptions, because they overlooked the essential thing – the importance of relationships – those developed between company reps and prescribers. These relationships did not just enable reps to offer incentives to doctors to prescribe Gador's products, but they also enabled reps to understand *why* doctors would prescribe a particular drug.'

This information was key, because while in the United States and Europe psychiatry had shifted towards a technological or biological approach that considered mental illness to be located in the brain, Argentinian psychiatrists still largely understood mental illness as resulting from social and political problems. 'Gador knew that selling drugs through images of "neurotransmission" and "selective receptors" as Eli Lilly was doing, wasn't the best way to get psychiatrists to adopt a given drug', continued Lakoff. 'You had to approach local doctors on their own political and epistemological footing. This meant in the case of Argentina you had to appeal to the psychiatrists' more socio-political understanding of why patients suffered from mental disorders.'

Gador therefore developed a marketing campaign that focused on suffering caused by globalisation. This campaign cleverly capitalised on an argument that resonated with local psychiatrists about how the challenges of globalisation were largely responsible for escalating economic and social misery. 'So Gador took advantage of the understanding the psychiatrists had adopted about why their patients were suffering, and they used that understanding in their campaign', said Lakoff. For instance, one advert featured a series of unhappy people traversing a map of the world, suffering from symptoms of globalisation: 'Deterioration of interpersonal relations', 'Deterioration in daily performance', 'Unpredictable demands and threats', 'Personal and familial suffering', 'Loss of social role', 'Loss of productivity'.[15] Here Gador explicitly appealed to the notion that their pills targeted the social suffering in terms of which most people articulated their distress; a message that had far greater resonance in Argentinian psychiatry than did references to neurotransmitters and serotonin levels.

Gador actively deployed this deeper cultural knowledge of the local language of distress to win local doctors over to their product. 'My sense is that Eli Lilly were not present on the ground in the same way Gador was', affirmed Lakoff. 'They didn't have the same long-term "experts in the field" doing the cultural work.' While Eli Lilly's campaign was based on bio-speak that did not resonate with Argentinian psychiatrists, Gador's message touched the heart of their socio-political beliefs. It was the deeper cultural knowledge Gador cultivated, in other words, that helped them win the greater market share.

Let's now fast-forward a year to another pharmaceutical campaign that Ethan Watters had been separately studying in Japan; to a time when Western pharmaceutical companies were becoming far more aware that you had no hope of capturing local markets unless your marketing campaigns chimed with local cultural meanings.

Watters describes a plush conference room in Kyoto, in which some of the world's leading academic experts in cross-cultural psychiatry were gathered.[16] The conference had been paid for and organised by GlaxoSmithKline, which had recruited experts from France, Britain, the

US and Japan to discuss the topic 'Transcultural Issues in Depression and Anxiety'. All the attending experts had been flown to Kyoto first class, and all had been accommodated in an exclusive city hotel. One attendee, Professor Laurence Kirmayer from McGill University, commented to Watters upon the lavishness of it all: 'These were the most deluxe circumstances I have ever experienced in my life, the luxury was so far beyond anything I could personally afford, it was a little scary. It didn't take me long to think that something strange was going on here. I wondered: what did I do to deserve this?'[17]

The clue was to be found dotted among the attendees: a handful of people dressed so slickly and expensively that they couldn't possibly be academics. But these were no ordinary company reps either, offering the usual sales patter about the virtues of their drug. No, these people were something else entirely, a whole new breed of company employee. 'Their focus was not on medications', Kirmayer recalled to Watters, 'they were not trying to sell their drugs to us. They were interested in what we knew about how cultures shape the illness experience.' Kirmayer said that what surprised him about these employees was their consummate capacity to understand and debate everything the experts discussed. 'These guys all had PhDs and were versed in the literature', said Kirmayer. 'They were clearly soaking up what we had to say to each other on these topics.' These private scholars, these company anthropologists, where obviously there *to learn*.

In order to find out what they wanted to learn, we first need some contextual background. In Japan before the 2000s, SSRI antidepressants like Seroxat were not considered viable treatments for the Japanese population. The cause seemed clear. At that time in Japan there wasn't really a recognised medical category for what is termed in the US or Europe as mild or moderate depression – the disorders most regularly treated with SSRIs. The Japanese category that came closest to depression was *utsybyo*, which described a chronic illness as severe as schizophrenia and for which suffers needed to be hospitalised. Thus huge swathes of the 'worried well', who were prescribed SSRIs in Europe and the US, simply resided outside the pool of people to whom companies could sell pills. The challenge for GlaxoSmithKline, then, was clear: how do you get these untreated people to think of their distress not only as 'depression' but as something to be helped by medications like Seroxat?

This was precisely why expensive conferences like the one in Kyoto were set up. Company officials needed to acquire a deep and sophisticated understanding of how to market the 'disease' and its 'cure'. They needed to learn how to convert the Japanese population to a more Anglo-American way of understanding and treating their emotional discontent. This was why Kirmayer believed he and his colleagues had been treated like royalty in Kyoto – GlaxoSmithKline need to solve a cultural puzzle potentially worth billions of dollars.[18]

Once that knowledge had been gathered, GlaxoSmithKline launched a huge marketing campaign in Japan. The images of depression it popularised in magazines and newspapers and on TV were intentionally vague, so that nearly anyone who was feeling low could interpret their experience as depression. These messages were also particularly targeted at the young, the smart, the aspiring, and avoided dwelling on the pills' dubious efficacy as well as their many known undesirable side-effects. The ads also focused on de-stigmatising depression, urging people not to suffer in silence, and encouraging them to take charge of their own condition and request a prescription. Alongside the ad campaigns, around 1,350 Seroxat-promoting medical representatives were visiting selected doctors an average of twice a week, priming them to prescribe the right treatment for the new malady.[19] Furthermore, the drug company created websites and web-communities for people who now believed they were suffering from depression, and these sites and communities gave the impression of being spontaneously growing grassroots organisations. Celebrities and clinicians appeared on these sites, endorsing and adding popular appeal to these online forums. What the patients and patient-carers using these websites didn't know was that behind all this web-information was GlaxoSmithKline, pulling the strings.

When I spoke to Ethan Watters about these company practices, he was frank: 'To suggest to any knowledgeable audience that drug companies would do this surprises no one. But what is harder to believe was how studiously were they doing this, how directed and calculated it all was. These private scholars who worked in this world of drug companies learnt everything you needed to know to market drugs successfully in Japan, and so what happened after wasn't just an ancillary outcome of two cultures colliding, or the inevitable product of globalisation – this was pulling levers and doing various nefarious things to change the cultural conception in Japan of where that line was between illness and health.'

Within a few years the efforts of GlaxoSmithKline had more than paid off. 'Depression' had become a household word and Seroxat sales had soared from $108 million in 2001 to nearly $300 million in 2003.[20] The companies had now learnt that culturally sensitive marketing was key to disseminating their drugs, even if this meant altering an entire culture's way of understanding and responding to their emotional discontent. As Koji Nakagawa, GlaxoSmithKline's product manager for Seroxat at the time, explained: 'People didn't know they were suffering from a disease. We felt it was important to reach out to them.' The company's message was simple: 'Depression is a disease that anyone can get. It can be cured by medicine. Early detection is important.'[21]

What marketing campaigns like GlaxoSmithKline's seemed to achieve was a recasting of many people's emotional struggles, which had once been understood and managed in terms indigenous to the population, into medical diseases requiring pharmaceutical treatments. As Kathryn Schulz put it when writing in 2004 on such promotional practice in Japan, 'for the last five years, the pharmaceutical industry and the media have communicated one consistent message: your suffering might be a sickness. Your leaky vital energy, like your runny nose, might respond to drugs.'[22] The depression contagion was not spreading because more people were getting sick, but because more and more were being taught to redefine their existing sufferings in these new disease-laden terms.

While these processes of medicalisation were being purposefully manufactured in Japan and Argentina, they were also being rolled out in many other new markets too.

For one final telling example, let's travel now to Latvia to be a fly on the wall of a psychiatrist's consulting room some time during early 2000.

A young woman visits her doctor complaining of *nervi* – a disorder of the nerves with symptoms similar to those we classify as 'depressive' in the West. The main difference with nervi, however, is that in Latvia it's mostly treated by doctors attending closely to the patient's life story and investigating the possible social and political meanings of their distress. Nervi is not therefore seen as a biomedical condition to be treated with drugs. But as this patient continues to relay her symptoms to her doctor, something unusual happens: the doctor tells her that she may not be suffering from nervi after all, but rather from something called 'depression' – a mental disorder that can be treated by a new wave of antidepressant pills.

At the same time as this young woman is hearing the surprising news, other victims of nervi around the country are receiving the same message: their nervi may be better understood and treated as depression. And as more and more cases of nervi are reconfigured as depression, the nation's rates of depression unsurprisingly increase. But what had happened to instigate this change? Why were local doctors now reading nervi differently? When the social anthropologist Vieda Skultans tried to unravel this mystery, what she found was that this shift coincided with two seminal events: the translation of the ICD (with a chapter containing the World Health Organisation's version of the DSM) into Latvian; and the organisation of conferences by pharmaceutical companies aimed at educating psychiatrists and family doctors about the new diagnostic categories.[23]

Skultans showed that once the new language of depression was made professionally available through the ICD, the pharmaceutical industry could then disseminate the new language to patients and the wider public through educational programmes. This shift away from understanding distress in the more socio-political terms of 'nervi' towards the more biological terms of depression not only meant that new markets opened up for pharmaceutical treatments: people also started to hold themselves responsible for their distress – no longer were they suffering from the strains of living in a fraught socio-political environment, but from a condition located within the internal recesses of their brains.

•

What happened in Argentina, Japan and Latvia provides just three examples of how pharmaceutical companies managed during the 2000s to capture new foreign markets throughout Asia, South America and Eastern Europe via directly transfiguring local languages of distress. What the multinationals had learnt was that you needn't wait for local symptom pools to become Westernised through spontaneous processes of globalisation – you could actually take the matter into your own hands by *intentionally* creating new markets, either by recasting existing local complaints and conditions in terms of Western mental health categories, or by giving labels to feelings for which local populations had no existing disease categories. By funding conventions and vast marketing offensives, by co-opting huge numbers of prominent psychiatrists and manufacturing the supporting science, increased sales could be almost guaranteed. I say 'almost' because there's always a risk an investment won't deliver. But the risk is worth it, as Watters put it: 'because the pay-off is remarkable when the companies get it right. And it seems that each new culture they go into, they get a little better at getting it right!'

To say that companies were behind many new and spreading mental health epidemics is not to deny the reality of psychological distress. Of course emotional suffering is universal, but we also know that it's susceptible to being culturally shaped and patterned by the meanings we ascribe to it. So if a company can convince enough local people that their way of understanding and treating distress needs a radical makeover, then the rewards can be staggering if locals take the bait. Just consider the facts: IMS, a provider of healthcare data, has shown that the global antidepressant market increased from $19.4 billion in 2009 to $20.4 billion in 2011, and the global antipsychotic market from $23.2 billion in 2009 to $28.4 billion in 2011. This means that the global psycho-drug market grew from $42.6 billion in 2009 to $48.8 billion in 2011 – an expansion of over $8 billion in just two years.[24] Of course, increased European and US consumption can partly account for this exorbitant rise, but it certainly can't account for it entirely. Consumption is rapidly escalating in developing, emerging and non-Western economies: in 2010 the Japanese antidepressant market, for example, had a value of $1.72 billion, up 10.7 per cent from 2009,[25] while in China the annual growth figures have been around 20 per cent for the last few years.[26] Recent estimates of antidepressant usage in Brazil now put the figure at 3.12 per cent of the entire population, a significant increase over previous years.[27] If reliable data were available for other foreign markets (Mexico, Argentina, Chile, India, South Africa, Thailand, etc.) we would no doubt witness similar escalating rates.

While the global expansion of Western psycho-drugs would hardly be possible without robust pharmaceutical and psychiatric sponsorship, there are other organisations that are giving this expansion a significant boost. In 2001 the World Health Organisation publicly backed the globalisation of psycho-pharmaceuticals by publishing a major report on the state of global mental health. After synthesising years of research on psychiatric problems in developed and developing countries, the report stated that depression will be the world's second-leading health problem after heart disease by the year 2020. The solution to this looming epidemic was making Western psycho-drugs more widely available. Poorer countries would save millions a year treating people with pills in the community rather than in costly hospitals. Pills would also stem the negative consequences of poor mental health on the economy: medicated people would be more likely to remain economically productive. On the other hand, if depression weren't treated the economic cost could, in the final analysis, be prohibitive.[28]

This all sounds very logical and perhaps even chivalrous, and of course when our Western psycho-technologies genuinely help it would be wrong to keep them for ourselves. But even if we accept that psycho-drugs can work in some cases, the jury is out on whether the over-medicating of vast swathes of the world's population helps anyone other than the drug companies themselves.

We have already heard in Chapter 4 how antidepressants work no better than placebos for the majority of people, but we also know there are serious problems with the more powerful antipsychotics. In fact, one of the most damning criticisms of the 2001 World Health Organisation report comes from data gathered some years earlier, ironically enough, by the very same organisation. This separate WHO study was undertaken by a team of over 100 psychiatrists who compared the recovery rates of psychiatric patients in developed countries (like the US, Denmark and UK) with patients being treated in developing countries (like Nigeria, Colombia and India).[29] The findings were troubling. In the two-year follow-up study after treatment, only *15.5 per cent of patients in the developed world* had completely clinically recovered, compared to a full *37 per cent of patients from the developing countries*. Also, a full *42 per cent* of patients in the developed countries experienced impaired social functioning throughout the follow-up period, whereas only *16 per cent* from the developing countries experienced the same social impairment. The most worrying statistic of all was that while patients in developing countries did far better than patients in developed countries, the latter were taking far more medication: *61 per cent* of patients in the developed countries were on continuous antipsychotic medication, compared to only *16 per cent* in the developing countries. So who was getting better quicker? Not the patients in developed countries like the UK and the US who were taking far more pills, but the patients in developing countries like Nigeria and India where psychiatric resources and pill-taking were comparatively meagre.[30] How do we explain this?

One possible reason is that we in the developed world are doing worse because we are under different kinds of social pressures. Maybe the social conditions of the contemporary West simply aren't conducive to good mental health: and indeed the authors of the study directly pointed to cultural differences being the most important factor in our poorer outcomes. Yet the differences they emphasised weren't only to do with differing levels of social stress (it would be churlish to argue that somehow life is far more difficult for *us*); rather, in non-Western communities there appeared to be better community support for the emotionally and mentally distressed. This insight accords with numerous studies showing how crucial good relationships, community acceptance and support are in recovery.[31] We already know that when people can be assisted in a non-hospital environment, closer to home, with lower doses of medication, their recovery is far better.[32] We also know from studies in Finland of new 'Open Dialogue' approaches (where treatment is focused on supporting the individual's network of family and friends, as well as respecting the decision-making of the individual) that community-based care works far better than conventional biochemically-heavy interventions.

Could research like this help explain why patients in developing countries are doing far better than their more medicated Western counterparts, for whom community relations are increasingly atomised, unsupportive and individualistic? If so, could the exportation of individualised chemical treatments and biological understandings of distress be to the detriment of these less individualist communities, especially because, as I discuss in the Appendix, the damaging long-term effects of these medications may help explain why clinical outcomes are less successful in places where they are most aggressively prescribed? Furthermore, could this be a biological vision so intimidating to most people that they feel there's nothing to be done other than hand over the sufferer to the experts so they can do their work?

Western psychiatry has just too many fissures in the system to warrant its wholesale exportation, not just because psychiatric diagnostic manuals are more products of culture than science (Chapter 2), or because the efficacy of our drugs is far from encouraging (Chapter 4), or because behind Western psychiatry lie a variety of cultural assumptions about human nature and the role of suffering of often questionable validity and utility (Chapter 9), or because pharmaceutical marketing can't be relied on to report the facts unadulterated and unadorned (Chapter 10), or finally because our exported practices may undermine successful local ways of managing distress. If there is any conclusion to which the chapters of this book should point, it is that we must think twice before confidently imparting to unsuspecting people around the globe our particular brand of biological psychiatry, our wholly negative views of suffering, our medicalisation of everyday life, and our fearfulness of any emotion that may bring us down. Perhaps, ultimately, we are investing vast wealth in researching and treating mental illness because, unlike many other cultures, we have gradually lost our older belief in the healing powers of community and in systems that once gave meaning and context to our mental discontent. This is a view that commentators like Ethan Watters urge the mental health industry to start taking very seriously: 'If our rising need for mental-health services does indeed spring from a breakdown of meaning, our insistence that the rest of the world think like us may be all the more problematic. Offering the latest Western mental-health theories, treatments and categories in an attempt to ameliorate the psychological stress sparked by modernization and globalization is not a solution; it may be part of the problem. When we undermine local conceptions of the self and modes of healing, we may be speeding along the disorienting changes that are at the very heart of much of the world's mental distress.'[33]

At the end of my interview with Watters, he had one final message he wanted to impart: 'I believe that the rest of the world has as much to teach us about how to live a healthy human life as we have to teach them', he said passionately, 'but we need a good deal more humility in order to understand that.' Without that humility, the flow of ideas will continue in only one direction. And even if that doesn't mean that the rest of the world will end up thinking just like us, it does mean that the rest of the world's way of understanding, managing and experiencing emotional suffering will imperceptibly change. How it will change will differ from place to place, but the best we can hope for is that these changes are undertaken with full awareness of the serious problems afflicting psychiatry in the West. Others realising that our so-called solutions have created vast new complications in the places where they were devised may be the only bulwark against the ill-advised rush to import a system that brings as many problems as it purports to solve.

13
How to fix the cracks?

Towards the end of my long series of interviews I walked through one of London's most exclusive neighbourhoods on my way to Belgrave Square. The sky lent a crisp blue backdrop to the tapestry of autumnal leaves rippling in the trees overhead. As I reached the end of Pont Street and turned into the grand regency square, there on my left, nestled against the Austrian embassy, sat the *grande dame* of British psychiatry – the Royal College of Psychiatrists. Like a posh wedding cake, it proudly ascended an elegant five storeys from the broad and leaf-dappled pavement, painted a creamy magnolia with Doric columns holding up the portico entrance. It was stately, elegant, oddly edible.

After a couple of failed attempts on the intercom system, I put my ear closer to the brass speaker and tried to decipher the whispered and garbled fizzing. At once the system kicked in. 'Push the door!' someone boomed. Shocked, I pushed far too hard, almost falling into the lobby. A demurely dressed receptionist smiled innocently: 'Can I help you?'

'I have an appointment with Professor Sue Bailey', I mumbled, rubbing my ear. 'Ah yes, Dr Davies', the receptionist smiled, 'please do wait in the members' room, she'll be with you shortly.'

Five minutes later, my hearing returned, I was escorted up five flights of stairs to Professor Bailey's office, neatly tucked away on the top floor. It's a modest office compared with what I had come to expect, and considering that Professor Bailey is, after all, the president of the Royal College of Psychiatrists.

Bailey is a straight-talking and no-nonsense psychiatrist with a grounded Manchester accent. Her handshake is firm, her voice steady, and I sensed right away when she said 'I know your work' that she wanted to cut to the chase.

I had come to discuss the future of psychiatry, and my starting point was a crucial event that was, at the time, about to occur in the profession: an editorial was soon to be published in the *British Journal of Psychiatry*, one of the most respected and widely read psychiatry journals internationally. The editorial had been written by 29 senior consultant psychiatrists, all of them members of the Royal College of Psychiatrists and all expressing deep concern about the current state of psychiatry. Their article is so significant because it runs counter to the growing professional belief, many times articulated in the same journal, that the current crisis in psychiatry can be best solved by reaffirming psychiatry's identity as a discipline essentially concerned with studying, diagnosing and pharmacologically treating 'brain-based' mental diseases.

Although the authors of the editorial do not deny that the brain sciences and psychopharmacology have a role to play in psychiatry, they insist that the dominant 'medical model', which sees the diagnosis of brain disorders and the prescription of drugs as psychiatry's primary task, has not only failed the test of science, but is not getting the clinical results it promised. They therefore insist that the 'medical model' must take a back seat to interventions and methods that really do work. In essence, the editorial requests a paradigm shift, away from the medical model and towards an approach that prioritises healing relationships with people, helping people find meaning in their lives, and using therapies and other social/humanistic interventions as the first line of treatment.

Once I had outlined the editorial's main arguments to Sue Bailey, I asked her whether she would like to comment.

'OK', said Bailey, sitting up presidentially, 'I prefer not to comment, because I think their vision is quite limited really. So while I am very fond of them, I think we can have a better vision than the vision they've got.' I gently pointed out that their position simply builds on the mounting evidence that the current medical model is under considerable strain. Firstly, while there are still no biological markers found for the majority of mental disorders, the medical model is also leading to the widespread over-medicalisation of our problems, and to the over-prescribing of often dangerous and ineffective drugs. I asked what she made of those charges.

'OK, let's pick those points off', said Bailey impatiently. 'It's quite interesting that over-medicalisation is levelled at psychiatry [i.e. the idea that psychiatry is wrongly recasting many normal and natural human responses into medical conditions requiring drug treatment]. It would be probably better levelled at primary care and GPs. When you go into a profession where you want to help people, and you don't have the tools to help them, the temptation is to medicalise them.'

I tried to ask Bailey why she held GPs responsible, when it was psychiatry that had put these drugs on the map, promoted their value to GPs, and dramatically expanded the number of mental disorders for which these pills can be prescribed – but as I began to speak, Bailey raised her hand, indicating she had more to say. And while what she said did not make for easy listening, it's still worth quoting in full:

'So let's focus back on the critical psychiatrists – they are saying that many problems [treated as mental health problems] are not medical issues. They may be right, but does it actually make any difference to the person who is in distress? The person is in distress for some reason, and that may be because they have had a bad day, it may be that they have been traumatised and abused by Jimmy Savile, for instance. And it's now in the newspapers and they are worried about it. Now, it may not need medical treatment but they need some support, to be listened to. I have no problem with that. I have a problem with [Bailey names a senior critical psychiatrist] accusing us with over-medicalising problems. But you'd need to talk to a neuroscientist about the fact that that there isn't much evidence about biomedical markers [for mental disorders]. I am more on the side of social science; that is what I do, I do qualitative research. But actually there is increasing evidence of biomedical markers. But it would be really useful if the neuroscientists on one end, the social scientists somewhere in the middle, and the critical psychiatrists at the other end would all get over themselves and actually look at this properly. You've got a human in front of you who has come to you for a reason, who wants help. And the job is to listen to them and to try and disentangle it, and some of it will be about social support, some will be about advice about how they are living their life, and some of them temporarily will have a distress – however that is diagnosed in the new classification system. Some of them will be sat there with a rancid depression that no one has taken any notice of. What we are about is a patient–doctor dyad that's trying to understand the dilemma that comes into the room, and that's what we have got. And I think that's what we do in mental health. We care and treat. So over-medicalisation, yes, maybe happening, but at the other end we've got [suffering people]. I mean this morning I've been to Deaths in Custody where 200 young people have committed suicide while in juvenile prisons. So the father of one of these very bravely came and told the young man's story, and probably the main reason why he committed suicide was that nobody recognised he had ADHD … So I suppose I don't have a lot of time for people who are fixed to one theory and one point of view. We are in the business of understanding human nature and then doing what we can, within the evidence base, whether it's from a medication evidence base, a talking therapies evidence base, an alternative therapies evidence base – we do the best we can.'

I took a deep breath. I wasn't sure where to go from here. I was struggling to understand what Bailey was actually saying – was she saying that GPs are medicalising our normal and natural responses to the problems of living, but not psychiatrists? And was she saying that the writers of the editorial are 'fixed in one theory' by arguing that psychiatry relies too heavily on the medical model, which privileges diagnosis and medication? As the interview continued, I therefore tried harder to pinpoint precisely where the institutional leader of British psychiatry stood. As we went back and forth what gradually emerged was that Bailey viewed the writers of the editorial as indeed 'fixed in one theory'; a theory that she felt contradicted her more eclectic vision: that we must use medication, diagnosis, the insights of social science, psychotherapy, neurobiology and social care as combined resources to help patients.

When I pointed out that the authors of the editorial also seemed to share this more eclectic view (aside from their request for the medical model to take more of a back seat), her eyes suddenly narrowed: 'I say I am different from them, because they are zealots in their own model. And I think any zealot-driven model is a bad idea.'

This seemed to me a strong statement to make. So I asked Dr Sami Timimi, a consultant psychiatrist, a Director of Medical Education in the NHS, and a contributor to the editorial, whether he felt such a statement was fair: 'Positioning critical psychiatry as extreme and zealous', replied Timimi coolly, 'seems to me to reflect a possible misunderstanding of our position. She seems to think that we are proposing an alternative one-dimensional model that can be applied across psychiatry. But that is what we are arguing against, because that is what the medical model has done: prioritised a narrow focus on the diagnosis of symptoms and prescribing. It also sounds like she is having great difficulty imagining that psychiatric services could exist if diagnosis, for example, didn't play a central role. Now as far as I can see, all the evidence says that diagnosis hasn't helped in terms of forwarding the science: there is virtually no concrete evidence linking our diagnostic categories to either biological or even psychological markers. But even if we put that to one side and look at how clinically useful our current diagnostic system is, all the evidence suggests that in terms of helping us make usefully clinical decisions the current diagnostic framework doesn't help at all. In fact it seems to do the opposite.'

What the evidence shows, according to Timimi, is that what matters most in mental healthcare is not diagnosing problems and prescribing medication, but developing meaningful relationships with sufferers with the aim of cultivating insight into their problems, so the right interventions can be individually tailored to their needs. Sometimes this means giving meds, but more often it does not. The problem with simply putting labels on people, Timimi believes, is that it ends up often medicalising problems that are not medical in nature, as we have seen. And this isn't helped by successive expansions of the DSM and ICD, which encourage practitioners to wrongly medicalise more and more emotional troubles as mental disorders that warrant only pharmaceutical treatments.

As this last criticism had been made by many other people I'd interviewed (you'll recall the chair of *DSM-IV*, Allen Frances, saying that *DSM-IV* created three new false psychiatric epidemics), I decided to ask Sue Bailey whether she agreed that the expansion of DSM and ICD was a driver of medicalisation. Bailey seemed irritated by the question: 'Look, I think there are frankly better things people should be doing with their time. I haven't actually got a lot of truck with these discussions if I am honest with you. The majority of people I look after are living in poverty, with inequality, and have experienced abuse – they've got undiagnosed, unrecognised mental illnesses. So I actually think that we should focus on the reality of what we can do as doctors, rather than having erudite discussions about what the various situations of what DSM should have done.'

Again, I was surprised to hear this. So I quoted Bailey's response to Dr Timimi. He was less surprised than incredulous: 'These debates about medicalisation are debates about *real things* that affect *real people* in everyday practice. I think what she said shows a staggering intellectual complacency, and a real desire to avoid thinking about the clinical implications of medicalisation.' After all, for the 29 authors of the editorial, the more people whose suffering is wrongly medicalised, the more will be prescribed often dangerous and inefficacious drugs, the more will suffer the stigma of unnecessarily being labelled 'mentally ill', and the fewer will be offered non-medical alternatives. For authors of the editorial like Timimi, then, Bailey's dismissal of medicalisation provokes incredulity because, as Timimi summarised, the evidence shows that the medical model (without which there'd be no medicalisation) is not working.

To illustrate this final point, Timimi revealed the results of some research he had recently undertaken. He compared two different mental-health teams working in the NHS. One team followed the usual medical model – where diagnosis and drug treatment took precedence – while the other team adopted a 'non-diagnostic' approach where medication is given only sparingly, diagnosis is hardly used at all, and individual treatment plans are tailored to the person's unique needs. Timimi then gave me two clinical examples of how the 'non-diagnostic' approach actually works in practice.

In the first example a young man enters the consulting room displaying behaviours that would traditionally warrant the diagnosis of ADHD. But rather than assign the diagnosis, the psychiatrist invites the mother in and takes some family history. It turns out that the son and mother had been living for many years with domestic violence until the abusive man eventually left. But the boy had been so scarred by the experience that his behaviour was now understandably chaotic. Rather than diagnosing and medicating his behaviour, the psychiatrist focused on helping the mother and son gain insight into why the boy was struggling. In one session, for instance, while the psychiatrist was reflecting on the mother's feelings of guilt and lack of confidence, the mother began to cry. Straight away the boy started rebuking the psychiatrist – he saw the psychiatrist as yet another man hurting his mother. This event opened up a conversation about how hyper-vigilant the boy had needed to become, and how this was hampering his life. By talking and working things through, together they developed an explanatory framework that began to make sense of why the boy might be struggling with authorities, and with being angry generally. And as this work continued, the boy, without drugs or a diagnosis, gradually began to improve. In the second example, the same psychiatrist met the family of a boy who had many learning difficulties but who had worked out how to cover this up, usually by acting the class clown. Again, rather than using the common approach of assigning a diagnosis and prescribing meds, the psychiatrist centred on working with the boy's local school. In the end, the psychiatrist helped the boy move to another school where more classroom support could be offered, and where he could enjoy a fresh start. Once again, this simple non-medical strategy worked to good effect.

The psychiatrist in both examples spent far more time with his patients than would have been required had he merely assigned a diagnosis and prescribed medication.

But the results were worth the additional time, effort and of course money. In fact, when Timimi assessed how well patients did in the non-diagnostic approach compared to those treated via the medical model, the differences were dramatic: Only 9 per cent of patients treated by the non-diagnostic approach continued needing treatment after two years, compared with 34 per cent of patients who were being treated via the medical model. Furthermore, only one person from the non-diagnostic approach ended up having to be hospitalised, whereas over fifteen people in the medical-model team were referred for in-patient hospital treatment. Finally, the non-diagnostic approach led to more people being discharged more quickly, and to the lowest patient 'no show' rate out of all the mental health teams in the county.

'So we know the non-diagnostic approach was effective because we measured the outcomes', said Timimi. 'It had the lowest use of medication, the lowest use of in-patient treatment, but the highest recovery rate. So research like this shows that a non-diagnostic approach can not only work, but it can work a lot better than the current medical one we have.'

This view was further confirmed for Timimi when, after his study, he became consultant to one of the less successful mental health teams in his county, where the medical model was firmly entrenched. What he found was that most patients had been in the service for many years and had become psychologically dependent upon their pills and thoroughly cultured into thinking of their problems as related to diagnoses like ADHD, bipolar disorder, depression and so on. The medical model seemed to be actually helping create patients who had chronic conditions; conditions that weren't products of their biology but of how their problems were being medically managed. The medical model was, in effect, creating the circumstances in which patients were staying unwell for longer.

Timimi's approach is not unique. Many of the psychiatrists contributing to the editorial embrace similar methods, but so too do increasing numbers of others. When I interviewed Dr Peter Breggin, another internationally renowned critical psychiatrist located in the US, it was clear he had long ago rejected the medical model, and to very good effect. 'The model I prefer to use is a person-centred team approach', said Breggin, 'where the prescriber and the therapist work with the family and the patient. This approach is centred around the person, and what the patient really wants, feels and needs.' For Breggin this did not mean simply diagnosing and medicating people outside their context, but side-stepping the medical model and focusing on the matrix of relationships in which the person habitually operates: 'If I get a child who is labelled ADHD and is on stimulants, I just work with the family in the office. I take the kid off the drug, and work with the family in an honest and caring atmosphere, which is something kids love, working out what went wrong. Even if the child is "psychotic", I guarantee that within time these problems can be fixed if we all work together responsibly, and we are getting amazing results.'

For Breggin, most problems are created by the contexts in which people live and therefore require contextual not chemical solutions. 'People who are breaking down are often like canaries in a mineshaft', explained Breggin. 'They are a signal of a severe family issue. And sometimes the one who is breaking down is being scapegoated, sometimes they are the most sensitive, creative member of the family, sometimes they are the one person in the family with a really different personality. You don't know what is going on often, but with work you can see the dynamics that have developed in the family that are pulling things down.' For Breggin, because the medical model fails to take context seriously – whether the family or the wider social context – it overlooks the importance of understanding and managing contexts to help the person in distress.

Another consultant psychiatrist and contributor to the editorial, Dr Pat Bracken, echoed the value of this more person-centred approach: 'One of the reasons psychiatry is in crisis is that we are simply over-prescribing meds. Lots of people say that the only thing they get from psychiatry is pills. But there are serious questions about whether this approach has delivered – has it alleviated distress, has it helped people enduring states of madness or depression, has it helped them to move on in their lives? There are serious people standing back from psychiatry, looking at the evidence and saying, hang on a minute here, there is no evidence that this massive expansion of drugs is working. In fact, there is growing concern that this enormous tidal wave of prescribing is actually causing major problems, not least of all by increasing mortality rates of people experiencing mental illness.' (For more information on this, please see the Appendix.)

Bracken argues, in keeping with the editorial, that psychiatry must therefore readjust its relationship to the usefulness of psychopharmacology. 'But this is not the same as being anti-drugs', Bracken was keen to emphasise. 'We are very clear in the editorial that there is a role for using medicine to ease human distress. Rather we believe we need to get balance back into the situation again.'

For Bracken, the balance will return only by dethroning the medical model from the helm of psychiatry, where problems are simply understood as symptoms and signs of underlying illnesses. But he also recognises this is a tall order. 'The medical model was established in the asylums in the early 20th century', continued Bracken, 'so it has been at the heart of psychiatry's identity for a long time. This could have changed in the 1970–80s when psychiatry moved out of the asylums. At this time the natural process would have been for psychiatry to have become more interested and involved with the social sciences, with efforts to look at what kind of environments are important for people to recover and flourish in. But instead, at that very moment, the pharmaceutical industry started to target psychiatry in way that has allowed the dominance of the medical paradigm to continue. In fact, I think the influence of pharma has made the medical focus in psychiatry even more narrow, largely because money speaks – when there is money to support academic departments, psychiatry departments, etc. that all promote this approach, well then, it's not surprising that is what continued.'

Bracken's message was clear: 'We are not saying there is no valuable practice going on in psychiatry. Our point is that when you actually look at how people are helped, it's not all about medication and diagnosis; we are rather focusing on issues to do with negotiation of meaning and context, prioritising relationships with people, working democratically with other agencies and service users. We are not abandoning our typologies in that move, but we are seeing the use of drugs, the use of therapies, the use of diagnosis even, as secondary to something more primary. And when psychiatrists in their individual practices do that, I think that's what people say is a good psychiatrist. So we should start turning the paradigm round, start seeing the non-medical approach as the real work of psychiatry, rather than as incidental to the main thrust of the job, which is about diagnosing people and then getting them on the right drugs.'

•

It was clear to me the direction in which psychiatry would go if the critical psychiatrists had the power. But as this group was on the institutional outskirts, what I now wanted to know was how the future would look for those with power at the centre. Would the future look anything like what the critical psychiatrists hope for, with their desire to relegate the medical model? I put this question to Sue Bailey, who once again offered a strong response: 'The risk [of challenging the medical model] is that we end up without a voice for mental health', she said. 'Despite the best efforts of some senior members of this college, mental disorder is still not recognised by the United Nations and World Health Organisation as a non-communicable disease [i.e. as a serious medical illness like heart disease, diabetes or cancer].'

Getting this recognition was crucial, Bailey believed, because it would finally force governments to take mental health issues seriously, which would in turn increase provision for mental healthcare. But so long as the profession remained internally divided, mental disorders were less likely to be granted this coveted disease status. 'By having the neuroscientists and the critical psychiatrists fighting', explained Bailey, 'I would go as far as to say they are causing harm, because our argument about the importance of mental health is as strong as cancer. But cancer specialists have these polarised debates in a closed room; and yes, a bit of blood is spilt on the carpet. But when they come out they speak about cancer in one voice. We do not speak about mental health in one voice; but until we do, with enough common ground, then mental health will not get the attention or service provision it deserves.'

The main problem with Bailey's quest for professional consensus is that the forces of disagreement are deeply entrenched. How can you get the brain-disease psychiatrists and the critical psychiatrists to agree on a common vision of mental distress, when their understandings of suffering, of aetiology, of treatment, of diagnosis are fundamentally at odds? It's like asking Buddhists and Christians to agree that their views of the afterlife are, at bottom, really the same. Furthermore, Bailey's request for professional agreement is hobbled by her aim for those critical of the medical model to help form a consensus that would ultimately allow mental disorder to attain 'disease status'. But why would the critical psychiatrists do that? Their whole point is that to think of mental suffering in 'disease terms' is to fundamentally misunderstand what we are dealing with.

•

Once I had closed the door of the Royal College of Psychiatrists behind me and stood outside again on

Belgrave Square, I felt a sudden and gloomy wave of certainty that Sue Bailey's position was an impossible one. In many ways I could understand her exasperation – the reconciliation she sought was so improbable that her solution offered very little hope. I therefore would need to turn to others I had spoken to, unconstrained by having to juggle many competing interests, who had thought through alternative ways in which psychiatry could be reformed. When summarising the various views I had heard, they broadly boiled down to four propositions. So let me state them here:

1. Psychiatry needs to develop greater modesty and humility about what it can actually hope to achieve.

2. There needs to be more thorough regulation and transparency regarding psychiatry's financial ties to the pharmaceutical industry.

3. The training of future psychiatrists must include instilling greater critical awareness of psychiatry's scientific failings and current excesses, as well as better awareness of how to manage patients outside of the medical model.

4. The public needs to become better informed about the current crisis in psychiatry. And if the industry does not reform, people need to be prepared to vote with their feet.

I realise that an entire book could be written for each of these propositions. But allow me to just give you a very brief summary of each of them in turn.

This first proposition I heard again and again. For example, I interviewed Professor Thomas Szasz, perhaps one of the most influential critical psychiatrists of the 20th century and author of the now classic *The Myth of Mental Illness*. As he had always argued that the biological philosophy of suffering underpinning psychiatry was causing more problems than it solved, I asked him what his philosophy looked like: 'My understanding of emotional suffering', answered Szasz in considered tones, 'and I hope I won't be misunderstood, is no different from the traditional understanding of the Jews, Christians or Muslims of emotional suffering. Suffering is life. God didn't put us on this earth, assuming that he did, to be happy. Life, as I put it humorously, is not a picnic. It makes no difference if you are a king or a pope or a tyrant.'

I asked Szasz what is it about our period that makes it normal for everyone to be medicated when misery strikes. Why do we believe as a culture that suffering must be removed chemically, rather than understood in many cases as a natural human phenomenon, and possibly something from which we can learn and grow if worked through productively?

'In one sentence, and my statement is not original, our age has replaced a religious point of view with a pseudo-scientific point of view', responded Szasz. 'Now everything is explained in terms of molecules and atoms and brain scans. It is a reduction of the human being to a biological machine. We don't have existential or religious or mental suffering any more. Instead we have brain disorders. But the brain has nothing to do with it, except that it is an organ necessary for thinking.'

'So by reducing everything to the physical', I clarified, 'have we distorted our understanding of the meaning and potential purpose of emotional discontent? We have turned it into a malady from which we need to be cured?'

'You put it perfectly. And that's why people keep looking to novels, to writers, to the cinema and to the theatre to see emotional stories acted out and lived out. They don't consult psychiatric textbooks.'

Sadly, a month after I interviewed Szasz he died at his home in Syracuse. He was 92. I was probably the last person to have interviewed him. But among what must have been some of his closing words on psychiatry, he leaves us with the following statements, which I summarise: it was hubris for medicine to try to manage realms of life it was never designed to treat. It had become deluded in its belief that its physical technologies, its ECT machines and laboratory-manufactured molecules, could solve the deeper dilemmas of the soul, society and self. Professional grandiosity had blinded both the industry and a growing public to psychiatry's serious philosophical and technical limitations, and this had been compounded by the demise of traditional systems of meaning that once provided alternative solutions to the riddles of human despair.

If Szasz were correct that psychiatry was misguided about what it could hope to achieve, I now wondered how our culture would alternatively respond to the millions of suffering people who each year seek out psychiatric drugs and explanations for their pain. I decided to put this difficult question to the consultant psychiatrist Pat Bracken, who had also written extensively on the limitations of the dominant biomedical approach:

'There are no easy answers', said Bracken with a sigh. 'This widespread suffering may actually be a social phenomenon. Go back a few decades and you would have seen a much more central role for the church. The Sri Lankan anthropologist, Gananath Obeyesekere, has talked about this a lot, about the crucial role of culture in handling people's distress, giving people words, giving people paths, giving people rituals through which they can find some peace in this world. And you know – religion has often played that role. But in a post-religious secular society, what happens when we don't have religion to do those kinds of things? What do we do then? While turning to medicine or therapy may be appropriate in some cases, this is a far bigger problem than can be answered by medicine or psychotherapy alone. What complicates things more is that we also live in a capitalist society, where there is always going to be someone trying to sell you something – whether a drug or a psychotherapeutic session. In fact, some people would argue that capitalism can only continue by constantly making us dissatisfied with our lives, so that there's always something new to sell us. It is constantly in the business of churning up our desires. You know, if everybody said I am very happy with my television, my car and everything else I've got, and I am perfectly content with my lifestyle, the whole economy would come shattering down around our ears. And that's one of the ironies of our current recession – we are constantly saying we must get the economy going, we must consume more, we must buy more, but this all relies on our dissatisfaction. So I don't have an easy answer for the question of what we can do with the huge numbers of the "worried well" who now rely on psychiatric drugs.

But what I am saying is that it's a vast sociological, anthropological and almost spiritual problem for human beings. So the idea that medicine is going to come up with a neat answer is far from the truth. In fact, the belief that it can is also behind the rise of antidepressants and other drugs. But the only people who have benefited from that are those working in the drug companies.'

Bracken felt that his many years working as a consultant psychiatrist had taught him that what we customarily call mental illness is not always illness in the medical sense. It's often a natural outcome of struggling to make our way in a world where the traditional guides, props and understandings are rapidly disappearing. Instead, our dominant worldview is now driven by barely perceptible capitalist imperatives: to work, to earn, to attain profit, to succeed, to consume. Not all mental strife is therefore due to an internal malfunction but often to the outcome of living in a malfunctioning world. The solution is not yet more medicalisation, but an overhaul of our cultural beliefs, a re-infusing of life with spiritual, religious or humanistic meaning with emphasis on the essential involvement of community, and with whatever helps bring us greater direction, understanding, courage and purpose. This is something way beyond what the medical model can offer, with its technological outlook and its financial entanglements with key industries in the capitalist machine.

'What may also be needed', said Ethan Watters, joining the discussion, 'is for people to become de-enthused'. So long as people continue to defer to psychiatric myths of biological breakdown and chemical salvation, the status quo in psychiatry will remain, including its many worrying excesses. 'So if psychiatry itself starts to lose some of its status', continued Watters, 'by having to start proving its legitimacy in terms of outcome studies, then that's all for the better, because consumers will know a little more about what they are getting, and the enthusiasms will weaken.' Watters' view is that as people become more aware of psychiatry's excesses, yes, it will lose some legitimacy, but insofar as this will bring public expectations back into line with what psychiatry can actually deliver, the change should be welcomed.

While it was interesting for me to hear these various pleas for greater professional modesty, it also struck me how at variance they were with what was actually happening on the ground. We now know, for example, that consecutive editions of the DSM and ICD keep expanding the number of diagnoses believed to exist. We know that psychotropic prescriptions are rising year-on-year. We know that public dependence on psychiatry is at an all-time high, and we know that alternative systems of meaning through which we once managed and understood our discontent (religious, philosophical, spiritual), no longer have their appeal for increasing numbers. So if a greater professional modesty doesn't seem to be on the horizon, where do we go from here?

This moves us on to proposition number 2: reforming the relationship between the pharmaceutical and psychiatric industries. We have seen how the medical model would never have attained such power and influence without the financial backing of the pharmaceutical industry. But we have also seen how the full extent of this patronage has not been made fully transparent to the public. Again and again I heard from critics a demand for this culture of concealment to end. And in this area at least there may be a smidgen of good news. I have already spoken about the Sunshine Act in the US, soon to be implemented by the Obama administration, where doctors will be increasingly forced to declare their pharmaceutical ties. This may discourage some of the excesses we have seen by shaming the unscrupulous into more ethical behaviour. In Britain the situation is less clear. Sue Bailey, for example, assured me that the EU has now formed an 'Ethical Life Science Group' that will keep better track of industry payments to institutions and doctors, and that the Royal College is now 'conducting its own internal survey asking members to report whether the organisation they work for receives industry money'.

These changes are to be welcomed. But do they go far enough? My belief is that until we have a national online register where you can freely check what a given psychiatrist, researcher, psychiatric department or mental health organisation is getting paid and by whom, internal surveys count for very little, because the figures will continue to remain a professional secret. After all, you have a right to know whether the psychiatrist who has just prescribed you or your child a powerful drug is being paid by the company that makes that drug. You also have a right to know whether a mental health organisation that speaks favourably about antidepressants receives yearly donations from antidepressant manufacturers. Until there are public websites where such payments are made fully transparent and that therefore enable the full extent of the problem to become clear, the real debates about how to reform industry ties won't even begin: should there be limits placed on what doctors receive yearly? To what extent should industry payments be donated to charity? To what extent should unpaid voluntary industry service be obligatory (for which companies then reimburse the NHS)? These are no doubt thorny issues that warrant long and hard debate. But right now these debates are not only avoided, they aren't even being proposed in the places that count.

This moves me on to proposition 3: the changes needed in the training of our future psychiatrists. At present in the UK, psychiatric training provides only cursory lip service to academic critiques of the bio-psychiatric world-view. Serious anthropological, sociological or philosophical critiques of the medical model are seen at best as interesting sidelines to what psychiatrists actually do. What is generally not imparted, in other words, is a thorough and lasting social, critical or historical awareness of what trainees are participating in, how they are participating in it, and in what ways this participation ultimately sustains practices disadvantageous to patients. In short, trainees are not educated to doubt or even question the system in any constructive way, but only to be certain in its application. As one trainee recently put it to me: 'The critiques are all very well, but I did not come into medicine to critique medicine but to do medicine.' The assumption here is that what one thinks has little bearing on what one does.

Until a new, critically reflective generation of psychiatrists emerges, nothing will change. But right now such robust critical thinking is far from being instilled in the new generation. As Pat Bracken said frankly: 'What I hear from the trainees working with me is that the exams are very much heavily skewed towards learning facts, diagnostic categories, causal models all framed in the medical model, as though you can teach psychiatry in the same way as you will teach respiratory medicine or endocrinology.' This point was also echoed by the consultant psychiatrist Duncan Double, who has studied psychiatric training in Britain. As he writes, in Britain today there is still 'an orthodox medical approach to the problems of interpreting and treating mental disorders', and 'any challenge to this orthodoxy is suppressed by mainstream psychiatry'. Double provided a couple of examples of how this orthodoxy plays itself out: he recalled a consultant psychiatrist who had a critical approach, but who confessed that he nevertheless trained his psychiatrists conventionally to enable them to prepare for the examination of the Membership of the Royal College of Psychiatrists. What troubled this psychiatrist most was not just that he was acting against his convictions, but that by the time these trainees had passed their professional tests their critical sensitivities had been eroded. Double also recalled a consultant in psychiatry who had once ruefully remarked that she had become 'irretrievably biological' in her approach to psychiatry. Although this was regarded as an acceptable outcome of her training, she felt she was not able to deal with any criticism of psychiatry. In short, her training had closed her off not only to the limits of what she was doing, but to any seriously considered non-biomedical alternatives.[1]

When I interviewed Duncan Double I asked him for more specifics, beyond the anecdotal, about how training looks today. I asked whether today's trainees are obliged to read, for example, works by Professor Irving Kirsch, Professor Joanna Moncrieff, Professor David Healy,

Professor Paula J. Caplan, Robert Whitaker and others. 'No, those sorts of books would largely be ignored', replied Double, as though I had said something very naive.

'But how about other critical perspectives?', I pressed. 'Would there be any critical scrutiny of, say, the construction of the DSM, psychiatry's relationship to the pharmaceutical industry, of the biomedical philosophy of suffering, of psychiatry's wider socio-cultural history?'

'There would be very little of this really', said Double, who then explained that a serious problem with introducing these perspectives is that outside criticism of the profession is often too readily dismissed by many as a kind of anti-psychiatry. 'The problem with this dismissive view is that young psychiatrists are often fearful of being identified with critical positions – because they think it may actually affect their progression in their career.'

If we accept that propositions 1, 2 and 3 are far from being realised, we could be forgiven for thinking that psychiatry's future will continue along the same lines as the present. And this is why the fourth and final proposition seems to many the most important of all: members of the public need to become better informed about the current state of psychiatry, and if the industry does not reform, be prepared to vote with their feet. Commentators on both sides of the Atlantic who despaired about the likelihood of internal reform raised this crucial point with me repeatedly. As Peter Breggin put it: 'The only thing that is going to change things is if people literally stop going. My own belief is that this is because psychiatry is a money-making, self-contained machine, which is by definition resistant to change from the inside.'

'Supposing you're right', I said to Breggin, 'then how do you get people to stop going? How is that going to happen?'

'I think we need braver journalists and authors, dissident psychiatrists and psychologists', answered Breggin. 'This has to be an educational movement, a political movement; we need grass-roots disillusionment among professionals, among consumers and the sciences. From this we can only hope there will be manifested new kinds of organisations, research and journals.'

Could this be the route to reform, then – a reliance on *us*? From everything I have learnt from all my encounters, I have to say, and as inadequate as this solution feels, it may well offer the best hope in the coming years. As Timimi put it: 'The things that get powerful institutions to change don't usually come from inside those institutions. They usually come from outside. So anything that can put pressure on psychiatry as an institution to critique its concepts and reform its ways must surely be a good thing.'

•

It's 2:00 on a Wednesday morning. I'm sitting alone at my kitchen table, the lights are dimmed, the shutters closed, and I'm writing these words with only a large pot of coffee to prop me up. My wife and baby daughter are tucked up safely in bed. I wish I were there too. But I know this will be a long night. My publisher expects this book by the morning. There have been too many nights like this in recent months, too much fretting, too much vacillation, too few hours to spare. Don't get me wrong: I have enjoyed the journey I have been on immensely; but even so, I'm now looking forward to a little rest, and most of all to spending more time with my family.

But even during those times when I have been away from them, during my various lockdowns in airport lounges, my disrupted nights in strange hotels, my long and uncomfortable journeys by car, plane and bus, I haven't in truth ever been entirely alone. Because you, the reader, have always been there. You have been at the front of my mind, as I have struggled to honestly and clearly communicate the revelations set down in these pages. I have known that everything I have said won't resonate with you, that you will formulate your own opinions. But I have also hoped that some of the facts here disclosed will leave their mark on your views and future actions. I believe that psychiatry is not the enemy; that the people I have disagreed with are not the enemy. No, I believe the only enemy is anything that actively tries to conceal the inconvenient facts. And the good news is that today in psychiatry the cell of concealment is cracking. The truths are finally seeping out. What role you choose to play in furthering this seepage is naturally a matter for you alone. But insofar as I have succeeded in making what is not generally known more freely available, then I have to admit it's with a lighter heart that I bring this book to a close and finally bid you goodnight …

Appendix
Antipsychotics (neuroleptics) – breaking the brain?

As I have not really discussed the effects of antipsychotic medications in the main body of this book, and because this is such an important topic, let me at the very least say a few brief words before I close. What follows can in no way do justice to the vast body of research pursuing the pros and cons of antipsychotic medication – their benefits, their side-effects and their harmful neurological effects. As I can provide only the most cursory survey here, I have placed a short list of useful books at the end of this Appendix for those interested in pursuing this topic further. In what follows I draw upon these books, but especially the excellent work of Robert Whitaker.

While it's true that antipsychotics can help certain people some of the time, inflated claims about their ability to 'cure' mental disorder are as unsubstantiated as are claims made for the 'curing' powers of antidepressants. Like the claims for antidepressants, those made in favour of antipsychotics must also be weighed against the facts. And any serious reading of the research literature on antipsychotics reveals that the facts are problematic.

Antipsychotics (or neuroleptics as they are more technically known) are administered for what are considered to be the more severe forms of mental disorder, including schizophrenia, bipolar disorder, delusional disorder and psychotic depression. These drugs are broadly classed under 'first-', 'second-' and 'third-generation' headings – 'third generation' being the newest wave of antipsychotic medications. All antipsychotics are said to work in a similar way, most purporting to block dopamine receptors in different brain pathways (the chemical thought responsible for psychotic experiences). However, it's important to note that, just as for the antidepressants, there is no research confirming that antipsychotics fix any known brain abnormality or that they 'rebalance' brain chemistry to some optimal level.[1] Rather, like any mood-altering substance, they simply alter the brain's functioning, and mostly in ways that are still largely opaque to researchers.

Despite the uncertainty as to how antipsychotics work neurologically, studies of their effects over the short term do reveal them to have moderately better results than placebos at reducing certain psychotic symptoms, helping people stabilise after a psychotic episode. That conclusion is now rarely disputed. What is disputed, however, is the precise value of this 'stabilised' state, especially for people who might have recovered spontaneously or responded well to other therapeutic support. For instance, using antipsychotics over the short term doesn't just lead to a reduction in the intensity of psychotic symptoms. Their effects are less specific than that: they also diminish other physical, emotional functions integral to all our mental activity. The psychiatrist Peter Breggin has referred to this state of diminished activity as 'deactivation'. To give a sense of what the very common experience of deactivation looks like for people taking antipsychotics, let me quote a patient's description of deactivation documented in the *British Medical Journal.* While this patient felt his psychotic symptoms had somewhat abated after antipsychotic use, he also bemoaned other disturbing changes: 'My personality has been so stifled that sometimes I think the richness of my pre-injections days – even with brief outbursts of madness – is preferable to the numbed cabbage I have now become … in losing my periods of madness I have had to pay with my soul.'[2]

It is of course up to the individual patient to decide whether paying with one's soul is an acceptable price for the mitigation of their symptoms, assuming, firstly, that the patient is in an able enough emotional state to make this decision for themselves, and secondly, that the patient has been provided by their doctor with the information necessary for making an informed decision (which generally does not happen).

So let's provide some of this information here, by way of assessing the *long-term* effects of antipsychotic treatment. Firstly, despite many claims that neuroleptics improve the outcome of schizophrenia, the actual evidence for this is scant.[3] On the contrary, research conducted over consecutive decades since the 1950s indicates that long-term usage may actually make outcomes worse for the majority of patients. A particularly pertinent suite of studies in the 1970s revealed this paradoxical conclusion. William Carpenter and Thomas McGlashan at the National Institute of Mental Health explored whether patients fared better off drugs. Their study, published in the *American Journal of Psychiatry,* showed that 35 per cent of the non-medicated group relapsed within a year after discharge, compared with 45 per cent of the medicated group. This finding was confirmed in a later study by Jonathan Cole published in 1977, also in the *American Journal of Psychiatry*, which reviewed all of the long-term studies on schizophrenic outcomes. It concluded that at least 50 per cent of all schizophrenia patients could fare well without drugs, and therefore requested a serious reappraisal of current prescription practices. This was quickly followed by a study in *International Pharmacopsychiatry* published in 1978 by Maurice Rappaport from the University of California. He followed 80 young males diagnosed with schizophrenia over a period of three years. All had been initially hospitalised, but not all had been administered antipsychotics. He showed that those not treated with antipsychotics again had by far the best outcomes: of those treated with antipsychotics a full 73 per cent were re-hospitalised, compared with only 47 per cent who were not given meds. Rappaport thus concluded that 'many unmedicated-while-in-hospital patients showed greater long-term improvement. Less pathology at follow-up, fewer rehospitalisations, and better overall functioning in the community than patients who were given chlorpromazine while in the hospital.'[4]

Studies like these gained further legitimacy in the 1980s when two researchers from the University of Illinois, Martin Harrow and Thomas Jobe, began a long-term study of 64 newly diagnosed schizophrenia patients. Every few years the researchers assessed their progress. They asked whether the patients' symptoms had decreased, whether they were recovering, how they were getting on with their lives and whether they still taking antipsychotics. After observing the patients for two years, they noticed that the experience of those still taking antipsychotics began to diverge from those who weren't. By 4.5 years into the study nearly 40 per cent of those who had stopped taking medication were 'in recovery' and more than 60 per cent were working. Whereas of those still taking medication only 6 per cent were 'in recovery' and few were working. As the years unfolded these dramatic differences remained: at the fifteen-year follow-up assessment 40 per cent of those off drugs were in recovery, versus 5 per cent of the medicated group. These results were published in 2007 in *The Journal of Nervous and Mental Disease*, and led the authors to conclude that patients who had remained on medication did far worse than patients who had stopped their medication – this latter group were more successful in their lives and at work.[5]

Research like this has raised many serious concerns that have often been sidelined by many working within psychiatry. One of particular importance pertains to the precise long-term damage that antipsychotics can cause the brain. This is to say – can the neurological changes that antipsychotics induce explain the worse outcomes of medicated patients?

The writer Robert Whitaker has closely investigated this question in his book *The Anatomy of an Epidemic*. He builds upon the research by two physicians, Guy Chouinard and Barry Jones from McGill University, which provides a neurological explanation for why patients taking antipsychotic medication long-term regularly fare worse than non-medicated groups. They start from the accepted position that antipsychotics work by blocking dopamine receptors in the brain, for which, they theorise, the brain then compensates by increasing the number of dopamine receptors (by up to 30 per cent). This then leaves the brain hypersensitive to dopamine once the medication is stopped; a hypersensitivity believed responsible for further psychotic experiences and thus further 'relapses'. Whitaker summarises the problem thus:

> Neuroleptics [antipsychotics] put a brake on dopamine transmission, and in response the brain puts down the dopamine accelerator (the extra D2 receptors). If the drug is abruptly withdrawn, the brake on dopamine is suddenly released while the accelerator is still pressed to the floor. The system is now wildly out of balance, and just as a car might careen out of control, so too the dopaminergic pathways in the brain. The dopaminergic neurons in the basal ganglia may fire so rapidly that the patient withdrawing from the drugs suffers weird tics, agitation, and other motor abnormalities, the same out-of-control firing is happening with the dopaminergic pathway to the limbic region, and that may lead to 'psychotic relapse or deterioration'.[6]

What Whitaker argues is that Chouinard and Jones' work had in theory ascertained why the outcomes of people taking antipsychotics were so comparatively low: medication escalates the likelihood of relapse by increasing dopamine activity once the person has ceased taking medication. As such relapses are then treated with yet more medication, which in turn raises the likelihood of yet another relapse, a vicious spiral of worsening mental health ensues.

It's not just the dopamine system that Whitaker has argued was being damaged by long-term antipsychotic use. Recent studies on macaque monkeys, for instance, have shown that after two years on either haloperidol or olanzapine there was an observable shrinkage in their brain tissue.[7] And similar structural changes in the brain have also been discerned in humans. One study showed that antipsychotics could increase the basal ganglia and, as with monkeys, reduce grey matter in certain brain regions.[8] Furthermore, there is no definitive research indicating that these brain changes are indeed in any way positive. Just like the brain changes sustained by long-term drug or alcohol abuse, they may well be both deleterious and irreversible. For example, some patients who take antipsychotics long-term develop what is called 'tardive dyskinesia' (TD), a gross motor dysfunction characterised by sudden, uncontrollable movements of voluntary muscle groups (e.g. constant movements of the mouth, tongue, jaw and cheeks; constant tongue protrusion or squirming and twisting). The problem with this condition is that it remains after the drugs are withdrawn, which has been taken as evidence for their causing permanent brain damage. Whitaker argues that antipsychotic usage may not therefore be curing the brain, but rather damaging the brain. This leads him to offer the following reflections:

> This does not mean that antipsychotics don't have a place in psychiatry's toolbox. But it does mean that psychiatry's use of these drugs needs to be rethought, and fortunately, a model of care pioneered by a Finnish group in western Lapland provides us with an example of the benefit that can come from doing so. Twenty years ago, they began using antipsychotics in a selective, cautious manner, and today the long-term outcomes of their first-episode psychotic patients are astonishingly good. At the end of five years,

> 85% of their patients are either working or back in school, and only 20% are taking antipsychotics.[9]

Outcomes for serious mental illness are disheartening, despite increasing use of antipsychotics. Many psychiatrists often blame these poor results on the nature of the disorder itself. As one senior psychiatrist put it to me: 'Schizophrenia and bipolar disorder are chronic life-long conditions, so relapses are to be expected.' This psychiatrist did not ask whether such chronicity could be partly or entirely drug-related, an interpretation supported by studies showing that schizophrenia often has much better outcomes in places where antipsychotics are less aggressively and frequently prescribed.

I have hardly been able to do full justice to the controversial and counter-intuitive points discussed above, but fortunately there are many sources that can help you explore these important matters further. Here are some particularly well-researched and trustworthy books:

Breggin, P.R. and Cohen, D. (1999), *Your Drug May Be Your Problem: How and Why to Stop Taking Psychiatric Drugs.* Massachusetts: Perseus Books.

Healy, D. (2008), *Psychiatric Drugs Explained.* London: Churchill Livingston.

Moncrieff, J. (2009), *The Myth of the Chemical Cure: a critique of psychiatric drug treatment.* London: Palgrave Macmillan.

Whitaker, R. (2010), *The Anatomy of an Epidemic.* New York: Broadway.

A final warning

While most psychiatric drugs have harmful side-effects, they also can have powerful withdrawal effects. Therefore, any precipitous or sudden withdrawal is always dangerous. It is therefore crucial that anyone deciding to withdraw from any kind of psychiatric medication do so under the supervision of an experienced physician who is, of course, well informed and thus able to respect fully any patient's desire to explore non-medication alternatives.

Acknowledgements

I have so many people to thank. First off, let me offer my sincere gratitude to many people who set aside time out of their busy schedules to grant me interviews. Without their generosity this book simply would not have been written. I also must thank those who closely read this book from beginning to end, holding me to task on every sentence. Particular thanks to Duncan Heath, my editor, Paula Caplan, Razwana Jabbin, and of course Alexandra Davies, my wife (I'll come back to her in a moment). I also benefited from informative conversations with so many trusted colleagues, including Rosie Rizq, Lyndsey Moon, Istvan Praet, Richard House, Del Loewenthal, Ann MacLarnon, Garry Marvin, Stuart Semple, Todd Rae, and many others in the areas of anthropology and psychology at the University of Roehampton. Others who left their mark, as always: Matias Spektor (the most positive force in so many ways), Benjamin Hebbert (sorry we didn't go for yellow), Richard Schoch (a mentor in the true sense of the term), Mark Knight (it goes without saying). Nancy Browner, James Wilkinson – I still think of you and the work we did (which has coloured every page – thank you). I must also especially thank Andrew Lownie, for your enthusiasm and belief – his support and advice means a great deal. Also, my sincere gratitude for the excellent team at Icon Books – Peter Pugh, Philip Cotterell, Andrew Furlow, Henry Lord, Rob Sharman, Madeleine Beresford, Stacey Croft and Nira Begum.

Finally, my gratitude to my students and clients, who have taught me so much; and to my loving and supporting family (Mike, Lyn, Alicia, Natalie, Helen, Andy, John, Alistair and Jean). Finally, my apologies to my wife, Alexandra, for writing yet another book! Without her love, support and brilliant editorial skills, I would not have got through. This book is dedicated both to her and to my daughter, Rose, the most joyous solace in difficult times.

Notes

Chapter 1: Psychiatry's early breakdown and the rise of the DSM

1. Carlat, D. (2010), *Unhinged: The Trouble with Psychiatry – a doctor's revelations about a profession in crisis*. London: Free Press (p. 52).
2. See: Cooper, J.E. et al. (1972), *Psychiatric Diagnosis in New York and London*. Maudsley Monograph, no 20. Oxford: Oxford University Press. Also see: *International Pilot Study of Schizophrenia* (1973), Geneva: World Health Organisation.
3. Such was the problem at the time that each psychiatrist had their own personal system of classification. See: Kendell, R.E. (1975), *The Role of Diagnosis in Psychiatry*. Oxford: Blackwell.
4. Caplan, P.J. (1995), *They Say You're Crazy*. New York: Da Capo (p. 53).
5. Quoted in Carlat, D. (2010), *Unhinged: The Trouble with Psychiatry – a doctor's revelations about a profession in crisis*. London: Free Press (p. 52).
6. Quoted in Kirk, S.A. and Kutchins, H. (1994), 'The Myth of the Reliability of DSM', *Journal of Mind and Behavior*, 15(1&2): 71–86.
7. Carlat, D. (2010), *Unhinged: The Trouble with Psychiatry – a doctor's revelations about a profession in crisis*. London: Free Press (pp. 53–4).
8. Spiegel, A. (2005), 'The Dictionary of Disorder: how one man revolutionized psychiatry'. *The New Yorker*, 3 January 2005.
9. Aboraya, A. (2007), 'Clinicians' Opinions on the Reliability of Psychiatric Diagnoses in Clinical Settings'. *Psychiatry*, 4(11): 31–3.
10. Aboraya, A. et al. (2006), 'The Reliability of Psychiatric Diagnosis Revisited'. *Psychiatry*, 3(1): 41–50. Also, for a summary of diagnostic reliability research undertaken in the 1980s and 1990s, please see: Caplan, P.J. (1995), *They Say You're Crazy*. New York: Da Capo (pp. 197–200).
11. Aboraya, A. et al. (2006), 'The Reliability of Psychiatric Diagnosis Revisited'. *Psychiatry*, 3(1): 41–50.
12. See: Andrews, G., Slade, T., Peters L. (1999), 'Classification in Psychiatry: *ICD-10* versus *DSM-IV*'. *British Journal of Psychiatry*, 175: 3–5.
13. NICE prefers *DSM-IV* because the evidence base for treatments refers, to a larger extent, to DSM criteria. See: www.cks.nhs.uk/depression/management/scenario_detection_assessment_diagnosis/assessment_and_diagnosis/basis_for_recommendation
14. Andrews, G., Slade, T., Peters, L. (1999), 'Classification in Psychiatry: *ICD-10* versus *DSM-IV*'. *British Journal of Psychiatry*, 175: 3–5.

Chapter 2: The DSM – a great work of fiction?

1. Caplan, P.J. (1995), *They Say You're Crazy*. New York: Da Capo (pp. 205–6).
2. Kutchins, H., Kirk, S.A. (1997), *Making us Crazy*. New York: Free Press.
3. Ibid.
4. Quoted in: Angell, M. (2009), 'Drug Companies & Doctors: A Story of Corruption', *The New York Review of Books*, 15 January 2009.
5. Spiegel, A. (2005), 'The Dictionary of Disorder: how one man revolutionized psychiatry'. *The New Yorker*, 3 January 2005.
6. Lane, C. (2009), *Shyness: how normal behaviour became a sickness*. New Haven: Yale University Press (p. 44).
7. Spiegel, A. (2005), 'The Dictionary of Disorder: how one man revolutionized psychiatry'. *The New Yorker*, 3 January 2005.
8. Andreasen, N.C. (2007), 'DSM and the Death of Phenomenology in America: an example of unintended consequences'. *Schizophr Bull*. 33(1): 108–12.
9. Macaskill, N., Geddes, J., Macaskill, A. (1991), '*DSM-III* in the Training of British Psychiatrists: a national survey'. *Int J Soc Psychiatry*. 37(3):182–6.

Chapter 3: The medicalisation of misery

1. Polanczyk, G. et al. (2007), 'The worldwide prevalence of ADHD: a systematic review and metaregression analysis'. *The American Journal of Psychiatry*, 164(6): 942–8.
2. Waddell, C. (2002), 'Child Psychiatric Epidemiology and Canadian Public Policy-Making: the state of the science and the art of the possible'. *Canadian Journal of Psychiatry*, 47(9): 825–32. Also see: Merikangas, K.R. et al. (2010), 'Prevalence and Treatment of Mental Disorders Among US Children in the 2001–2004 NHANES'. *Pediatrics*, 125(1): 75–81.
3. Kessler R.C., (2005), 'Prevalence, severity, and comorbidity of twelve-month *DSM-IV* disorders in the National Comorbidity Survey Replication (NCS-R)'. *Archives of General Psychiatry*, 62(6): 617–27.
4. Singleton, N., Bumpstead, R., O'Brien, M., Lee, A., Meltzer, H. (2001), 'Psychiatric Morbidity among adults living in private households', *The Office for National Statistics Psychiatric Morbidity report*, London: TSO.
5. For interview, see Adam Curtis's BBC documentary *The Century of the Self* (2002).
6. This discussion is paraphrased from my book: *The Importance of Suffering* (Davies, 2012).
7. *DSM-IV* was published in 1994, while a slightly revised edition called *DSM-IV–TR*, under the chairmanship of Frances, was issued in 2000.
8. See *The Lancet*: www.thelancet.com/journals/lancet/article/PIIS0140-6736(12)60248-7/fulltext

9. See: www.ipetitions.com/petition/DSM5/

Chapter 4: The depressing truth about happy pills

1. While I have long been aware of Kirsch's research, I am grateful for an excellent piece on Kirsch by CBS News, entitled 'Treating Depression: is there a placebo effect?' Their interviews with Walter Brown and Tim Kendall prompted me to interview them for this book.
2. I gathered this biographical information from Wikipedia, which I have double-checked for its accuracy.
3. For original graph, see: Kirsch, I. (2009), *The Emperor's New Drugs: exploding the antidepressant myth*. London: Bodley Head, (p. 10).
4. Ibid., p. 54.
5. Ibid., p. 62.
6. Kirsch, I., (2008), 'Challenging Received Wisdom: Antidepressants and the Placebo Effect'. *McGill J Med.*, 11(2): 219–22.
7. Khan, A., Redding, N., Brown, W.A. (2008), 'The persistence of the placebo response in antidepressant clinical trials'. *Journal of Psychiatric Research*, 42(10): 791–6.
8. After asking the MHRA about the number of trials needed to approve an antidepressant, they responded: 'As a general rule a minimum of two studies is required to prove efficacy of a drug. A single study will have to demonstrate very compelling results to be considered sufficient alone to demonstrate efficacy.' In other words, it's possible for a drug to be approved on the basis of only one study.
9. Mojtabai, R. and Olfson, M. (2011), 'Proportion of Antidepressants Prescribed Without a Psychiatric Diagnosis is Growing', *Health Affairs*, 30(8): 1434–42.
10. Blanchflower, D.G. and Oswald, A.J., (2011), 'Antidepressants and Age'. IZA Discussion Paper no. 5785. Available at SSRN: ssrn.com/abstract=1872733 (accessed September 2011).
11. The total number of prescriptions dispensed in 2012 was 50,167,201 for all types of antidepressants, up 7.5 per cent on 2011 (when totals were 46,677,813). The cost of antidepressant prescription was £211,145,435 in 2012. Health and Social Care Information Centre, Prescriptions Dispensed in the Community, Statistics for England (2002–2012); www.hscic.gov.uk/catalogue/PUB11291

Chapter 5: Dummy pills and the healing power of belief

1. PMDD was originally called 'late luteal phase dysphoric disorder' (LLPDD). It was renamed PMDD by the American Psychiatric Association in its May 1993 revision of the *DSM-IV*.

2. Eli Lilly TV broadcast advertisement (aired 2000). As part of its routine monitoring and surveillance programme, the Division of Drug Marketing, Advertising, and Communications at the FDA reviewed this advertisement and concluded that it was misleading, lacking in fair balance, and therefore in violation of the Federal Food, Drug, and Cosmetic Act and its applicable regulations. Unfortunately, this advert was widely aired before the DDMAC requested its removal.
3. Nathan Greenslit makes this point. See: Greenslit, N. (2005), 'Depression and Consumption'. *Culture, Medicine and Psychiatry*, 29: 477–501.
4. Quoted in ibid.
5. Ibid.
6. Ibid.
7. Ibid.
8. Meyer, B. et al. (2002), 'Treatment Expectancies, Patient Alliance, and Outcome: Further Analyses From the National Institute of Mental Health Treatment of Depression Collaborative Research Program'. *Journal of Consulting and Clinical Psychology*, 70(4): 1051–5.
9. The meaning that the healing environment has for the patient has been shown to increase the placebo effect to varying degrees. See: Moerman, D.E. (2002), *Meaning, Medicine and the 'Placebo Effect'*. Cambridge: Cambridge University Press. The presence of a doctor also increases expectancy, which in turn increases therapeutic outcome, especially if the doctor is warm and/or enthusiastic about the treatment. In one study, the response to a placebo increased from 44 per cent to 62 per cent when the doctor treated them with 'warmth, attention, and confidence'. See: Kaptchuk, T.J. et al. (2008), 'Components of Placebo Effect: randomised controlled trial in patients with irritable bowel syndrome'. *British Medical Journal*, 336(7651): 999–1003. My statement 'up to 40 per cent' is based on the likely outcome of adding doctor/patient expectancy to environmental expectancy. Admittedly, not all patients will experience 40 per cent placebo improvement, but most will react positively to environments triggering expectations for recovery. For an extended analysis of expectancy, see: Kirsch, I. (1985), 'Response Expectancy as a Determinant of Experience and Behavior'. *American Psychologist*, 40(11): 1189–1202.
10. Experiment cited in: Moerman, D.E. and Jonas, W.B. (2002), 'Deconstructing the Placebo Effect and Finding the Meaning Response'. *Ann Intern Med*, 136: 471–47.
11. Branthwaite, A. and Cooper, P. (1981), 'Analgesic effects of branding in treatment of headaches'. *British Medical Journal*, 282: 1576–8.
12. Moerman D.E and Harrington, A. (2005), 'Making space for the placebo effect in pain medicine', *Seminars in Pain Medicine*, 3: 2–6.

13. Anton de Craen, J.M. et al. (1996), 'Effect of Colour of Drugs: systematic review of perceived effect of drugs and of their effectiveness', *British Medical Journal*, 313: 21–8.

Chapter 6: Mental oddities and the pills that cause them

1. See: Adam Curtis's BBC documentary, *The Century of the Self* (2002).
2. Recent research has shown that the most commonly reported drug-induced psychoactive effects of the antidepressants Fluoxetine and Venlafaxine were sedation, impaired cognition, reduced libido, emotional blunting, activation (feelings of arousal, insomnia and agitation) and emotional instability. See: Goldsmith, J. and Moncrieff, J. (2011), 'The Psychoactive Effects of Antidepressants and their Association with Suicidality'. *Current Drug Safety*, 6(2): 115–21. Also see: Healy, D. (2006), *Let Them Eat Prozac*. New York: New York University Press (Chapter 7).
3. Simon Sobo's article makes this point – that drugs don't heal us but alter us. See: simonsobo.com/a-reevaluation-of-the-relationship-between-psychiatric-diagnosis-and-chemical-imbalances
4. Price, J., Cole, V., Goodwin, G.M. (2009), 'The Emotional Side-Effects of Selective Serotonin Reuptake Inhibitors: qualitative study'. *British Journal of Psychiatry*, 195: 211–17.
5. See Sobo, S. (2001), 'A Reevaluation of the Relationship between Psychiatric Diagnosis and Chemical Imbalance'. See: simonsobo.com/a-reevaluation-of-the-relationship-between-psychiatric-diagnosis-and-chemical-imbalances

Chapter 7: Bio-babble?

1. I am also grateful to David Davis' article in the *LA Times Magazine* for filling in some factual gaps, some of which I paraphrase. See: Davis, D. (2003), 'Losing the Mind', *LA Times Magazine*, 26 October 2003.
2. Quotations from MindFreedom website. See: www.mindfreedom.org/kb/act/2003/mf-hunger-strike/hunger-strike-debate/scientific-panel-1st-reply-to-apa
3. See 'APA Statement on "Diagnosis and Treatment of Mental Disorders"'. Website: www.mindfreedom.org/kb/act/2003/mf-hunger-strike/hunger-strike-debate/apa-2nd-reply-to-mfi
4. Schildkraut, J.J. (1965), 'The Catecholamine Hypothesis of Affective Disorders: a review of supporting evidence'. *American Journal of Psychiatry*, 122: 509–22.
5. Healy, D. (1999), *The Antidepressant Era*. Cambridge MA: Harvard University Press.
6. Coppen, A. (1967), 'The Biochemistry of Affective Disorders'. *British Journal of Psychiatry*, 113: 1237–64.

7. Moncrieff, J. (2009), *The Myth of the Chemical Cure: a critique of psychiatric drug treatment.* London: Palgrave Macmillan (p. 132).
8. Ruhé, H.S., Mason, N.S., Schene, A.H. (2007), 'Mood is Indirectly Related to Serotonin, Norepinephrine and Dopamine Levels in Humans: a meta-analysis of monoamine depletion studies'. *Molecular Psychiatry*, 12: 331–59.
9. Booij L., Van der Does, A.J., Riedel, W.J., (2003), 'Monoamine Depletion in Psychiatric and Healthy Populations: review'. *Mol Psychiatry*, 8(12): 951–73.
10. Carlat, D. (2010), *Unhinged: The Trouble with Psychiatry – a doctor's revelations about a profession in crisis.* London: Free Press (pp. 79–80).
11. Belmaker, R.H., Agam, G. et al. (2008), 'Major Depressive Disorder', *New England Journal of Medicine*, 358: 55–68.
12. Tsankova, N., Renthal, W., Kumar, A., Nestler, E.J., (2007), 'Epigenetic Regulation in Psychiatric Disorders'. *Nature Reviews Neuroscience*, May, 8(5): 355–67.
13. Kaffman A., Meaney, M.J. (2007), 'Neurodevelopmental Sequelae of Postnatal Maternal Care in Rodents: clinical and research implications of molecular insights'. *J Child Psychol Psychiatry*, 48(3–4):224–44. A really good journalistic account of this study can be found here: Zimmer, C. (2010), 'The Brain: The Switches That Can Turn Mental Illness On and Off', *Discover Magazine*, published online, 16 June 2010.
14. McGowan, P.O. et al. (2009), 'Epigenetic Regulation of the Glucocorticoid Receptor in Human Brain Associates with Childhood Abuse'. *Nat Neurosci*, 12(3): 342–8.
15. Jacob Peedicayil, J. (2007), 'The Role of Epigenetics on Mental Disorders'. *Indian J Med Res*, 126: 105–11; Tsankova, T., Renthal, W., Kumar, A., Nestler, E.J. (2007), 'Epigenetic Regulation in Psychiatric Disorders'. *Nature Reviews Neuroscience*, May, 8(5): 355–67.
16. Olopade, O.I. et al. (2008), 'Advances in Breast Cancer: Pathways to Personalized Medicine'. *Clinical Cancer Research*, 15 December 2008, 14: 7,988–99.
17. ASCO website: www.cancer.net/patient/All+About+Cancer/Genetics/Genetic+Testing (accessed May 2012).
18. See: Joseph, J., Ratner, C. (no date), 'The Fruitless Search for Genes in Psychiatry and Psychology: Time to Re-examine a Paradigm?' Website: www.councilforresponsiblegenetics.org/pageDocuments/1NX6VC0254.pdf (accessed September 2011).
19. Caspi, A. et al. (2003), 'Influence of Life Stress on Depression: Moderation by a Polymorphism in the 5-HTT', *Gene Science*, 301(5631): 386–9.
20. Quoted in Carlat, D. (2010), *Unhinged: The Trouble with Psychiatry – a doctor's revelations about a profession in crisis.* London: Free Press (p. 80).

21. World Health Organisation, 'Mental Health and Substance Abuse, Facts and Figures Conquering Depression'. Website: www.searo.who.int/en/Section1174/Section1199/Section1567/Section1826_8101.htm (accessed August 2010).

Chapter 8: Money and power ruling head and heart

1. Reid, S., 'Child Victims of the Chemical Cosh: boy who killed himself after taking Ritalin'. *Daily Mail.* See: www.dailymail.co.uk/health/article-2002856/Harry-Hucknall-10-killed-taking-Ritalin.html (updated 13 June 2011).
2. See: www.metro.co.uk/news/859706-mick-hucknalls-cousin-harry-was-a-victim-of-prescribed-drugs
3. Healy. H. and Whitaker, C. (2003), 'Antidepressants and suicide: risk–benefit conundrums'. *J Psychiatry Neurosci.*, 28(5): 331–7.
4. See: www.bbc.co.uk/news/uk-england-cumbria-17348819
5. Khan, A., Warner, H.A. and Brown, W.A. (2000), 'Symptom Reduction and Suicide Risk in Patients Treated with Placebo in Antidepressant Clinical Trials: an analysis of the Food and Drug Administration database', *Arch Gen Psychiatry*, 57: 311–17. Kirsch, I. (2009), *The Emperor's New Drugs: exploding the antidepressant myth.* London: Bodley Head. Khan, A., Redding N., and Brown, W.A. (2008), 'The Persistence of the Placebo Response in Antidepressant Clinical Trials', *Journal of Psychiatric Research*, 42(10): 791–6.
6. I quote the following examples in my recent article for *Therapy Today*, from which I paraphrase. See: Davies, J. (2012), 'The Deceptions of the Pharmaceutical Industry'. *Therapy Today*, 23 (8): 18–21.
7. Kondro, W. and Sibbald, B. (2004), 'Drug company experts advised to withhold data about SSRI use in children'. *Canadian Medical Association Journal*, 170: 783.
8. Reported in: www.nytimes.com/2009/02/26/business/26drug.html?_r=2&ref=business
9. Eyding, D. et al. (2010), 'Reboxetine for Acute Treatment of Major Depression: systematic review and meta-analysis of published and unpublished placebo and selective serotonin reuptake inhibitor controlled trials', *British Medical Journal*, 341: 4737.
10. Turner, Erick H. et al., (2008), 'Selective Publication of Antidepressant Trials and Its Influence on Apparent Efficacy', *New England Journal of Medicine*, 17 January 2008: 252–60.
11. Ibid.
12. Spielmans, G.I. and Parry, P.I. (2010), 'From Evidence-based Medicine to Marketing-based Medicine: evidence from internal industry documents', *Bioethical Inquiry*, 7: 13–29.

13. See: House of Commons Health Committee Report (2004–05), 'The Influence of the Pharmaceutical Industry'. Website: www.parliament.the-stationery-office.co.uk/pa/cm200405/cmselect/cmhealth/42/42.pdf (accessed December 2011).
14. Quoted in Spielmans, G.I. and Parry, P. I. (2010), 'From Evidence-based Medicine to Marketing-based Medicine: evidence from internal industry documents', *Bioethical Inquiry*, 7: 13–29.
15. Smith, R. (2005), 'Medical Journals Are an Extension of the Marketing Arm of Pharmaceutical Companies'. *PLoS Med*, 2(5): e138.
16. Quotations from ibid.
17. Quoted in Spielmans, G.I. and Parry, P.I. (2010), 'From Evidence-based Medicine to Marketing-based Medicine: evidence from internal industry documents', *Bioethical Inquiry*, 7: 13–29.
18. Quoted in ibid.
19. Goldacre, B. (2010), 'Drug Firms Hiding Negative Data are Unfit to Experiment on People'. The Guardian, 14 August 2010. Website: www.guardian.co.uk/commentisfree/2010/aug/14/drug-companies-bury-negative-research (accessed December 2011).
20. Spielmans, G.I., Biehn, T.l., Sawrey, D.L. (2010), 'A Case Study of Salami Slicing: pooled analyses of duloxetine for depression', *Psychother Psychosom*, 79: 97–106.
21. See: Fournier, Jay C., DeRubeis, R.J. et al. (2010), 'Antidepressant Drug Effects and Depression Severity: a patient-level meta-analysis'. *The Journal of the American Medical Association*, 303(1): 47–53. Please also see: Jackson, G. (2005), *Rethinking Psychiatric Drugs*. London: AuthorHouse.
22. Lexchin, J., Bero, L.A., Djulbegovic, B., Clark, O. (2003), 'Pharmaceutical Industry sponsorship and research outcome and quality'. *British Medical Journal*, 326: 1167–70.
23. Smith, R. (2005), 'Medical Journals Are an Extension of the Marketing Arm of Pharmaceutical Companies'. *PLoS Med*, 2(5): e138.
24. Angell. M. (2008), 'Industry-Sponsored Clinical Research: A Broken System', *The Journal of the American Medical Association*, 300 (9): 1069–71.

Chapter 9: But they make us rich

1. Campbell, E.G., Weissman, J.S., Ehringhaus, S. et al. (2007), 'Institutional Academic-Industry Relationships'. *The Journal of the American Medical Association*, 298(15): 1779–86.
2. See: House of Commons Health Committee Report (2004–05), 'The Influence of the Pharmaceutical Industry'. Website: www.parliament.the-stationery-office.co.uk/pa/cm200405/cmselect/cmhealth/42/42.pdf (p. 44).

3. The money they received was for research (42 per cent), for consultancies (22 per cent) and for talks and presentations (16 per cent). See: Cosgrove, L., Krimsky, S., Vijayaraghavan, M., Schneider, L. (2006), 'Financial Ties between *DSM-IV* Panel Members and the Pharmaceutical Industry'. *Psychother Psychosom*, 75: 154–60.
4. See the *DSM-5* website: www.DSM5.org/MeetUs/Pages/TaskForce Members.aspx
5. http://www.propublica.org/article/dollars-for-docs-the-top-earners
6. See: Carlat, D. (2010), *Unhinged: The Trouble with Psychiatry – a doctor's revelations about a profession in crisis*. London: Free Press (p. 135).
7. For full breakdown and coverage of all these exposures, see Senator Grassley's government website: www.grassley.senate.gov/about/Disclosure-of-Drug-Company-Payments-to-Doctors.cfm
8. See: www.pharmapolitics.com/birgenau.html
9. Timimi, S. (2008), 'Child Psychiatry and its Relationship with the Pharmaceutical Industry: theoretical and practical issues'. *Advances in Psychiatric Treatment*, 14: 3–9.
10. Harris, G., Carey, B. and Roberts, J. (2007), 'Psychiatrists, Children and Drug Industry's Role'. *New York Times*: 10 May 2007. Website: www.nytimes.com/2007/05/10/health/10psyche.html (accessed June 2011).
11. See: http://www.amsascorecard.org/
12. Such services include 'speaking at and chairing meetings, involvement in medical/scientific studies, clinical trials or training services, participation at advisory board meetings, and participation in market research where such participation involves remuneration and/or travel'.
13. See: www.pmcpa.org.uk/files/sitecontent/ABPI_Code_2012.pdf
14. A similar response was given by UCL when I asked: 'Please provide all figures regarding monies received from the pharmaceutical industry by any individual faculty member (records going back three years).' They responded: 'This information is not held. Whilst individuals are required to declare any interest, they are not specifically required to declare the payments received.'
15. Davies, J. (2009), *The Making of Psychotherapists: an anthropological analysis*. London: Karnac.
16. I started working voluntarily as a trainee, but continued to do so after my training had been completed. So while I can't guarantee I will always work voluntarily, if I ever took fees my paid hours would be few and my fees affordable for the average person. I have the luxury of taking this position, because I earn my living from my university post in social anthropology.

Chapter 10: When science fails, marketing works

1. See House of Commons Health Committee Report (2004), 'The Influence of the Pharmaceutical Industry'. Website: www.parliament.the-stationery-office.co.uk/pa/cm200405/cmselect/cmhealth/42/42.pdf (p. 58).
2. I here recreate Daniel Carlat's story from a combination of his reported experiences in his article 'Dr Drug Rep', published in the *New York Times* (25 August 2007), and the information I gathered from my interview with him. In parts of my account I paraphrase from his NYT article.
3. Paraphrased from Carlat's *New York Times* article, 'Dr Drug Rep'.
4. Kimberly Elliott, quoted in Daniel Carlat (2010), *Unhinged: The Trouble with Psychiatry – a doctor's revelations about a profession in crisis.* London: Free Press (p. 125).
5. In fact, in 2007 nearly three-quarters of antidepressants in the US were prescribed by non-psychiatrists. See: Mojtabai, R. and Olfson, M. (2011), 'Proportion of Antidepressants Prescribed Without A Psychiatric Diagnosis Is Growing'. *Health Affairs*, 30 August 2011, 30(8): 1434–42.
6. See: B. Grant (2009), 'Merck Published Fake Journal'. *The Scientist* (30 April 2009).
7. Timimi, S. (2008), 'Child Psychiatry and its Relationship with the Pharmaceutical Industry: theoretical and practical issues'. *Advances in Psychiatric Treatment*, 14: 3–9. doi: 10.1192/apt.bp.105.000901.
8. NHS Report (2012), 'Prescriptions Dispensed in the Community: England, Statistics for 2001 to 2011'. Published by The Health and Social Care Information Centre. Website: www.ic.nhs.uk/webfiles/publications/007_Primary_Care/Prescribing/Prescriptions%202001%20to%202011/Prescriptions_Dispensed_2001_2011.pdf (accessed August 2012).
9. This approximate figure is based on taking relative population sizes into account. There were 46.7 million prescriptions of antidepressants dispensed in 2011 in Britain (UK population is 62.6 million), and 254 million prescriptions of antidepressants dispensed in 2011 in the United States (US population is 311.6 million). The US figure was sourced from: 'Antidepressants: a complicated picture'. Published online by the National Institute of Mental Health. Website: www.nimh.nih.gov/about/director/2011/antidepressants-a-complicated-picture.shtml (accessed July 2012).
10. By the late 1990s pharmaceutical companies were spending about $700 million on direct-to-consumer advertising each year. But by 2005 they were spending more than $4.2 billion a year according to the United States GAO (Government Accountability Office, 2006). See: Sufrin, C.B. and Ross, J.S. (2008), 'Pharmaceutical industry marketing: understanding its impact on women's health'. *Obstet Gynecol Surv*, 63(9): 585–96.

11. Quoted in Lacasse, J.R. and Leo, J. (2006), 'Questionable Advertising of Psychotropic Medications and Disease Mongering'. *PLoS Med*, 3(7): e321. doi:10.1371/journal.pmed.0030321. Website: www.plosmedicine.org/article/info:doi/10.1371/journal.pmed.0030321
12. Lacasse, J.R. and Leo, J. (2005), 'Serotonin and Depression: A disconnect between the advertisements and the scientific literature'. *PLoS Med*, 2(12): e392. doi:10.1371/journal.pmed.0020392. Website: www.plosmedicine.org/article/info:doi/10.1371/journal.pmed.0020392
13. Promotional video, American Psychiatric Association website: www.healthyminds.org/ (accessed February 2011).
14. Foster, Juliet L.H. (2010), 'Perpetuating Stigma?: Differences between advertisements for psychiatric and non-psychiatric medication in two professional journals'. *Journal of Mental Health*, 19(1): 26–33. See: cambridge.academia.edu/JulietFoster/Papers/441956/Perpetuating_Stigma_Differences_between_advertisements_for_psychiatric_and_non-psychiatric_medication_in_two_professional_journals
15. Quoted in Glibody, S., Wilson, P. and Watt, I. (2004), 'Direct-to-Consumer Advertising of Psychotropics: an emerging and evolving form of pharmaceutical company influence'. *British Journal of Psychiatry*, 189: 1–2.
16. Lacasse, J.R. and Leo, J. (2005), 'Serotonin and Depression: A disconnect between the advertisements and the scientific literature'. *PLoS Med*, 2(12): e392. doi:10.1371/journal.pmed.0020392. Website: www.plosmedicine.org/article/info:doi/10.1371/journal.pmed.0020392
17. Donohue, J. and Berndt, E. (2004), 'Effects of direct-to-consumer advertising on medication choice: The case of antidepressants'. *J Pub Pol Marketing*, 23: 115–27. Also see: Rosenthal, M.B., Berndt, E.R., Donohue, J.M., Epstein, A.M. and Frank, R.G. (2003), 'Demand Effects of Recent Changes in Prescription Drug Promotion', *Frontiers in Health Policy Research*, Vol. 6, D.M. Cutler and A.M. Garber, eds. Cambridge, MA: MIT Press, 1–26.
18. Kravitz, R.L., Epstein, R.M., Feldman, M.D., Franz, C.E., Azari, R. et al. (2005), 'Influence of patients' requests for direct-to-consumer advertised antidepressants: A randomized controlled trial'. *JAMA*, 293: 1995–2002.
19. Glibody, S., Wilson, P. and Watt, I. (2004), 'Direct-to-Consumer Advertising of Psychotropics: an emerging and evolving form of pharmaceutical company influence'. *British Journal of Psychiatry*, 189: 1–2.
20. Gray, R. (2011), 'When Talking Pills can be Better than Talking'. www.bbc.co.uk/news/health-12716742 (accessed August 2011).

Chapter 11: The psychiatric myth

1. This chapter brings together and articulates some arguments made in my previous book, from which I occasionally quote and paraphrase. See:

Davies, J. (2012), *The Importance of Suffering: the value and meaning of emotional discontent*. London: Routledge.

2. See: Porter, R. (1996), *A Social History of Madhouses, Mad Doctors and Lunatics*. London: NPI.
3. Moncrieff, J. (2009), *The Myth of the Chemical Cure: a critique of psychiatric drug treatment*. London: Palgrave Macmillan (p. 32).
4. Ibid.
5. Ibid.
6. Ibid.
7. See: Squire, L.R. and Slater, P.C. (1983), 'Electroconvulsive therapy and complaints of memory dysfunction: a prospective three-year follow-up study'. *British Journal of Psychiatry*, 142: 1–8. See also: Breggin, P. (2007), 'ECT Damages the Brain: Disturbing News for Patients and Shock Doctors Alike'. *Ethical Human Psychology and Psychiatry*, 9(2): 83–6. Finally, see: Andre, L. (2009), *Doctors of Deception: What They Don't Want You to Know About Shock Treatment*. New Brunswick, NJ: Rutgers University Press.
8. Bracken, P. et al. (2012), 'Psychiatry Beyond the Current Paradigm', submitted to the *British Journal of Psychiatry*, 201: 430–34.
9. I have slightly altered this quotation. See: Davies, J. (2012), *The Importance of Suffering: the value and meaning of emotional discontent*. London: Routledge (p. 50).
10. This discussion of different cultural repsonses to voice hearing is paraphrased from my earlier book, as in the note above.
11. See: Bentall, R.P. (2010), *Doctoring the Mind: why psychiatric treatments fail*. London: Penguin (p. 106).
12. For an excellent article that critiques this position, see: www.nytimes.com/2010/01/10/magazine/10psyche-t.html?pagewanted=all
13. Angermeyer, M. and Matschinger, H. (2005), 'Causal beliefs and attitudes to people with schizophrenia: trend analysis based on data from two population surveys in Germany'. *British Journal of Psychiatry*, 186: 331–4.
14. Mehta, S. (1997), 'Is being "sick" really better? Effects of disease view of mental disorder on stigma'. *Journal of Social and Clinical Psychology*, 16(4): 405–19.
15. See: Timimi, S. (2011), 'Campaign to Abolish Psychiatric Diagnostic Systems such as ICD and DSM'. See: www.criticalpsychiatry.co.uk/index.php?option=com_content&view=article&id=233:campaign-to-abolish-psychiatric-diagnostic-systems-such-as-ICD-and-DSM-timimi-s&catid=34:members-publications&Itemid=56. For further summary of studies, see: Watters, E. (2010), 'The Americanization of Mental Illness', *New York Times* (8 January 2010).

16. See argument by Ethan Watters in 'The Americanization of Mental Illness'. *New York Times*, 8 January 2010.
17. See: Burton, N.L. (2006), *Psychiatry*. Oxford: Blackwell.
18. Dowrick, C. (2004), *Beyond Depression: a new approach to understanding and management*. Oxford: Oxford University Press (p. 69).
19. Sharfstein, S.S. (2005), 'Big Pharma and American Psychiatry: the good, the bad, and the ugly'. *Psychiatric News*, 40(16): 3.
20. Davies, J. (2012), *The Importance of Suffering: the value and meaning of emotional discontent*. London: Routledge.
21. Ibid.
22. Ibid.

Chapter 12: Psychiatric imperialism

1. For a full account of Watters' exploration of anorexia in Hong Kong, the account from which I draw here, see his excellent study: Watters, E. (2011), *Crazy Like Us: the globalization of the Western mind*. London: Robinson Publishing.
2. Ibid., p. 52.
3. These facts are from Janis Whitlock's (et al.) unpublished paper: 'Media and the Internet and Non-Suicidal Self-Injury'. For a similar published version, see: Whitlock, J.L., Purington, A. and Gershkovich, M. (2009),' Influence of the media on self injurious behavior'. In *Understanding Non-Suicidal Self-Injury: Current Science and Practice*, M. Nock (ed.). American Psychological Association Press (pp. 139–56).
4. See: news.bbc.co.uk/1/hi/health/3580365.stm
5. See: www.bbc.co.uk/newsbeat/10059733
6. See: news.bbc.co.uk/newsbeat/hi/health/newsid_8563000/8563670.stm
7. Blanchflower, D.G. and Oswald, A.J. (2000), 'Well-Being Over Time in Britain and the USA'. See: www.dartmouth.edu/~blnchflr/papers/Wellbeingnew.pdf
8. 'The Well-being of Children in the UK' (2004). University of York. See: www.york.ac.uk/inst/spru/wellbeingsummary.pdf
9. These facts are from Janis Whitlock's (et al.) unpublished paper: 'Media and the Internet and Non-Suicidal Self-Injury'. For a similar published version, see: Whitlock, J.L., Purington, A. and Gershkovich, M. (2009), 'Influence of the media on self injurious behavior'. In *Understanding Non-Suicidal Self-Injury: Current Science and Practice*, M. Nock (ed.). American Psychological Association Press (pp. 139–56).
10. As above, these facts are from Whitlock, J.L., Purington, A. and Gershkovich, M., unpublished paper: 'Media and the Internet and Non-Suicidal Self-Injury'.

11. See: Watters, E. (2011), *Crazy Like Us: the globalization of the Western mind*. London: Robinson Publishing (p. 33).
12. Ibid.
13. Harrington, A. (2012), 'Being Human: individual + society & morals + culture'. See presentation: fora.tv/2012/03/24/Being_Human_Individual__Society__Morals__Culture
14. See: Watters, E. (2011), *Crazy Like Us: the globalization of the Western mind*. London: Robinson Publishing (p. 65).
15. Lakoff, A. (2004), 'The Anxieties of Globalization: antidepressant sales and economic crisis in Argentina'. *Social Studies of Science*, April 2004, 34: 247–69.
16. For a full account of these events, which I paraphrase here, please see Chapter 4 in Watters, E. (2011), *Crazy Like Us: the globalization of the Western mind*. London: Robinson Publishing.
17. Ibid.
18. Paraphrased from ibid., p. 211.
19. See the following article on Japan and depression in the *New York Times*: www.nytimes.com/2004/08/22/magazine/did-antidepressants-depress-japan.html?pagewanted=all&src=pm
20. Ibid.
21. Ibid.
22. Ibid.
23. Skultans, V. (2003), 'From Damaged Nerves to Masked Depression: inevitability and hope in Latvian psychiatric narratives'. *Social Science and Medicine*, 56(12): 2421–31.
24. For 2009 figures, see: www.imshealth.com/ims/Global/Content/Corporate/Press%20Room/Top-line%20Market%20Data/2009%20Top-line%20Market%20Data/Top%2015%20Global%20Therapeutic%20Classes_2009.pdf. For 2010 figures, see: www.imshealth.com/ims/Global/Content/Corporate/Press%20Room/Top-Line%20Market%20Data%20&%20Trends/2011%20Top-line%20Market%20Data/Top_20_Global_Therapeutic_Classes.pdf
25. See: www.reuters.com/article/2011/04/22/lundbeck-japan-idUSLDE73L03X20110422
26. See: www.pharmatimes.com/article/10-12-16/Lundbeck_sees_China_as_land_of_opportunity_for_Lexapro.aspx
27. See: www.woncaeurope.org/content/p05263-use-antidepressants-primary-health-care-brazil
28. Ecks, S. (2005), 'Pharmaceutical Citizenship: antidepressant marketing and the promise of demarginalization of India'. *Anthropology and Medicine*, 12(3): 239–54.

29. Jablensky, A. et al. (1992), 'Schizophrenia: manifestations, incidence and course in different cultures. A World Health Organisation ten-country study'. *Psychological Medicine Monograph Supplement 20*. Cambridge: Cambridge University Press.
30. Bhugra, D. (2006), 'Severe Mental Illness Across Cultures'. *Acta Psychiatrica Scandinavica*, 113, 429: 17–23.
31. Middleton, H. et al. (2011), 'The Dodo Bird Verdict and the Elephant in the Room: A service user-led investigation of crisis resolution and home treatment'. *Health Sociology Review*, 20(2): 147–56.
32. Mosher, L.R. (1999), 'Soteria and Other Alternatives to Acute Psychiatric Hospitalization: A personal and professional review'. *Journal of Nervous and Mental Disease*, 187: 142–9.
33. Watters, E. (2010), 'The Americanization of Mental Illness'. *New York Times*, 8 January 2010.

Chapter 13: How to fix the cracks?

1. Double, D.B. (2001), 'Integrating critical psychiatry into psychiatric training'. In Newnes, C., Holmes, G. and Dunn, C. (eds), *This is Madness Too*. Ross-on-Wye: PCCS Books.

Appendix: Antipsychotics (neuroleptics) – breaking the brain?

1. Whitaker, R. (2010), *The Anatomy of an Epidemic*. New York: Broadway.
2. Moncrieff, J. (2009), *The Myth of the Chemical Cure: a critique of psychiatric drug treatment*. London: Palgrave Macmillan (p. 115).
3. Ibid.
4. Whitaker, R. (2010), *The Anatomy of an Epidemic*. New York: Broadway (pp. 101–02).
5. Harrow, M. and Jobe, T H. (2007), 'Outcome and Recovery in Schizophrenia Patients'. *The Journal of Nervous and Mental Disease*, Vol. 195, No. 5.
6. Whitaker, R. (2010), *The Anatomy of an Epidemic*. New York: Broadway (pp. 105–06).
7. Dorph-Petersen, K.A. et al. (2005), 'The influence of chronic exposure to antipsychotic medications on brain size before and after tissue fixation: a comparison of haloperidol and olanzapine in macaque monkeys'. *Neuropsychopharmacology*, 30(9): 1649–61.
8. Vita, A. and De Peri, L. (2007), 'The Effects of Antipsychotic Treatment on Cerebral Structure and Function in Schizophrenia'. *International Review of Psychiatry*, 19(4): 429–36.
9. Robert Whitaker: www.huffingtonpost.com/robert-whitaker/anatomy-of-an-epidemic-co_b_555572.html

Index